The Power of the Machine

For Sara and Christoffer

The Power of the Machine

Global Inequalities of Economy, Technology, and Environment

Alf Hornborg

ALTAMIRA
PRESS

A Division of
ROWMAN & LITTLEFIELD PUBLISHERS, INC.
Walnut Creek • Lanham • New York • Oxford

ALTAMIRA PRESS
A Division of Rowman & Littlefield Publishers, Inc.
1630 North Main Street, #367
Walnut Creek, CA 94596
www.altamirapress.com

Rowman & Littlefield Publishers, Inc.
4720 Boston Way
Lanham, MD 20706

12 Hid's Copse Road
Cumnor Hill, Oxford OX2 9JJ, England

British Library Cataloguing in Publication Information Available

Library of Congress Cataloging-in-Publication Data

Hornborg, Alf.
 The power of the machine : global inequalities of economy, technology,
and environment / Alf Hornborg.
  p. cm.
 Includes bibliographical references and index.
 ISBN 0-7591-0066-7 (c. : alk. paper) — ISBN 0-7591-0067-5 (p. : alk. paper)
 1. Technological innovations. 2. Technology—Economic aspects. I. Title.
HC79.T4 H67 2001
338'.064—dc21   2001035413

Printed in the United States of America

♾ ™ The paper used in this publication meets the minimum requirements of
American National Standard for Information Sciences—Permanence of Paper for
Printed Library Materials, ANSI/NISO Z39.48-1992.

Contents

Part 2   Money, Modernity, and Personhood

Figures and maps

Preface

The chapters of this book were written over a period of ten years and in very diverse contexts, but they all pursue a basic set of intuitions about power and human-environmental relations that have preoccupied me since the early 1970s. It is never an easy task to argue for an interpretation of the world that goes against the grain of the everyday discourse of the people around you. To see reality in a new way means adopting an unfamiliar language for talking about it. It also means identifying "problems" other than those defined by conventional debate. Such new understandings will thus be frustrating to most people: by being "difficult" to read and by not being immediately useful in solving the seemingly self-evident "problems" at hand. There is also the risk that a reconceptualization of power structures and global inequality—even if explicitly not aiming to demonize the individual inhabitants of the affluent North—for many people would imply wedging an onus of guilt into their everyday lifestyle. All in all, it is not hard to understand the kinds of factors that select for pragmatic "knowledge" in the sense of perspectives that are *easy to live with*. But pragmatism is socially defined, and societies change. Globalized media now provide the rich and the poor with increasingly vivid images of each other's everyday lives. The social and psychological costs of denying or rationalizing the polarizations and tensions of world society are mounting. There is a chance that we are approaching a point where significant numbers of people on both sides of the North-South divide will be demanding more credible narratives than neoclassical economic theory and the rhetoric on "sustainable development."

[margin handwritten note: new]

[margin handwritten note: narrative *]

The research on which this book is based has been supported by the Swedish Council for Research in the Humanities and Social Sciences (HSFR) and the Swedish Council for Planning and Coordination of Research (FRN). The case study presented in chapter 12 was funded by The Bank of Sweden Tercentenary Foundation.

ix

Several of the chapters in this book have previously appeared in journals or edited collections of articles. Revised versions are reproduced here
with permission of the following journals and publishers: chapter 1:
Knowledge and Policy 6:37–45 (1993); chapter 3: *Ecological Economics*
25:1:127–136 (1998); chapter 4: *Journal of World-Systems Research* 4(2):169–
177 (1998); chapter 5: Routledge (R. Denemark et al., eds., *World System
History: The Social Science of Long-term Change*, pp. 235–252, 2000); chapter
6: *Man* (N.S.) 27:1–18 (1992); chapter 8: *Anthropological Theory* 1:4 (2001);
chapter 9: *Journal of Material Culture* 4(2):143–162 (1999); chapter 10:
Routledge (P. Descola & G. Pálsson, eds., *Nature and Society: Anthropological Perspectives*, pp. 45–62, 1996); chapter 11: Lund University Press
(A. Hornborg & G. Pálsson, eds., *Negotiating Nature: Culture, Power, and
Environmental Argument*, pp. 133–152, 2000), chapter 12: *Canadian Review
of Sociology and Anthropology* 31:245–267 (1994). My thanks to these journals and publishers, and also to Dorothy Smith, Erin McKindley, A. J.
Sobczak, and Rosalie Robertson for competently and efficiently turning
my manuscript into a book.

A very large number of people have, in various discussions over the years,
helped me to refine the arguments I present in this book. Most of them—
students, lecture audiences, anonymous reviewers—must go unmentioned.
Although inevitably far from complete, the list of colleagues to whom I feel
indebted for productive discussions on topics discussed in this book includes Kaj Århem, Zygmunt Bauman, Hugh Beach, Sing Chew, Gudrun
Dahl, Philippe Descola, Kajsa Ekholm-Friedman, Karl-Erik Eriksson,
Gunder Frank, Jonathan Friedman, Maurice Godelier, Stephen Gudeman,
Thomas Håkansson, Ulf Hannerz, Tim Ingold, Mikael Kurkiala, William
McNeill, Robert Paine, Gísli Pálsson, Bryan Pfaffenberger, the late Skip Rappaport, Andrew Sherratt, and Mathis Wackernagel. None of them, however,
has read more than fragments of this book, and few have been in complete
agreement with me about the little they have read. I thus assure the reader
that the responsibility for any remaining shortcomings is entirely my own.

My thoughts also go to friends and neighbors in several communities
in different parts of the world who, for longer or shorter periods, have
shared their homes with me and helped me begin to fathom the variety
of perspectives on the world as well as the fundamental commonalities of
human existence. For this I am indebted to the villagers of Huahuapuquio
and their relatives in Lima; to residents of the Mi'kmaq communities of
Eskasoni, Membertou, and Whycocomagh; and to longtime friends in the
Swedish parish of Västrum.

Finally, I continue to be grateful to my wife, Anne-Christine, and my
children, Sara and Christoffer, for providing me with a meaningful context and the requisite peace of mind with which to dare my excursions
into the abstract and the global.

Introduction

※

The Machine As Emperor

The last quarter of the second millennium A.D. saw the rise to power of the machine. Like all power structures, the machine will continue to reign only as long as it is not unmasked as a species of power. This book is intended as a contribution to such an unmasking.

⌐Power⌐is here understood as a social relation built on an asymmetrical distribution of resources and risks. Power relations are culturally constructed but masquerade—to the powerful and powerless alike—as inevitable and natural. To reveal their arbitrary foundation is thus an epistemologically arduous task. It involves not only exposing conventional perspectives as mystifying but necessarily also presenting an alternative and more credible interpretation of social reality. This has become increasingly difficult in the intellectual climate of postmodern social science. Deconstruction becomes toothless when all it finally adds up to is a philosophy of "anything goes."

To unmask the power of the machine, we need to be as open to thermodynamics as to semiotics. It is one thing to say that the machine is culturally constituted, that is, that our perception of it is symbolically mediated. It is something else to say that, beyond this cultural lens, the *actual* machine contradicts our everyday image of it—that there is something outside our conventional representation of it that we now need to acknowledge. To make both kinds of arguments in the same book is not very common these days. Researchers in the human sciences tend to be either constructivists or objectivists, and the two discourses usually are kept separate if not antagonistic. But to expose the special character of machine power requires that the two kinds of discourse can be articulated, for machines rely for their very existence as much on symbols as on thermodynamics.

The title of this book is intentionally ambiguous. The book's central argument is that three possible meanings of machine "power" that we conventionally would distinguish—power to conduct work, power over other people, and power over our minds—are really aspects of a single, social phenomenon. It seeks to show that the foundation of machine technology is not primarily know-how but unequal exchange in the world system, which generates an increasing, global polarization of wealth and impoverishment. The main challenge has been to achieve a distanced view of the everyday, cultural categories and assumptions which continue to reproduce this asymmetric, global power structure. One of the strategies that I use is to juxtapose the modern power of the machine with premodern power structures such as that embodied in the Inca emperor.

When I argue in chapter 8 that the machine and the emperor are comparable (as instances of Marxian fetishism), I mean it in all the three senses of "power" referred to above. Both imply power over other people and power over their minds, but also, simultaneously and concomitantly, power that actually *works*. It is precisely the illusory distinction between symbolic communication and technical efficacy that prevents us from recognizing the machine as a social institution no less culturally constituted than Inca ritual. In both cases, the efficacy hinges on the symbolic codes that mobilize the masses. As I argue in chapter 9, we cannot hope to understand the material agency of humans in the biosphere if we are not prepared to juxtapose materialist perspectives, on one hand, with symbolic analysis and phenomenology, on the other. Chapter 9 focuses on the semiotics of money and modernity, phenomena without which the machine would not be possible.

Although the chapters in this book range widely in terms of theoretical perspectives and empirical case material, they all pursue the fundamental intuition that the environmental crisis of modern society is a problem of power, culture, and epistemology. The underlying concern is to show that the objective and the subjective dimensions of human-environmental relations are inseparable. In particular, I hope to reveal how the material existence of modern, industrial infrastructure (i.e., "development") ultimately relies on certain cultural notions about production and exchange, and on the unequal flows of resources that these notions mask and repro-

duce. My main thesis is that we are caught in a collective illusion about
the nature of modern technology. We do not recognize that what ultimately keep our machines running are global terms of trade. The power
of the machine is not *of* the machine, but of the asymmetric structures of
exchange of which it is an expression.

This work could perhaps be viewed as an additional chapter in the critical, cultural analysis of capitalism inaugurated by Karl Marx. Throughout *Marx*
part 1, I try to show that the most central "fetish" of capitalism is nothing
less than the industrial machine. To make this clear, it is necessary to uncover the material asymmetries implied in contemporary patterns of
global trade. I argue that these asymmetries are systematically concealed
from view by the hegemonic, economic vocabulary. It is only in making
these material dimensions of exchange transparent that it becomes possible for us to assess the *moral* dimensions of the global market economy. *morality*
A cultural critique of industrial capitalism might begin by recognizing
that economic exchange (and the vocabulary and institutions that orchestrate it) is *a part of the technology.*

I am trained in cultural anthropology, and many of my theoretical and
empirical reference points indeed derive from anthropology. In strug- *human*
gling with the transdisciplinary field of human ecology, however, I have *ecology*
ventured into the literature of neighboring disciplines such as sociology,
archaeology, economic history, geography, and development studies. My
argument represents a conjunction of perspectives from the humanities,
social sciences, and natural sciences. It is polemical in relation to most
conventional discourse on "sustainable development," ecological economics, and similar topics in suggesting that solutions to our ecological
predicament will have to be much more profound and radical than is usually envisioned in the environmental debate. I argue for a *defamiliarization*
of our conventional conceptions of technology and development, that is,
a fundamental distancing from the cultural categories through which the
modern economic system operates, and in terms of which most policy
negotiations are conducted. Above all, I argue that we must recognize the
global, *distributional* aspects of development, technology, and environmental issues. The intellectual ancestry of these ideas can be traced to the
underexplored interfaces between world system theory, political ecology,
ecological economics, economic anthropology, fetishism theory, and semiotics. An important aspect is to connect political ecology and political
economy with the anthropological concern with *culture.*

In part 2, I thus relate the phenomenon of machine fetishism to the
wider, cultural and existential context of modernity, focusing on processes of semiotic abstraction. If I confuse readers by juxtaposing arguments from thermodynamics and semiotics in one and the same book,
it is because both are part of the world we live in, and both are of

significance for the problems of sustainability which confront us as we
enter the third millennium. If the phenomenology of modern personhood
seems totally unrelated to questions of natural resource management, it
is only because our Cartesian compartmentalization of knowledge produces such illusions. It is in fact deluding to separate scientific discourses
on the "reality" of environmental problems from humanistic discourses
on the *representations* of such realities, simply because the representations
(including all our discourse) tend to be active ingredients *in* reality. This
condition is powerfully evoked in much post-structuralist thought as well
as in the Marxian concept of fetishism, which is a central point of departure for this study.

This book, in short, is about the epistemology of exchange. I believe
that many of the intuitions that have guided it ultimately derive from my
previous struggles with anthropological theories of kinship and marriage
(Hornborg 1988, 1993, 1998b). Fundamental to both inquiries has been a
concern with "underlying" structures of exchange masked or veiled by
the cultural constructions of the participants. The difference between
what Lévi-Strauss (1969) referred to as elementary and complex structures of kinship is cognate to the difference between primitive and modern money. The transformation in both cases is in the semiotics of reciprocity. Direct marriage exchange resembles the exchange of primitive
valuables such as the Melanesian *kula* or the ancient Andean *mullu* (*Spondylus* shell), discussed in chapter 5, in that both represent a culturally *restricted* interchangeability. The transitions to complex structures of marriage and to general-purpose money entailed a successive *generalization* of
exchange in time and space.

Whereas Malinowski's "pure gift" tolerated delayed reciprocity only
within a restricted social space (cf. Sahlins 1972), money purchases (ficti-
tiously) present themselves as immediate reciprocation and are thus able
to extend the social range of exchange beyond the reach of personal, face-
to-face relations. Money capital is an institution for delaying and extending the archaic, gravitational pull of reciprocity. It is the conceptual and
institutional transmutations of this "pull" that make possible increasingly
asymmetric exchanges between distant populations and ecosystems. The
extension in time and space of such gravitational fields is achieved
through a process of semiotic abstraction that is at the heart of what we
know as modernity. My use of the metaphor of "gravitation" here is not
fortuitous, for it refers to the capacity of money signs to *make matter move*.
These processes clearly interlace the semiotic and the material, culture
and nature, the subjective and the objective. In fact, as I show in chapter
11, their very fulcrum is the phenomenology of the modern person.

The connection between money and modern personhood constitutes a
fulcrum in an epistemological sense as well. Parts 1 and 2 in this book

illustrate two diametrically opposite ways of transcending the kind of conventional, Western dualism that regards nature as *material* and society as *communicative*, and the two as mutually exclusive domains of reality. Conventional ecological science approaches nature as flows of matter and energy, whereas economic science approaches society as flows of money signs. This book consistently tries to transcend this dichotomy, part 1 by arguing that society is also material (involving flows of matter and energy), part 2 by arguing that nature is also communicative (involving flows of signs). The anthropological study of money—and the modern persons whose configurations it shapes—must bring these putatively separate domains together, because money simultaneously organizes material *and* semiotic flows in nature *and* society. An anthropological study of money should help us overcome the illusory abyss between studies of the social construction of nature and studies suggesting a natural science of society.

If the word "power" in the title is ambiguous, so also perhaps, ultimately, is the word "machine." My concern with modernity and the social consequences of abstraction finally addresses modernist rationality as a *machination* in the widest sense. Although my primary argument is that the machine is social, it is embedded in reflections about the inverse observation that our modern social system functions like a machine. It has been observed that it was precisely this modernist rationality which made the atrocities of the Holocaust possible (Horkheimer and Adorno 1944 [1972]; Bauman 1989). We can only hope that humanity shall one day be able to look back with the same horror and indignation at the global inequalities of the present age.

Mechanization of Society

I

TECHNOLOGY AND UNEQUAL EXCHANGE

1

Technology and Economics: The Interfusion of the Social and the Material

After several decades of strong public awareness that industrial civilization is moving in an unsustainable direction, there is an uneasy feeling that all this talk is not going to help. The concerned scientists, the "green" politicians, the uncounted thousands of activists around the world: will all their awareness ever have a real impact on the grinding wheels of the world economy? Why do so many of us remain skeptical? Is it, perhaps, because the recipes themselves seem contradictory? How, for instance, can engineers be expected to come up with increasingly complex technologies that are simultaneously cleaner *and* less expensive? How can economists be expected to devise "green taxes" which will both discourage consumption *and* stimulate growth? How is it possible to organize "development aid" that will stimulate production for export and yet increase local self-sufficiency? These are some of the impossible tasks specialists are being confronted with, should they try to implement the dominant, contemporary doctrine, as codified, for instance, in the Brundtland Report (World Commission on Environment and Development [WCED] 1987). As long as the concept of development continues to hinge *growth* on growth, the notion of "sustainable development" remains an oxymoron.

In very general terms, I argue in this book, the problem is our way of conceptualizing the relationship between sociocultural constructions and

9

material processes. We seem to have difficulties understanding exactly in which sense human ideas and social relations intervene in the material realities of the biosphere. Rather than continuing to approach "knowledge" from the Cartesian assumption of a separation of subject and object, we shall have to concede that our image-building actively participates in the constitution of the world. Our perception of our physical environment is inseparable from our involvement in it.

In this and the next seven chapters, I wish to challenge the fragmentarized worldview that treats "technology" and "economy" as if they were separate parts of reality. My argument is a plea for holistic perspectives on technology as a total social phenomenon, but it follows a somewhat different track from the "social constructivist" approach (cf. Bijker, Hughes, and Pinch 1987). It is not enough to say that the specific *forms* of technology are socially constructed; ultimately, the whole idea of a technological "realm," so to speak, rests on social relationships of exchange. This implies that what is technologically feasible cannot be distinguished from what is socially (i.e., economically) feasible. If, since Newton, the machine has served as a root metaphor for the universe, an advocate of a less mechanistic worldview might begin by demonstrating that even the machine is an organic phenomenon.

TECHNO-ECONOMICS

Seen as a total phenomenon, industrial technology represents the conjunction of three different factors, or levels of reality: (1) thermodynamics and other properties of matter and energy, or *nature*, for short; (2) technical *knowledge*, or ideas about how to assemble various components and substances so as to exploit such material properties; and (3) economics, defined as sociocultural institutions for *exchange* between individuals and groups. In sum, machines are part nature, part knowledge, and part exchange.

I hope to show that the worldview of industrial society does not properly reckon with the interrelatedness of these three levels. If we were to recognize how nature, knowledge, and exchange interact to generate industrial technology, machines would assume a quite different appearance than as indices of "progress" and "development." We would see that technology is not just a matter of applying technical knowledge to nature, for in order for this knowledge to result in anything at all, the components and substances to which it refers must be *socially accessible*. For the machines to continue running, specific components have to be provided, and at specific *rates*. It could be argued that this is what the world market is really all about. Although it is theoretically conceivable to keep the machines supplied with fuels and raw materials through some other mode of extraction, such as keeping colonies of slaves, the market has proven a more successful institution because it requires fewer soldiers and has made the *exploitative* nature of the extractive process less obvious.

Calling world trade exploitative, I insist, is more than a value judgment. It is an inference based on the Second Law of Thermodynamics. If production is a dissipative process (Georgescu-Roegen 1971), and a prerequisite for industrial production is the exchange of finished products for raw materials and fuels, then it follows that industrialism implies a *social* transfer of entropy. The sum of industrial products *represents* greater entropy than the sum of fuels and raw materials for which they are exchanged. The net transfer of "negative entropy" to industrial centers is the basis for techno-economic "growth" or "development." In other words, we must begin to understand machines as thoroughly *social* phenomena. They are the result of asymmetric, global transfers of resources. The knowledge employed to keep them running would be infertile if the world market did not see to it that the industrial sectors of world society maintain a net gain in "negative entropy" (or in *exergy*; see chapter 3). Inversely, the non-industrial sectors experience a net increase in entropy as natural resources and traditional social structures are dismembered. The ecological and socioeconomic impoverishment of the periphery are two sides of the same coin, for both nature and human labor are underpaid sources of high-quality energy for the industrial "technomass." Perhaps I should add that I use the concepts of center/periphery and industrial/non-industrial sectors in an abstract sense, to denote a structural relationship rather than discrete geographical areas or political units (cf. Frank 1966). The polarization of "developed" and "underdeveloped" countries is an expression of this structural relationship but does not exhaust it.

In not reckoning with the intimate connection between economics and technology—the social and the material aspects of industrialism—we tend to talk as if technology were primarily a matter of knowledge. We imagine that education and "technology transfer" might solve problems of "underdevelopment," forgetting, as it were, that new centers of industrial growth require new peripheries to exploit, and that peripheries are already in so high demand that, looking East, we are seeing former centers turn into peripheries rather than vice versa. The science of technology is not simply a matter of applying rational thought to nature, for the "natural" conditions for matter-energy conversions in privileged, so-called developed areas have been transformed by world trade. Technological science deals with the *management* of resources locally accumulated within such restricted areas through unequal, global exchange. It *presupposes* such accumulation, which implies that its own applicability is socially re-

*exchange value
as the only
real value*

stricted. Conventional economics, in recognizing no other concept of value than exchange value, tends to conceal this inequality.

If technology is nature plus knowledge plus exchange, we tend to forget the last part of the equation. The social processes through which its components are supplied are visualized as external to the definition of technology. Our machines fool us into thinking that they can exist without the socioeconomic premises that I have just outlined, and that they are simply revealed regularities of nature, to be approached as *non-social* phenomena. This illusion is related to our conception of the "material" world as natural, nonnegotiable, open to scientific revelation and manipulation, but in its fundamentals immune to contamination by human thought and society. We seem to have difficulties understanding that machines, being material structures, for their very existence depend on social relations. Machines occupy an ambiguous position in the Cartesian scheme: they are material, yet products of mind. This is probably why we have such a hard time grasping them as the social phenomena that they are.

The environmental debate increasingly focuses on ways in which economics and ecology do not harmonize. The argument in this book, however, is that industrial technology is a *product* of this disharmony. Its power to conduct work "in itself," as it were, is a cultural illusion. It is the productive potential of the fuels and other raw materials which is at work in our machines, not the machines "in themselves." The accessibility of such resources hinges on the socially constructed discrepancy, in world trade, between material qualities and price, ecology and economics; thus, social distribution is necessarily prior to production, and global terms of trade are a crucial "productive force" or "factor of production."

One way of grasping the nature of this illusion is to think in terms of how industrialism has shifted the boundary between negotiable and non-negotiable aspects of human production systems. If we exclude local barter of bulk goods, most pre-industrial trade was in items the primary value of which was symbolic, for instance as magic sources of fertility or indicators of social prestige. Because work generally was manual, the local exchange value of such items corresponded to their productive potential—the rate at which they could be converted into human labor. To say that the local exchange value of a long-distance import was proportional to its productive potential would be tautologically true for such economic systems. Whenever an object of exchange carries an *intrinsic* (thermodynamic) productive potential, however, there is a chance that exchange value and productive potential are not proportional; that is, that a unit of productive potential is underpaid relative to the product into which it is transformed. As we shall see in chapters 4 and 5, such underpayment can occur in the context of several different kinds of production systems. Nevertheless, the delegation of work from human bodies to machines introduced historically new possibilities for maintaining a discrepancy between exchange value and productive potential, which in other words means encouraging new strategies for underpayment and accumulation.

Whereas traditional, long-distance trade conveyed symbols, the productive potential of which was defined by the ratio according to which they could be converted into local labor, modern trade increasingly has conveyed the productive potential itself in the form, for instance, of fossil fuels. Whereas the productive potential of traditional trade goods was defined by local value systems and subject to negotiation, technology renders the productive potential of fossil fuels a locally unnegotiable aspect of reality. Yet—and this is my main point here—this unnegotiably "material" appearance is a cultural illusion, for the technology itself is contingent on the rates at which products can be exchanged for fuels and raw materials—that is, on world market prices. World market prices, of course, are as negotiable and socially constructed as any local evaluations. It is by having been removed from the local and personal level and delegated to the global and impersonal that market evaluations—and the technologies that they make possible—have assumed the appearance of natural law. "Growth" is not something that technology generates in a purely material sense, but a consequence of how industrial products are evaluated in relation to fuels and raw materials. Growth and technology are thus not primarily material parameters but sociocultural constructions. To move beyond the self-contradictions of conventional recipes for sustainability, we will need to avoid reifying such socially constructed and value-based phenomena as if they were more "real" and binding— and less negotiable—than the ideas that generate them. We will need to reach a holistic understanding of how human ideas and social institutions in a very tangible sense intervene in material reality. Only then can we begin to see the options realistically open to the human species.

Karl Marx visualized an egalitarian society based on advanced, industrial technology. The collapse of the Soviet Union ultimately reflects the failure of Marxist thought to escape the illusions of what I refer to in this book as "machine fetishism." The communist alternative has proven unviable, but it would be unwarranted to simply conclude that the mainstream economists were right, for the so-called free world may well be next in line for economic collapse. The industrialized sectors have to sell in order to survive because selling is their means of drawing fresh resources from their peripheries. Because of the dissipative character of industrial production, however, this is an inherently contradictory relationship. There is a constant pressure to keep prices of fuels and raw materials low, yet the periphery must have the revenue to transfer—through purchase of industrial products—enough money back to industry to grant it continued access to those resources. If industrial growth were generative of "productive potential" rather than dissipative, this would not be a problem. Then industrial sectors could be content with domestic markets, and the sums gained from sales would not have to exceed the sum of costs. Then, also, growth would be able to "spill over" into peripheral areas in the form of rising prices for natural resources and increasing amounts of "development aid." To believe in such a vision, however, is to disregard the Second Law of Thermodynamics. As the "technomass" of industrial sectors grows, so does its thermodynamic costs of maintenance, not only in terms of the amounts of fresh resources required in the center but also in terms of the inputs of resources required to extract increasingly inaccessible resources in the periphery. Faced with this predicament, industry would not have been able to survive and expand for two hundred years were it not for the curious cultural institution we know as *money*.

INDUSTRIALISM AND THE LOGIC OF MONEY: THE ALGORITHM OF DESTRUCTION

Money in itself is merely an idea about the interchangeability of things and about the mutability of the rates at which things are exchanged. In practical, social life, it is a regulation of people's claims on one another. Against the thermodynamic background I have just outlined, it is clearly the very vacuity of money that has propelled industrial expansion, and the claims on non-industrial sectors have grown in proportion. This has been achieved in several ways:

1. Most fundamental is the fact that, by and large, prices must be inversely related to the productive potential of the traded products. This becomes apparent once we realize that production is dissipative rather than generative. It is simply a logical consequence of what the idea of money implies in a universe complying with the Second Law of Thermodynamics. Any stage in the production process aiming to enhance the utility of the substances thus transformed will reduce the sum of their productive potential (e.g., the availability of energy). A process of production based on exchanging manufactured products for the fuels and materials essential for that process must consequently assign the traded substances prices that—longitudinally, within this production process—are inversely proportional to their productive potential. An item produced from oil and metal ores

must be priced as if it were more valuable than the oil and the ores that were destroyed in making it, or the process could not go on. This in turn amounts to a constant *rewarding* of the continued destruction of oil and ores by giving industry access to increasing amounts of oil and ores to destroy.

2. A second expression of the appropriation of productive potential is the imperative that the sum gained from sales must be kept higher than the sum of costs, which generates inflation and, by extension, reveals the incapacity of the industrial sector to constitute its own, self-sufficient market. Industry's need of monetary profits expresses its incapacity to generate structural growth on its own because the profits simply represent a claim on new fuels and materials from the outside. As long as there are new populations to draw into the market, increased production ("growth") is the major strategy for resource appropriation. If such advantageous exchange rates were *not* fundamental to the viability of industrialism, we should ask why there should be so much concern about "underconsumption" (cf. Brewer 1990), or, in the 1970s, about the threat of higher oil prices. It is time to consider what this vulnerability could be telling us about the social nature of machinery—that is, about the ultimate thermodynamic dependency of industrial on non-industrial space.

3. Also important is the difference in paces of inflation for different goods—that is, the falling prices of most raw materials relative to those of finished products. This clearly amounts to falling prices per unit of productive potential, from the vantage point of industrial sectors, while implying rising costs for non-industrial ones, permitting exchange ratios to increasingly favor the former. The relative fall of prices for raw materials is one way for industry to continue procuring accelerating imports of resources when increased production is no longer as feasible a strategy, that is, when markets are becoming saturated and industry is faced with the pervasive specter of "underconsumption."

4. Grafted to the idea of money—and related to the fact of inflation—is the notion that it decreases in value over time and, if loaned, compensation should be paid in the form of interest. Interest rates, however, are as shifting and socially constructed as other prices, and the international credit institutions have encouraged Third World countries into taking loans with escalating debt payments, coercing them into higher rates of exploitation (Körner, Maass, Siebold, and Tetzlaff 1984 [1986]; Altvater, Hübner, Lorentzen, and Rojas 1987 [1991]). More than serving as acts of charity, the loans extended to "underdeveloped" sectors not only stimulate continued, unequal exchange but also provide "developed" sectors with substantial financial in-

come, further augmenting their claims on peripheral resources. Figures on falling prices of raw materials and on rising Third World debt payments are alarming in themselves, but even more so if we consider the thermodynamic realities orchestrated by these sums of money. Because the quantity of productive potential that can be purchased per dollar is higher in the periphery than in the center, the sums loaned to "underdeveloped" countries will be able to purchase less such potential per dollar (in the form of produce from the center) than the interest repaid to "developed" countries (used to purchase produce from the periphery). In a similar line of reasoning, Odum and Arding (1991) have estimated that credits extended from the United States to Ecuador yield an interest rate of 360% if energy rather than dollars is taken into account.

It seems apparent that this process of accumulation cannot continue forever. Perhaps we need not be as worried about the depletion of natural resources in absolute terms as about the inherent social limitations in the whole industrial arrangement. The inevitably falling capacity of the periphery to pay for what the center must sell—in order to cover rising, thermodynamic costs of maintenance—suggests an ultimately insoluble equation. The fact that the Soviet Union ran into these constraints of industrialism prior to the "free" world may largely be the result of the considerable extent to which its economic tentacles had confined themselves within the political borders of a single national community. National borders have not constrained industry based in the United States, Japan, or Western Europe. Making a market economy out of the former Soviet Union essentially means giving inequality—between centers and peripheries—freer rein.

Any centralized production process must maintain a net appropriation of productive potential. It must see to it that the suppliers of labor and natural resources contribute more productive potential than they receive. A market economy is simply the most elegant way of giving such asymmetries free rein. The notion of a "correct" price conceals the implications of the fact that what is being exchanged are intact resources for dissipated ones. Finished products and natural resources are incommensurable values because, from a thermodynamic point of view, products are not "refined" but degraded resources. How can we ever say what a fresh apple is worth in apple cores? Should it not be equally unreasonable to evaluate a gallon of oil in terms of products representing oil already dissipated? And, concomitantly, to reward the combustion of oil with more oil to dissipate? Does not the free exchange of industrial products for fuels and raw materials, by means of the logic of money, quite obviously encourage an accelerating destruction of natural resources?

Much recent literature suggests that ecology and economics study related and ideally congruent phenomena. Indeed, both biomass and "technomass" represent positive feedback processes of self-organization, where the system's use of harvested resources is "rewarded" with new resources in a continuing cycle. Both are dissipative structures, requiring inputs higher than outputs and subsisting on the difference. A crucial difference is that biomass is a sustainable process whereas technomass is not. For biomass, energy resources are virtually unlimited, and entropy—in the form of heat—is sent out into space. For technomass, resources are ultimately limited, and we are left with much of the entropy in the form of pollution. For biomass, growth is a morally neutral reward granted by nature itself, whereas for technomass it is a reward resulting from human ideologies and generating unequal, global relations of exchange. Considering also the fact that technomass *competes* with biomass for living space on our planet, it is essential that we reach a more profound understanding of the cultural concepts through which we intervene in nature, so as perhaps to be able to consciously generate less destructive ideas with which to replace them.

Such a reconceptualization of technology may also have to imply acceptance of the dependency of the global technomass on the combustion of fossil fuels (which presently accounts for 90% of world energy use) and abandonment of the vision of a technical means of harvesting solar energy more efficient than photosynthesis. If modern technologies for generating electricity from renewable sources (sun, water, and wind) were not in fact extensions of the mainstream infrastructure and thus subsidized by the global appropriation of fossil fuels, what do we mean by saying that the "underdeveloped" countries cannot "afford" these technologies? And what makes them so "unprofitable" even in "developed" countries? When the destructive nature of our economic system is emphasized, economists will often reply by expressing confidence in better technologies, but when technologists are asked why these have not yet been introduced, they tend to refer to faulty economics. These mystifications are founded on a conceptual dichotomy between "technology" and "economy," that permits us to shift back and forth between two presumably independent levels of reality, without grasping the techno-economic logic through which they are connected. New, environmentally benign technologies that are more expensive than conventional ones will automatically be the prerogative of a global minority, and thus also a means of generating an unequal distribution of environmental quality, drawing on resources in the periphery to keep the center clean and "green."

In fact, any discussion of how to make the economy sensitive to ecological requirements is severely constrained as long as it is couched in conventional, monetary terms such as the "costs" of environmental protection or revenue gained from emission permits. "Costs" and "gains" are relations between people, not between people and nature. They are ultimately a matter of relaxed or intensified claims on the periphery by the center or on the center by the periphery. Unless we are prepared to reorganize society in a much more fundamental way, it seems that any "green taxes" or other brakes on the system substantial enough to have a real impact on consumption would lead to economic decline, the most obvious sign of which would be rising unemployment rates, in the face of which any government would very quickly retract its "green taxes." More likely, the "green taxes" would never reach the magnitude at which such effects would follow, in which case they would remain symbolic and pointless. Mainstream economists are right in that industry cannot be burdened with too heavy a tax burden if it is to survive, but for reasons of which they are not themselves quite aware. There is a determinacy in the logic of money itself that outrules the conventional recipes, no matter how high we raise our voices. Neoclassical economics may have completely misunderstood ecology and thermodynamics, but it understands money. As long as the system is challenged on its own terms, the logic of money will be invincible. Our only hope is to replace that logic with a new systemic orientation, which requires a transformation of money itself.

This certainly also requires a transformation of economic science. In closing itself to the realities of physical processes, the peculiarly self-referential, neoclassical paradigm outrules the very idea of unequal exchange. Its axiom of intersubstitutability conceals the irreversibility and inequity of the industrial process. If technology is the science of managing accumulated natural resources, economics can thus be seen as the science of accumulation itself.

TECHNOLOGY AS SALVATION OR CURSE:
A VIEW FROM 1962

If, as I have indicated, industrial technology presupposes asymmetric exchange and accumulation, it is important to ask why we are having such difficulties perceiving machines as the thoroughly *social* phenomena that this would imply they are. Conventional discourse fails to recognize precisely *why* industrial technology remains the privilege of a global minority. This failure protrudes somewhat more clearly if we go back four decades to the records of the "Encyclopedia Britannica Conference on the Technological Order" in 1962 (Stover 1962). The pages of this special issue of *Technology and Culture* codify the major strands of discourse on technology that remain with us today. Among the participants were Jacques Ellul, Aldous Huxley, Lynn White, and Walter Ong.

On the optimistic side, Professor Zvorikine of the U.S.S.R. Academy of Sciences proclaims that

> the possibilities of technology depend upon the level of man's knowledge of the laws of nature. Modern technology is the material embodiment of the knowledge garnered by man in the struggle to subdue the forces of nature, the struggle to dominate them. (Stover 1962:444)

He goes on to say that the Communist Party "envisages unprecedented scientific and technical progress" (*Ibid.*:445). He claims that Lenin showed that whereas "imperialism turns technical achievements against mankind . . . only socialism uses technology for the well-being of the people" (*Ibid.*:449). He assures us that energy sources for industry are "practically inexhaustible" (*Ibid.*:453). Finally, he offers the eerily prophetic conclusion that "Soviet science has done more than just open wide the door of nature's treasure house. It is transforming nature" (*Ibid.*:454). In the records of the conference discussions, Zvorikine is reported to have said that as a member of "the other side," he would not try to give the West "the secrets of Russia's success" (*Ibid.*:634). At one point he exclaims, "How can technique be harmful to man?" (*Ibid.*:483).

Another version of optimism is represented by Arthur Goldschmidt of the United Nations' Department of Economic and Social Affairs (*Ibid.*:581) In his very first paragraph he introduces the implicit assumption that efforts to "improve the economic and social conditions in the less-developed countries of the world" are synonymous with efforts to "transfer technology." He proclaims that "there have been enormous successes" but observes that there are great obstacles to overcome and argues, in effect, for a technology for transferring technology. His general outlook is best reflected in his observation that "the conditions of rural life that make for ignorance, prejudice, and resistance to change are . . . repugnant to those trained people whose presence is needed to break down that resistance" (*Ibid.*:587).

Mr. Vu Van Thai, having served as economic advisor to the presidents of Vietnam and the Republic of Togo, shares Zvorikine's and Goldschmidt's technological image of development. He adopts an admonishing posture:

> The peoples of the underdeveloped countries want the fruits of technology without recognizing the cost, or being willing to pay it. Yet they must pay the price. They must make a synthesis between their own culture and the technological order. They must integrate technology and make it their own.

The developed countries cannot carry their technological cross for them. (*Ibid.*:623)

Zvorikine, Goldschmidt, and Thai spoke the same language, but the Soviet professor was less ready to admit to problems. According to the records of the discussion, Goldschmidt asked Zvorikine about problems of technology transfer within Russia, and the latter replied that "local people adjusted quite easily and rapidly to the technologies thus brought to them," and that "no special problems" seemed to be involved (*Ibid.*:484).

On the pessimistic side, of course, was Jacques Ellul's image of *la technique* as an autonomous and self-determining "accumulation of means which have established primacy over ends" (*Ibid.*:394). Ellul's (1954 [1964]) critique of technology, it will be recalled, is a critique of rationality, of the modern ambition to render accountable everything that is subconscious, and to quantify everything that is qualitative. Its major concern, in other words, is with technology's detrimental impact on humanistic and spiritual values, and with humanity's lack of control over it.

Another kind of pessimism was expressed by Aldous Huxley, the only one at the conference who addressed the impact of technology on the natural environment. "The relationship of technology to nature has deeply concerned me," he says.

> We are part of the natural order and must conform to the rules of that order. . . . It is absurd to attempt—to use that dreadful old-fashioned phrase—to conquer nature. . . . If there is a general industrialization, resources will be eaten up even faster. When the rest of the world is consuming as fast as America the acceleration in the destruction of raw materials will be enormous. (*Ibid.*:636, 638, 640)

But Huxley would not turn his back on technology. He adds that "these tremendous problems have developed because technology accomplished something intrinsically good." He says that "Gandhi's prescription is absurd" and assures his audience that

> if we went back to the spinning wheel four-fifths of the human race would die in about two years. We must go on. But we have somehow to see that we don't destroy our planet. . . . The problems are enormous, and we have just the next few years to meet them. (*Ibid.*:641)

Lynn White said that he hoped that the "relatively new notion of ecology" might enable man to regain some of the psychic unity with nature of which Christianity had deprived him, and he was seconded by the Reverend Walter Ong (*Ibid.*:647).

Much has happened in the world since 1962. The collapse of a modern, technological empire based on Marxian theory, a widespread disillusionment with the concept of development, the retreat of humanist critiques of rationality, and an extensive, industrial co-optation of the ecology movement: all these transformations demand that we resume the philosophical scrutiny of technology and examine how such changes have prompted new interpretations of the global predicament.

Ten years after the above-mentioned conference, at the 1972 United Nations conference in Stockholm, there was a widespread concern that the developed countries, far from carrying a "technological cross" for the underdeveloped ones, were in fact building their "development" on the impoverishment of the Third World. Twenty years further on, however, the 1992 WCED conference in Rio de Janeiro succeeded in establishing a widespread consensus that there was no inherent contradiction between economic growth and global sustainability, but rather the opposite. In the following chapter I will discuss the ambivalence about our global future that continues to shape contemporary public debate, as exemplified by media in the thoroughly "developed" country of Sweden.

2

Cornucopia or Zero-Sum Game: The Epistemology of Sustainability

On the very first days of the new millennium, newspapers in Sweden—as elsewhere—devoted some editorial space to assessing the state of the world. The leading daily *Dagens Nyheter* expressed puzzlement over a survey showing that a large percentage of Swedish youth were not particularly optimistic about the future. Why this worry about global ecology, the editor asked, now that the pessimistic prophecies of the Club of Rome could be dismissed once and for all? Yet, the previous day, in the same newspaper, an environmental journalist had observed that the state of the world environment is considerably worse than most people in the richer countries realize. The problem, he said, is that these people can choose to stay ignorant about the South's environment simply by switching television channels. Here were thus two very different messages on global ecology offered in the same newspaper.

Similarly contradictory were its assessments of global inequality. On New Year's Eve, an editorial proclaimed that the Marxist notion that the affluence of the rich is based on other people's impoverishment can be decisively dismissed. In the very same issue of *Dagens Nyheter*, however, an entry with the heading "Renaissance for Marx" reports that a new biography of Karl Marx is the season's best-seller in Britain. The next day, there is a two-page interview with the Marxist sociologist Manuel Castells, introduced as "the hottest intellectual in the world," who perceives the present as characterized by a process of unprecedented social polarization and warns that the conflict may soon become critical. How are we to understand these schizophrenic messages on global environment and development that surround us as we enter the third millennium?

Judging from mainstream public discourse, faith in technology and economic growth seems stronger than ever. The WCED conference in Rio de Janeiro in 1992—the climax of three decades of negotiations on global issues—solidified an official creed suggesting that growth is the general solution to environmental problems (WCED 1987). The key concept, of course, became "sustainable development." This creed is now often referred to as "ecological modernization" (Hajer 1995). Meanwhile, however, there remains a widespread countercurrent of skepticism, passive and invisible for the most part, but remarkably powerful when demonstrating strength enough to overturn the important World Trade Organization (WTO) meeting in Seattle on the eve of the old millennium. Many people must be asking themselves today if the critics in the 1970s were really so completely wrong about the conflict between growth and environment and if WCED's interpretation of global issues is really the only one possible. The 1970s saw a widespread concern that the economic growth of industrial sectors occurred at the expense of the Third World and the global environment. According to the WCED paradigm, however, growth is of benefit for both the global economy *and* global ecology. We may refer to the two paradigms as "zero-sum game" versus "cornucopia" theories of growth.

It might seem as if the choice between zero-sum game and cornucopia models should be a simple empirical question. What do the data say? It no longer seems feasible, however, to identify "simple empirical" questions in the social sciences. The global interconnections are too complex. The opposite camp generally seems to be able to turn each specific piece of information inside out by putting it in a different context and approaching it from a different perspective.

In a book the translated title of which would be *The True State of the World*, Danish statistician Björn Lomborg (1998) contradicts Worldwatch Institute, Greenpeace, and the World Wide Fund for Nature by suggesting that what have been perceived as global problems of inequality and environmental deterioration are mostly illusions. One by one, he dismisses all our worries about resource depletion, per capita food production, increasing gaps between rich and poor, deforestation, acidification, species extinction, chemical pollution, and global warming. The conclusion that not just some of but *all* these worries are illusory is indeed remarkable. It is obvious that both the compilation and the interpretation of statistics to a large extent boil down to whether we *wish* to see this or that pattern. This is not a simple question of manipulation, but of a fundamental human desire to see verified by data the patterns we imagine to exist in the world. But how do we choose these patterns or interpretations to begin with?

To the extent that we do *choose* our models, it is evident that our considerations are not concerned solely with the criterion of credibility. We like to think that our most fundamental criterion for "truth" is whether a specific interpretation of causal connections can explain the most aspects of our global predicament, but the widespread paradigm shift that has occurred since the 1970s instead suggests that a more crucial consideration is which interpretation *we can live with*. In the industrialized nations in the 1960s and early 1970s, there was an existential space, so to speak, for radical criticism. Especially among younger people, there was a widespread faith in the capacity of collective, social movements to transform fundamental structures in society. When faith in the future and collective change withered in the mid-1970s, a great many people in the North probably found the idea that their affluence was based on the impoverishment of the South and the global environment unbearable and thus impossible to accept. An important factor underlying this shift was the increasing mobility of globalized capital. Faced with the threat of unemployment, local populations everywhere grew more careful in their criticism of power (cf. Bauman 1998). To the extent that some of the indignation over environmental problems and global inequality persisted, it was generally transformed from revolutionary fervor to resignation. Globalization thus implied contradictory impulses that condemned both the embittered in the South and the conscience-stricken in the North to a predicament of perpetual cognitive dissonance. Through media they came into ever closer contact with global inequalities, while at the same time it seemed increasingly evident to them that there was virtually nothing they could do about them.

This may explain some of the market for the new genre of "green-bashing," counter-environmentalist books like Lomborg's. Many readers probably felt comfortable with Lomborg's wholesale denial of environmental concern. But there are more subtle ways of disarming indignation than simple denial. What ecological modernization has achieved is a neutralization of the formerly widespread intuition that industrial growth is at odds with global ecology. The environmental concern of young people is now being redirected into special educational establishments designed to promote the message that the adverse effects of economic growth can best be amended with more growth. The discursive shift since the 1970s has been geared to disengaging concerns about environment and development from the criticism of industrial capitalism as such. But the central question about capitalism should be the same now as it was in the days of Marx: Is the growth of capital of benefit to everybody, or only to a few at the expense of others? However much contemporary debate tries to sweep this question under the carpet, it will continue to reappear, albeit in new forms. Since Marx's time, it has been extended primarily in two directions. On one hand, questions of injustice and unequal exchange have transcended the local relation between worker and capitalist and been applied to the global exchange between industrial centers and their peripheries; on the other hand, there have been attempts to include global ecology in the same analysis.

Judging from much contemporary public discourse, asking questions about unequal exchange would seem obsolete or irrelevant for today's world. Concepts like "imperialism" and "exploitation" have well nigh vanished in the *sustainababble* following the Rio conference. Yet Marx's basic intuitions seem impossible to eradicate, however hard the neo-liberal discourse of the 1980s and 1990s has tried. Björn Hettne (1990) shows how thinking about global development has oscillated through the past century. In the mid-twentieth century, the dominant paradigm was based on a Eurocentric concept of modernization that, through the work of Walt Rostow and others, translated global inequality into a temporal axis that defined the future for the "underdeveloped" countries. "Development aid" was viewed as a global, Keynesian welfare policy that in the end would be of benefit both to the poor and to the rich. In the 1970s, the dependency theory of Gunder Frank, Samir Amin, and others gained prominence in connection with demands for a "New Economic World Order" and the success of the Organization of Petroleum Exporting Countries (OPEC) in bargaining oil prices. It argued for a kind of zero-sum perspective, in which the affluence of the "metropolis" or "core" was to be understood as based on the impoverishment of the "satellite" or "periphery." In the 1980s, however, a neo-liberal "counterrevolution" swept away both Keynesianism and dreams of a new world order. Milton Friedman, the World Bank, and the International Monetary Fund (IMF) redefined poverty as mismanagement and opened the world to an even tougher brand of capitalism. In 1990, Hettne believed that a new counterpoint may have been emerging in the form of "anti-modern" and marginalized groups such as environmental movements, feminists, peasants, indigenous peoples, and the unemployed. In the decade that followed, however, the most publicized criticism of unfettered capitalism came from multimillionaire George Soros, who expressed deep worries about the omnipotence of money and the growing vulnerability of globalized capitalism. Nevertheless, by the end of the decade, it seemed that Hettne's prediction was perhaps being substantiated by the globalized, motley alliance of anticapitalist demonstrators who captured the headlines in Seattle.

THE ZERO-SUM PERSPECTIVE:
FAILURES AND PROSPECTS

It is valid to ask why dependency theory has lost so much of its former influence in development studies. Was it because the development strategy it inspired—isolationism—proved such a failure? Hettne (1990) reminds us that the attempts of Chile and Nicaragua at "de-linking" were soon countered by measures from more powerful nations aiming at "destabilization" of these deviants. Meanwhile, the Newly Industrialized Countries of southern Asia were rewarded for their opportunism and willingness to submit to the conditions of global capital. Instead of dismissing dependency theory, we might refer to Wallerstein's (1974) observation that "development" is to advance from periphery to semiperiphery. Conversely, we can understand the current "underdevelopment" of major parts of the former Soviet Union as a process of peripheralization. Seen in this perspective, development and underdevelopment are the results of movements of capital in the world system, and the shifts of affluence in the 1980s and 1990s can be seen as a confirmation not of the recommendations of dependency theory but of its fundamental, zerosum model. There is evidently an inclination to dismiss the theoretical understanding of the dynamics of the world system—like the Marxist perspective as such—as soon as the practical implications someone has derived from it prove a failure. This is tragic, because it should be quite feasible to arrive at a correct analysis of a problem without (yet) having developed a good solution.

Brewer (1990) lists several major types of criticism that have been directed at dependency theory. According to Brewer, the argument that core areas have a "monopoly" and that they "exploit" their peripheries does not include explicit theoretical definitions of these concepts, but rather amounts to tautology. It is particularly problematic that the theory does not define a central concept like "surplus" or explain in which ways metropolis-satellite relations are to be seen as projected in geographical space. Brewer argues that nations are not really relevant entities in this context. He also criticizes dependency theory for not being able to explain why certain countries seem to be able to break free from their dependency.

The critics are right in that there is an element of tautology in dependency theory as long as the "core" or "metropolis" is defined as the place where accumulation occurs, while "accumulation" is defined as what occurs in the core. There are, however, more substantial specifications, such as the focus of the Prebisch-Singer theorem on the structural logic of exchange relations between industrial sectors and those sectors that deliver their raw materials. It is nevertheless true that the concept of "surplus"—

that which is transferred from periphery to core—is not defined in a clear manner. For more or less self-sufficient subsistence economies, Paul Baran (1957) offered a simple definition of "surplus" as the difference between what is produced and what is consumed, but for societies engaged in production for the market, it is necessary to refer to some measure other than money (market prices) to be able to argue that a particular exchange is exploitative. To solve this problem and produce a more rigorous argument, dependency theory could build on concepts from the natural sciences such as energy (see below).

Brewer is also right in that nations are not relevant units, simply because core-periphery relations cannot in any but the crudest manner be represented in terms of spatially demarcated areas. Gunder Frank (A. G. Frank 1966) instead argued that they were to be conceptualized as polarizing exchange relations at different levels of scale both within and between countries. These polarized flows can be traced even in local contexts such as the exchange between a hacienda owner and his workers. This geographical indeterminacy has been accentuated by the increasing globalization of capital flows, which make it all the more difficult to identify the "core" as a spatially distinct social unit or actor. There is no necessary congruity between the spaces where the appropriated resources are accumulated, where the capitalists live, and where they have their bank accounts.

Yet capital continues to generate obvious spatial patterns, as anyone can see on nightly satellite photos. Such images lend concrete, visual support, for instance, to statistics which say that the average American consumes 330 times more energy than the average Ethiopian. When new parts of the world system succeed in attracting capital—that is, when they "develop"—it shows clearly in the satellite images, as in the strong contrast between the dark northern and luminous southern half of the Korean peninsula. It must be of relevance to world system theory that the United States' share of world energy consumption is 25%, while 20% of the world's people do not have access to enough energy to successfully maintain their own body metabolism. This obviously also has an environmental dimension. The richest 20% of the world's population consume 86% of the aluminium, 81% of the paper, 80% of the iron, and 76% of the lumber (Brown 1995). Per capita carbon dioxide emissions in 1990 were around five tons in the United States but only 0.1 tons in India. (Remarkably, however, many people in the industrialized North continue to believe that it is their mission to educate people in the South on how to live and produce sustainably, as if the North was setting a good example, and as if environmental problems in the South were the result of ignorance rather than impoverishment.)

If rates of energy dissipation are an essential component in the inequitable dynamics of the world system, it must be a central theoretical challenge to integrate perspectives from the social and natural sciences to achieve a more complete understanding of capital accumulation. An explicit attempt to connect dependency theory and energy flows is Stephen Bunker's (1985) study of underdevelopment in the Amazon. He shows how the "extractive" economies of peripheral Amazonia are at a systematic disadvantage in their exchange with the "productive" economies of industrialized sectors. The flows of energy and materials from the former to the latter tend to reduce complexity and power in the hinterland while augmenting complexity and power in the core. Extractive economies generally can not count on a cumulative development of infrastructure as can the productive economies in the core, because economic activities in the former are dispersed and shifting according to the location of the extracted materials. As the stocks of natural resources become increasingly difficult to extract as they are depleted, an intensification of extraction will tend also to increase costs per unit of extracted resources, instead of yielding the economies of scale associated with intensification in the industrial core. Bunker's analysis suffers from his inclination to view energy as a measure of economic value (see next chapter), but in other respects his underlying intuition is valid. The luminous agglomerations of industrial infrastructure in the satellite photos are the result of uneven flows of energy and matter, and these processes of concentration are self-reinforcing, because the increasingly advantageous economies of scale in the center progressively improve its terms of trade and thus its capacity to appropriate the resources of the hinterland. Extractive economies are thus pressed to overexploit nature, while those parts of the landscape in industrial nations that have not been urbanized can instead be liberated from the imperative to yield a profit and rather become the object of conservation programs. Environmental quality is thus also an issue of inequitable global distribution. "Environmental justice" is merely an aspect of the more general problem of justice within the framework of world system theory.

THE CORNUCOPIA MODEL: IS GROWTH REALLY GOOD FOR THE ENVIRONMENT?

The preceding arguments to me seem logically coherent, credible, and persuasive. I am thus all the more curious about the alternative interpretation—what I refer to as the "cornucopia" model, that is, the currently hegemonic worldview that declares capital accumulation in the core completely innocent with regard to poverty and environmental problems in the South. An unusually accessible and instructive example of this worldview comes from Swedish economist Marian Radetzki (1990, 1992), whose essays address the overarching question of whether there is a positive or negative correlation between economic growth and environmental quality. He observes that the worst environmental destruction occurs in the poor rather than the richer countries and concludes from this that environmental quality improves as the economy grows and becomes "denser." The explanation, says Radetzki, is that the intensity of environmental damage decreases as per capita GNP increases. This intensity is defined as the quantity of "environmental resources" that are expended to generate one unit of GNP. Intensity of environmental wear is reduced because with growth there is a tendency for "material intensive" production to be replaced by the production of services. Meanwhile, there is an increase in the willingness of consumers to pay for a clean environment the more affluent they become, and environmental policies in wealthier nations encourage the development of new environmental technologies. Instead of intensifying the consumption of "environmental utilities," these nations can substitute services from "human and physical capital" for those of natural resources. For this reason, forests and other natural resources are *not* diminishing in the industrialized countries. Instead, much of the landscape is reverting to something approaching a "natural state." Growth and technological development make it possible to invest, for example, in aquaculture instead of depleting wild fish stocks, plantations instead of cutting down rain forests, and swimming pools instead of exploiting natural beaches. Radetzki concludes that it is thus possible to maintain continued economic growth, and that there is in fact an *unlimited* potential for "sustainable growth."

Radetzki's texts are useful reading because they summarize, in a nutshell, the logic of an economist's approach to the relation between growth and environment in a way that makes it very clear how the basic assumptions of the cornucopia model differ from those of the zero-sum game model. An essential difference is evidently Radetzki's assumption that an economic activity and its environmental consequences coincide geographically. If environmental quality is relatively high where growth is high (and vice versa), he concludes that growth reduces environmental damage, instead of (or perhaps without hesitating at?) the equally feasible interpretation that the environmental consequences of growth have been *shifted* to other parts of the world system. It is in fact unclear if Radetzki discusses the "environment" as a local or a global phenomenon. It seems unlikely that he would consider it a *solution* to environmental problems to have them shifted to someone else's backyard, but some of his arguments leave it an open matter. He writes, for instance, that growth makes it feasible to legislate so as to increase production costs for polluting industries, which has led to "a considerable shift of environmentally damaging activities from richer countries to poorer, where costly environmental policies are absent" (Radetzki 1990:38–39; my translation). "The environment," he continues, "is to a very large extent a concern of the wealthy." It is to be noted that this reasoning is offered in a context where he argues for growth as a solution to environmental problems. If we assume that Radetzki is *not* advocating a continued shifting of pollution to poorer countries, as some prominent economists actually have done (see chapter 4), we must draw the conclusion that his vision of the future is that all people in the world shall be "wealthy." This strikes me as impossibly naïve, considering that the gap between rich and poor continues to widen. Between 1947 and 1987, the ratio of per capita income between the richest and the poorest countries increased from 50:1 to 130:1 (N. A. Adams 1993).

Not only is the growth recipe in a global perspective politically naïve, but it also disregards the fundamental objection that processes of resource depletion and environmental destruction will increase with wealth, after all, even if they are shifted to other locations and thus vanish from sight. We have already mentioned emissions of carbon dioxide, which are 50 times higher for the average American than for the average citizen of India. Mathis Wackernagel and his colleagues have estimated that if all the people in the world were to reach the same standard of living as that in the richest countries, they would require three additional Earths (Wackernagel and Rees 1996; Wackernagel et al. 1997). Although the global access to "ecoproductive" land decreased from 5 to 1.7 hectares per capita between 1900 and 1990, the per capita "footprints" of the richer countries increased from 1 to between 4 and 6 hectares (*Ibid.*). To accumulate money is ultimately to be able to increase one's claims on other people's resources. It is evident that these claims cannot increase indefinitely, because the resources are not unlimited.

When Radetzki argues that there is a positive connection between economic growth and environmental quality, we must ask what this connection looks like. Does growth simply dissolve environmental problems as such (and not just locally), or does it shift them to poorer areas? Again and again we are inclined to interpose the crucial question: *"Where?"* Where is environmental quality improved? Where is it realistic to build artificial micro-environments (such as swimming pools) that reduce wear on the local environment, and where are the natural resources procured with which to build them? Where can the landscape revert to a "natural state," and from where are the resources appropriated that substitute for its former yields?

Two fundamental objections can be directed at Radetzki's argument, both of which concern the capacity of the market and monetary measures to conceal other dimensions of economic processes. When he claims that intensity of resource use decreases as per capita GNP increases, we may forget that whereas resource use is a physical reality, GNP is "only" a symbolic reality. GNP is ultimately a measure of the terms of trade (world market prices) that a country has been able to secure for its products and services in exchange for those of other countries. GNP is thus a measure that reflects a country's position in socially negotiated global exchange relations. Rather than say that intensity of resource use decreases per unit of GNP per capita, we can just as well say that the prices of a nation's products increase faster than its resource use. This could be understood as an expression of increasing margins of profit in industrial sectors as a consequence of increasingly advantageous terms of trade vis-à-vis the raw materials sectors. To conclude, from what Radetzki says about the relation between resource consumption and GNP, that growth is good for the environment would be tantamount to saying that it does not matter if environmental damage increases, as long as GNP increases *faster*. But the crucial question, of course, should be whether environmental damage increases in *absolute* terms.

The second objection can be directed at the claim that growth and technological development make it possible to substitute the services of "human and physical capital" for those of nature. The issue boils down to what we mean by "substitute." From a local perspective it might appear possible to "substitute" labor and capital for land; this approach became fundamental to industrial society from the very start. But to the (large) extent that these extra inputs of labor and technology are made possible by utilizing natural resources from another part of the world system (e.g., by importing food for the labor force or fossil fuels for the machines), it is questionable if it is valid to claim that labor and capital really can "substitute" for land. From a global and physical perspective it is to a very large extent an illusion that the stocks of natural resources can be increased with the help of more labor and capital. The faith in "substitution" shows the extent to which economic science has emerged as a local (originally British) perspective that really does not ask questions about the global management of resources beyond the territory of the individual nation.

As long as the primary knowledge interest of a science is to generate growth strategies for individual companies or nations, it is only natural that its fundamental assumptions should differ from those required of a science of global resource management. Only when the world is viewed as a finite and in certain respects closed system are we able to discover that what is locally perceived as a cornucopia may in fact be a component in a global zero-sum game. This discovery must be allowed to shake the very foundations of the two centuries-old assumptions of economics. We must finally ask ourselves whose knowledge interests our research is to serve: the individual corporation, the individual nation, or all of humanity?

To build an understanding of global interconnections between ecology and economy that serves the knowledge interests of global resource management and environmental justice, rather than national or corporate growth, we need to reconceptualize several aspects of development theory. Instead of visualizing nations as autonomous territories the environmental condition of which reflects, in a simple and immediate way, their own economic activities, we must learn to think of the world as a *system*, in which one country's environmental problems may be the flip side of another country's growth. Those of us who live in the privileged, affluent core would be amiss to use our green forests and fertile fields as evidence that worries about global ecology are unfounded, because the liberation and recovery of previously impoverished landscapes to a large extent has been made feasible by the import of resources from peripheral areas both within and between nations. The most difficult but perhaps also most important point is to learn to view technological development as an expression of capital accumulation, and thus ultimately of unequal relations of exchange with less "developed" sectors of world society. Growth and technological development in some parts of the world system are thus organically linked to underdevelopment and environmental deterioration in others. If we want to work for global environmental justice, we first need to develop a new theoretical understanding of technology as a redistribution of resources made invisible by the vocabulary and ideology of the market. This unequal exchange of resources can be made visible only by identifying, beneath the flows of monetary exchange value, measures of real resources such as energy, labor time, and hectares of productive land.

I am inclined to think that our preparedness to abandon the "cornucopia" model of growth and technology for a "zero-sum game" perspective will be connected to wider, existential concerns. It would probably be naïve to think that a majority of people in the wealthier nations, out of a pure quest for truth and solidarity with the distant and anonymous masses of the South, would choose an interpretation of reality that could be expected to subject them to deep and continuous ethical conflict. Perhaps their own affluence would first have to be seriously jeopardized in order for such a paradigm shift to occur at any substantial scale. Above all, we may assume that the zero-sum game perspective will be acceptable only if accompanied by a concrete and attractive vision of how the fundamental logic of capital accumulation can be transformed or domesticated in the name of global solidarity. For a large part of the twentieth century, the Marxist worldview offered *one* such vision that attracted a substantial part of humanity. Very few would today deny that that vision was incomplete and misguided in several respects. If we were to endeavor a new vision, it would probably have to proceed further in its questioning not only of the market, but of even more fundamental modern institutions such as money and technology. To domesticate the market, a long-term aim might be to split it horizontally so as to render local subsistence and global communication two parallel but distinct and incommensurable domains. Changes in that direction could amount to an immunization of local ecosystems and human life-worlds vis-à-vis the ravages of global capital flows. This would also serve to restrain the unevenly distributed growth of technological infrastructure, so that the machinery of the wealthier nations does not continue to expand at the expense of the very life-space of the global poor.

3

✷

The Thermodynamics of Imperialism: Toward an Ecological Theory of Unequal Exchange

President George H. W. Bush pioneered the current discourse on sustainability by claiming that "successful economic development and environmental protection go hand in hand; you cannot have one without the other" (quoted in Corson 1990:309). Whether serving to advocate restraint or increased economic and technological ambition, superficial environmental arguments can be used to underpin the present world order. Philosophers such as Naess (1973 [1989]) and Evernden (1985) have criticized the mainstream environmental movement for participating in a discourse on terms defined by the industrial establishment. Naess argues that the superficial environmentalist discussion that pervades the discourse on global development might function as yet another means of imperialist domination: the message that we are "all in the same boat (or spaceship)" is not true; there are at least two boats, and one of them is pulling the other toward catastrophe.

Emerging concepts of "political ecology" and "environmental justice" recognize that environmental problems are socially *distributed*. But the problem of how human societies distribute ecological risks should not be separated from the problem of how they distribute resources. The two problems are, so to speak, opposite sides of the same coin. Martinez-Alier and O'Connor (1996) have suggested a distinction between political economy, which studies "economic distribution conflicts," and political ecology, which "would study ecological distribution conflicts." Ultimately, however, such a dichotomy needs to be transcended, and ecology recognized as part and parcel of any attempt to understand political economy. It is only by looking at the ecological conditions of human economies that we can adequately conceptualize the mechanisms that generate inequalities in distribution. The focus of this chapter is on how an ecological perspective might provide us with an analytically more precise way of defining "unequal exchange."

UNEQUAL EXCHANGE: PROBLEMS OF CONCEPTUALIZATION

Unequal exchange has been a central concern of various strands of Marxist social theory, including early theories of imperialism, the dependency and world system perspectives of Frank (1967, 1978) and Wallerstein (1974, 1974–1989), and more orthodox Marxist arguments focused on "modes of production" and the international appropriation of labor value (for a review, see Bunker 1985:38–48). None of these approaches has been able to convince conventional economists that free market trade may entail such a thing as "unequal exchange." Considerations of monopoly aside, neoclassical economic ideology has dispelled all possible criteria for assessing a market transaction as unequal or unfair. Economists are generally simply not able to see how there could be a standard that would allow one to speak of some participant in market exchange as being undercompensated. This is indeed the conceptual predicament that conventional economics forces upon us.

Brewer (1990) observes that Marx viewed capitalism as a system that can exist by itself, without necessarily having to expand geographically. It was Rosa Luxemburg (1913 [1951]) who presented the thesis that a capitalist system cannot constitute its own market but is condemned to expansion, and thus in the long run to destroying its own conditions of existence. Some years earlier, in 1902, John A. Hobson had argued that monopoly conditions and capital accumulation reduced demand and encouraged export of capital, and that the incentive to protect foreign investments and markets generated "imperialism," defined as territorial expansion. From his exile during the First World War, V. I. Lenin in 1916 suggested that the best paid workers of the industrialized nations (the "labor aristocracy") could be perceived as implicated in the exploitation of poorer sections of the global working class. It was Lenin who coined the expression that imperialism was the "highest stage of capitalism."

Decades later, Paul Baran (1957) followed Luxemburg in arguing that capitalist economies must suffer from a chronic deficit in demand and concomitant "underconsumption," because the purchasing power of the workers is always bound to be less than the value of the produce that has to be sold in the market. This is the incentive toward capturing new, external markets in areas that, as a result, become structurally incapable of "development." This zero-sum perspective was particularly distinct in Gunder Frank's (1966, 1967) influential analysis of underdevelopment in Latin America as a result of its exchange with Europe and North America. Samir Amin (1974) showed how an unequal international division of labor can be founded in historical disparities in productivity and production costs, which have restricted the competitiveness of peripheral areas to the raw materials sector. To dependency theorists like Frank, it was evident that "underdevelopment" was not to be seen as a survival from an earlier stage—a question of lagging behind—but the result of economic relations of dependency between "metropoles" and "satellites" at various scales of geographical inclusiveness. Another important contribution from the dependency school is the so-called Prebisch-Singer theorem, according to which differences in the elasticity of demand between raw materials and industrial products has a tendency to undermine the bargaining position of the periphery and the market prices of raw materials vis-à-vis those of industrial products.

Inspired by dependency theory, Immanuel Wallerstein (1974, 1974–1989) elaborated *world system theory*, arguing that economic history could be understood in terms of uneven relations of exchange and power between core areas, semi-peripheries, and peripheries. Wallerstein connects to Luxemburg's ideas about the necessary exchange between capitalist and noncapitalist modes of production, and he explicitly suggests that the distribution of "surplus" in an economic system is a zero-sum game. Arghiri Emmanuel (1972) showed how wage disparities between different countries generate an "imperialism of trade" in the sense of an unequal exchange of hours of labor, because a low-wage country has to export more products in exchange for a given volume of imports from a high-wage country than it would have needed to if the wage level had been uniform.

Most of these contributions can be seen as offshoots of the basic Marxist tenet that the growth of capital involves a transfer of surplus from one category of people to another, even if the shift of perspective from the local factory to global trade relations generated considerable theoretical antagonism between the more and the less orthodox Marxists. The common denominator of this Marxist tradition, widely defined, is the observation that a relation of exchange, even when it has been entered voluntarily, can generate a systematic deterioration of one party's resources, independence, and development potential. Eric Wolf (1982) has shown how Europe's trade relations with the Americas, Africa, and Asia through several centuries implied precisely this for the majority of societies that were drawn into this exchange.

World system theories and more orthodox Marxist perspectives are vulnerable to criticism in opposite ways. The former are unable to provide adequate definitions of key notions such as "core/periphery," "exploitation," and "accumulation" as long as they do not relate to factors specified independently of the premises of the model itself. As noted in the previous chapter, there is an obvious risk of tautology when concepts of core/periphery relationships and accumulation are used reciprocally to define each other—that is, core as the locus of accumulation and accumulation as what goes on in the core. The more traditional Marxist model, on the other hand, does specify exploitation independently, by referring to the quantifiable appropriation of labor value, but is immediately contradicted by the poor empirical correspondence between the economic value of goods and the quantities of labor time invested in them (cf. Bunker 1985:44–45; R. N. Adams 1988:96–97). To extend this specification to the appropriation of "energy values" (Bunker 1985), though intuitively valid, remains conceptually misleading. This chapter will argue that energy transfers are indeed crucial to understanding unequal exchange, but that energy and values should not be confused.

An alternative approach would be to ground notions of underpayment and unequal exchange not in some (contestable) theory of value (whether based on bullion, land, labor, or energy), but in the proportion of a manufacturer's or manufacturing center's total finished product that is continuously returned to the suppliers of energy and raw materials in the context of various institutional arrangements. This proportion defines how much of the productive potential of energy and materials is permanently being transferred to the manufacturing center and likely to be accumulated in its own, expanding infrastructure. One way to assess the occurrence of unequal exchange may be to look at the direction of net flows of energy and materials (concrete, productive potential), but *without* falling into the trap of equating productive potential with economic value. On the contrary, as was suggested in chapter 1, it can be analytically demonstrated that unequal exchange emerges from a kind of inverse relationship between productive potential and value. Logically, in accordance with the Second Law of Thermodynamics (cf. Georgescu-Roegen 1971), the productive potential of a given set of resources *diminishes* as it is being converted into a product, that is, as its value or utility *increases*. Thus, it leads to confusion when Bunker (1985) argues that energy is a value and then goes on to say that "additional value is created when extracted materials are transformed by labor" (*Ibid*.:45). We cannot have it both ways. To pursue the implications of this paradox means building bridges between world system theory and the discourse on "ecological economics."

One of the most sophisticated statements of ecological economics to date is Martinez-Alier's (1987) book with that title. His point of departure seems to have been to find a meeting point between Marxism and ecology. In his research, he discovered that a Ukrainian *narodnik* by the name of Serhii Podolinsky (1850–1891) had tried to convince Marx and Engels to bring natural science into their theories on surplus value, but that they would not listen. More than a hundred years later, we are still struggling with the same problems of transdisciplinary communication. Although basically sympathetic to the world systems perspectives of Frank and Wallerstein, specifically mentioning Frank's (1959) work on the correlation between the growth of capital stocks and energy consumption in the United States and United Kingdom, and observing that dependency theory helped "prepare the terrain" for ecological critique, Martinez-Alier twice reproaches them for paying too little attention to ecology (Martinez-Alier 1987:15, 238).

Theories of labor value, like energy theories of value (e.g., Bunker 1985; Odum 1988; Costanza 1980), belong to a tradition of ideas that goes back to Aristotle's distinction between "real" economics (*oikonomia*), concerned with the management of concrete use values, on one hand, and *chrematistics*, or the art of making money, on the other (cf. Daly and Cobb 1989). The operation of human economies, however, can be understood only in terms of the *interfusion* of objective, material conditions and subjective, cultural constructions. The history of economic thought reflects a systematic incapacity to deal with this mutual interpenetration of the material and the social. Its two recurrent pitfalls are either (1) to attempt to specify objective criteria of value (such as labor or energy), or, inversely, (2) to more or less ignore, like the neoclassicists, the objective substratum of the human economy.

The recent discourse on ecological economics, although increasingly explicit about its aspiration to overcome such difficulties, still has to find a way of adequately handling the recursive (positive feedback) links between material conditions and cultural constructions. A recurrent problem is an inability to deal with cultural valuation, social institutions, and thermodynamic laws as analytically separate levels of reality. There is a concern with calculating "correct" prices and even establishing energy theories of value, endeavors that, it will be argued, represent a confusion of what Bertrand Russell called logical types. A meeting of world system theory and ecological economics, however, could be a very productive one, because each could contribute something that the other is missing.

World systems theorists generally have been as unconscious about thermodynamics as ecological economists have been naïve about imperialism.

The perspective of anthropology, finally, should provide an ideal setting for such a meeting. No other science has a tradition of handling the comparative, cross-cultural study of human economies, technologies, and ecologies. Nor has any other science proceeded as far in conceptualizing the recursive interfusion of cultural categories and material circumstances. One of the central ambitions of anthropology is to "defamiliarize" aspects of Western civilization by means of "cross-cultural juxtaposition" (Marcus and Fischer 1986:138). If we are ever to escape from the cultural categories that continue to govern our rapacious industrial economy, this may be a strategy that we shall have to pursue (cf. Sahlins 1976; Godelier 1986; Gudeman 1986).

"EMERGY" AND VALUE

Theories of value should be of a different logical type than valuation itself—that is, the assigning of values to things by market actors. They should be descriptive—that is, they should tell us why people value things the way they do. This is, in fact, what neoclassical economic theory does. Even if the argument is tautological ("people find things useful because of their utility"), it is logically coherent. Labor or energy theories of value, however, are not primarily descriptive but normative. They propose to establish the "real," objective value of goods and services. In effect, what they are doing is not telling us how people value things but how they *should* value them. In other words, they insert themselves on the same logical level as the phenomena they are to explain. This is what qualifies them as confusions of logical types. Valuation must be recognized as a subjective, cultural, and contextual phenomenon (cf. Sahlins 1976), not to be conflated with the material aspects of production. It is only by keeping these levels analytically separate that we can develop a scientific, non-normative theory of unequal exchange. Instead of trying to reduce economics to thermodynamics, we should show how the two are connected.

Probably the most famous theory of unequal exchange based on thermodynamics is that of Howard T. Odum (1988; Odum and Arding 1991). His point of departure is the concept of "emergy" (with an *m*), which originally was meant to stand for "embodied energy." Formally, it is similar to Marx's concept of labor value in that it denotes the amount of energy that has been invested in a product. Odum is an ecologist, and the idea of embodied energy ultimately derives from studies of ecological food chains. In other words, he uses a food chain metaphor to understand production processes. Top predators such as eagles, wolves, or humans represent the embodied energy of all the lower trophic levels all the way down to the plants.

The problem for Odum was that it was simply incorrect to speak of all the energy consumed as remaining, as it were, "embodied" in the top predators or, by extension, finished industrial products (cf. R. N. Adams 1988:96). Most of the energy, of course, would have been dissipated on the way. So in 1984, he decided to keep holding on to the concept of emergy, but to give it a new definition (Odum 1988:1139 n. 11). Henceforth, it would not stand for "embodied energy" but "energy memory." Eagles and electric toothbrushes would thus carry within themselves the memory, so to speak, of all the energy spent to produce them. But the concept is obviously a metaphysical one. Let us only mention two problematic implications. One is that two identical craft objects should have different emergy values depending on the efficiency of the craftsman. Another is that the emergy value of a junk car, having been subjected to years of maintenance, should be higher than that of a brand new one. If the early definition of emergy was downright mistaken, the latter is metaphysical. Emergy is not a property of the items exchanged. The notion that the dissipated energy is somehow still there in the object only confuses things.

Odum (1988:1136) has explicitly argued that emergy provides us with a theory of value. He and his associates have demonstrated correlations between the amounts of energy expended in production and the price of the product (cf. Costanza 1980). It remains unclear, however, whether an emergy theory of value proposes to be (1) descriptive, (2) normative, or (3) both? In other words, does it propose to explain how people actually do evaluate things (as reflected in prices) or how they *ought* to evaluate things? The emergy/price correlations suggest that it is descriptive, but Odum clearly also considers it normative. He undoubtedly feels that energy memory *should* be a measure of value. But if it is *both* descriptive *and* normative, it would seem to amount to nothing less than a way to legitimate, by and large, world market prices as they are. Industrial products, of course, have a higher emergy value than the fuels and raw materials from which they were produced.

On the other hand, Odum is very much concerned with exposing the unequal exchange of emergy between nations and regions. He suggests that there are differences in the emergy/dollar ratio in different parts of the world system, and he discusses trade between different countries in terms of their "emergy exchange ratio" (Odum and Arding 1991). Odum believes that the periphery is being underpaid for the emergy content of its natural resources because these are free gifts of nature and thus not properly evaluated on the market. In this part of his argument, the emergy theory of value is presented as normative, but *not* as descriptive.

Global trade policies, he concludes, should be directed at achieving "emergy equity." From a world systems perspective, however, this concept suggests no less of an oxymoron than does "sustainable development." If a major rationale of international trade is precisely the transfer of energy and other resources from peripheries to centers of accumulation, the commendable principle of "emergy equity" would amount to nothing less than to deprive world trade of its *raison d'être*.

"EXERGY," PRICES, AND THE SOCIAL FOUNDATIONS OF TECHNOLOGY

It has been suggested that "emergy" is a metaphysical concept. There is, however, another concept, building on thermodynamics, that is useful for our purposes because it does say something about the properties of the items exchanged. This is the concept of "exergy" (with an x), which is the *quality* of energy in a particular substance or context, or, in other words, that part of the energy which is available for mechanical work (cf. Wall 1986; Kåberger 1991; Månsson and McGlade 1993). Strictly speaking, there is no consumption of energy anywhere, only of its quality and accessibility (that is, exergy). Exergy is closely related to the concept of negative entropy. A nonmathematical interpretation might describe it as the potential for work that is inherent in any physically manifest information, order, structure, or contrast. When such material structures or contrasts are neutralized, for example in combustion, some of the energy that once generated them can be unleashed as work.

The concept of exergy can give us a completely different perspective on the relationship between energy and trade than can Odum's concept of emergy. Briefly, if emergy and price are positively correlated, exergy and price are not. In fact, there is a specific sense in which they are *negatively* correlated: Up to the point where the final product is sold, there is a negative correlation between price and the proportion of the original exergy that is left in a set of processed substances. The more of the original exergy that has been dissipated, the higher the price. We shall return to this matter shortly.

Another perspective that needs to be introduced at this point is Ilya Prigogine's concept of "dissipative structures" (Prigogine and Stengers 1984; cf. also R. N. Adams 1982, 1988). Dissipative structures are systems that stay far from thermodynamic equilibrium by continually drawing in exergy (negative entropy) from the outside and exporting the entropy, or disorder, they produce in the process. Erwin Schrödinger (1944 [1967]:79) suggested that "the device by which an organism maintains itself stationary at a fairly high level of orderliness (= fairly low level of entropy) really consists in continually sucking orderliness from its environment." This interpretation can be extended from biological to social systems (cf. R. N. Adams 1982, 1988). Societies also maintain their internal structure by drawing order from their environments. For hunter-gatherers this is generally a matter of exploiting other species in a fairly local ecological context. For cities or world system centers, however, the maintenance of structure relies on exchange with other, peripheral social sectors more directly involved in the extraction of exergy from nature. This social dimension of exergy appropriation has proven very difficult to conceptualize in terms that can be integrated with the perspectives of thermodynamics. Bunker (1985:33) observes, for instance, that Adams (1982) has "not fully realized the sociological implications of his essentially physical formulation."

The question we must address is this: If organisms draw order into their systems by eating, and export disorder by discharging waste materials, heat, and so forth, how do cities go about doing it? How do world system centers do it? The answer must be all around us, like water to fish. It is just a matter of getting our eyes on it and permitting ourselves the naïveté of a first encounter. The reader may have anticipated that *market prices* are the specific mechanism by which world system centers extract exergy from, and export entropy to, their peripheries. It would be impossible to understand accumulation, "development," or modern technology itself without referring to the way in which exchange values relate to thermodynamics, that is, the way in which market institutions organize the net transfer of energy and materials to world system centers.

For a century and a half, ecologists and economists have been trapped on opposite sides of a dualistic cosmology. Ecologists have looked for objective foundations for subjective, cultural phenomena, as when the Technocrats of the 1930s and later H. T. Odum offered their different versions of an energy theory of value. Economists, on the other hand, continue to assume that objective phenomena should be reckoned with in terms of subjectively founded criteria such as "willingness to pay." In the former case, there is an attempt by natural science to subsume the economy by suggesting that prices should reflect energy flows. In the latter case, there is an attempt by economics to subsume nature by suggesting that ecology can be evaluated in terms of prices. Herman Daly (1992:211–223) calls these two perspectives "ecological reductionism" versus "economic imperialism." Neither position, it seems, properly accounts for the way in which ecology and economics—nature and society—are actually interfused.

The conundrum for ecological economics boils down to two seemingly contradictory and irreconcilable observations. The first is that prices are cultural constructions that do not measure or reflect real, material flows.

This observation was emphasized by pioneers such as Patrick Geddes (1854–1932), Alfred Lotka (1880–1949), and Frederick Soddy (1877–1956), and it continues to be a point of departure for ecological economics (Martinez-Alier 1987:13, 90–91, 128–143). The second, which should have become evident during the so-called oil crises of the 1970s, is that prices are real determinants of local, material conditions for production. In the first sense, prices are not coupled to real, material conditions; in the second sense, they are. They thus seem to be unreal and real at the same time.

Another way of approaching this conundrum is by juxtaposing certain conclusions of ecological economics into a logical syllogism, the pursuit or spelling out of which seems to have been effectively blocked by the Cartesian matrix. On one hand, it has long been observed that the feasibility of technology ("productivity" or "productive forces") is a matter of energy availability (Martinez-Alier 1987:226–227). On the other hand, it is equally evident that energy availability is a matter of prices (*Ibid.*:4, 187, 210). To complete the syllogism, then, we would have to conclude that *the feasibility of technology is a matter of prices*. Systematic ratios of exchange and energy appropriation are at the very foundation of our industrial infrastructure. Unequal exchange in the world system is what reproduces machines, and machines are what reproduce unequal exchange. But does this agree with our everyday conception of technology as an application of inventive genius to natural resources? In some important sense it seems as if we have not yet grasped what technology really *is*. Not even the Marxist understanding of "capital" or "productive forces" seems to have pursued the syllogism to its distinctly post-Cartesian conclusion.

CAPITAL ACCUMULATION AND THE APPROPRIATION OF ENERGY

Technology has always represented a junction of the subjective and the objective (the mental and the material), but capital refers to those specific kinds of technologies that are dependent not only on human knowledge but also on human *evaluations* regarding the social exchange of labor time and other energy resources. In other words, capital represents the interfusion of technology and economics. The recursive relationship between technology and economy is well exemplified by modern transport technology (railways, steamboats, etc.), which neutralized the ancient distinction between distantly traded luxuries and locally traded bulk goods. In suddenly rendering long-distance transport of bulk goods rational, nineteenth century technology thus also reinforced the accumulative process of which it itself was a manifestation.

All infrastructure founded on an asymmetric exchange of energy between different social categories represents an *appropriation* of productive potential (cf. Borgström 1965; Rees and Wackernagel 1994). Our intuitive, everyday understanding of modern technology, however, is generally not that it is inherently exploitative. We are aware that it consumes energy (or exergy, to be precise), but what seems to escape us is the social logic by which it inexorably *provides itself* with ever increasing amounts of this energy. Yet this is crucial to an understanding of the very nature of modern technology. Industrial technology does not simply represent the application of inventive genius to nature but is equally dependent on a continuous and accelerating social transfer of energy organized by the very logic of market exchange.

It may seem trivial to point out that New York and Tokyo are net importers of energy. Yet we rarely reflect on why this must be the case. From a purely thermodynamic perspective, cities "must" be net importers of energy because, like all other dissipative structures (such as biomass), their techno-industrial infrastructures require continuous inputs of energy in order to maintain their structure. But this explanation is only one side of the story: a retrospective account in which the presence of urban technomass is taken as a self-evident point of departure. From another perspective, we can turn the question around and observe that the import of energy to industrial sectors is *an inexorable consequence of market exchange*. If industrial processes necessarily entail a degradation of energy (Georgescu-Roegen 1971), the sum of products exported from an industrial center must contain less exergy than the sum of its imports. But in order to stay in business, of course, every industrialist will have to be paid more money for his products than he spends on fuels and raw materials. At an aggregated level, then, this means that the more resources that have been dissipated by industry today, the more new resources it will be able to purchase tomorrow.

If we consider, longitudinally along the production process, any given set of fuels and raw materials destined to be transformed into a given product plus waste, its content of available energy will be inversely related to its price—that is, the more of its original energy that has been dissipated, the higher its price. The significance of this correlation is that it defines the logic of an expanding cycle of past, present, and future exchanges. We can completely disregard the subjective "utility" of the products, which is more or less arbitrary and ephemeral anyway—arbitrary because it is culturally defined (cf. Sahlins 1976), and ephemeral because it diminishes rapidly with use—and observe that if a finished product is priced higher than the resources required to produce it, this means that "production" (i.e., the dissipation of resources) will continuously be rewarded with even more resources to dissipate.

In the past few centuries, this logic has given the industrial sectors ac-

cess to accelerating quantities of energy of various kinds. So blinded are
we by the miraculous "discoveries" and "achievements" of technology
that we generally fail to appreciate the extent to which the development
of new technologies in itself is a manifestation of this increasingly intensive, social appropriation of energy. It has become everyday knowledge
that a minority of the world's population consumes an increasing proportion of its energy resources, but because technology and economy tend to
be conceived as separate domains, this unequal distribution of resources
is attributed to the "requirements" of industrial technology (i.e., an advanced level of "development") rather than to the accumulative tendencies inherent in market exchange, and *which made industrial technology possible to begin with.*

One way to achieve an illuminating, distanced view of modern, techno-
industrial growth may be to compare it with other modes of accumulation in pre-modern cultures. This complies with the method that Marcus
and Fischer (1986:138) refer to as "defamiliarization by cross-cultural juxtaposition." Such a comparison will need to consider three factors that
enter into any process of accumulation: (1) the social institutions that regulate exchange, (2) the symbolic systems that ultimately define exchange
values and exchange rates, and (3) the thermodynamic and other physical
circumstances that allow us to discern the direction of net flows of energy
and materials.

To support themselves, notes Norman Yoffee (1988b), centers of civilization must be able to *disembed* from their peripheral sectors those goods
and services that they require for their metabolism. A pervasive aspect of
such appropriation is that it is *represented as a reciprocal exchange* (Godelier
1986). The Inca emperor, for instance, engaged local populations to work
in his maize fields by offering them *chicha* (maize beer) and mimicking
traditional labor exchange. We can assess the exploitative nature of such
arrangements by observing that the *chicha* with which he appeased his
laborers could only have represented a fraction of the harvest that he
gained from their labor. It is from the same perspective that we must view
modern market exchange. Increasingly with modern technology, however, the productive input that is being underpaid is resources rather than
labor. We can observe that the resources imported to industrial centers
are transformed into quantities of products vastly greater than the fraction that is returned to their peripheries. We must ask by what ideological
means this unequal exchange is represented as reciprocal exchange. The
answer, as we have seen, is the very notion of "market price."

The concept of capital conjures two images, one relating to abstract
wealth, or purchasing power, the other to a technological infrastructure
of some sort. *Because* capital is both symbolic and material in constitution,
economists and ecologists are equally handicapped in their struggle to

account for it. In a very general, cross-cultural, world-historical sense, capital accumulation is a recursive (positive feedback) relationship between technological infrastructure and the symbolic capacity to make claims on other people's resources. Such a general understanding of capital accumulation would be as applicable to agricultural terraces in ancient Peru as to the textile factories of eighteenth-century England. In both cases, *the infrastructure is used to produce an output that is culturally transformed into more infrastructure.* The important thing is not whether this transformation is conducted by means of maize beer parties hosted by the Inca emperor or by the sale of British textiles on the world market. The important thing is that, in both cases, the material operation of a technological system presupposes specific rates of exchange that ultimately rest on human evaluations and that guarantee a minimum net transfer of energy from one social sector to another. Whether this energy is in the form of labor, food, fodder, draft animals, or fuels is also secondary to the essential logic of unequal exchange underlying capital accumulation itself.

The notion of a reasonable market price conceals the fact that what is being exchanged are intact resources for products representing resources already spent. This argument is not to be confused with an energy theory of value. It would be nonsensical to offer an "exergy theory of value" because it would systematically contradict the valuations that people actually make. Most attempts at achieving a dialogue between ecology and economics are deeply entrenched in the ambition to envisage principles for ecologically correct pricing that will guarantee long-term sustainability, and thus ultimately in the faith that such principles can be devised. But to pursue the logical implications of such a policy must lead to the discovery that it runs counter to those structural imperatives on which the very viability of industrialism is founded. The industrial sectors of world society subsist precisely on that discrepancy between the material and the symbolic that the more perspicacious versions of ecological economics are in the process of exposing. It is no coincidence that the emergence of modern industrialism, for which the discrepancy between price and productive potential is so crucial, was accompanied by an ideology (neoclassical economics) that rendered this very discrepancy invisible.

Because valuation is an altogether cultural phenomenon, a discussion of the objective aspects of industrial resource management that does not examine the assumption that finished products have a higher value than the raw materials for which they are exchanged remains imprisoned by the very cosmology that it should try to account for. A thorough analysis must struggle to distance itself from the cultural categories through which the system operates. As "prices" are socially negotiated exchange relationships between human beings, it is useless to search for their correlates in the material world. Only when we stop looking for a real measure of value, which should correlate with price, and recognize the impossibility of such a congruity, can we appreciate the profundity of the problem and perhaps begin to envisage ways of transcending it.

If human evaluation is viewed, as it were, from the outside, as a component in socio-ecological systems, we can achieve a clearer grasp of the way in which economic institutions allow human subjectivity to impinge on objective processes. Then we might also begin to discern how the very framework of human transactions will have to be modified so as not to permit this impingement to ruin the conditions for human survival. This is not the place for visions of remedies, but in a very general sense the core of the problem is perhaps to find other ways of compensating manufacturers for the value they have added to the raw materials than to give them access to increasing volumes of the same materials, which tends to generate an accelerating destruction of resources. In a society where everything is not interchangeable (i.e., a society without general-purpose money), a manufacturer conceivably could be compensated in other spheres of exchange than that in which his raw materials are conveyed, an arrangement that might curb the incentive to accelerate production.

The ideology of prices and money fetishism continues to confuse us in many ways, not least in the contemporary debate on ecology and sustainable development. In the Brundtland Report, even the adverse effects of economic growth are marshaled to reinforce our faith in it. But in representing exchange relations, money cannot repair damages to the biosphere, only redistribute them in the world system. Ecological issues and distributional issues are truly inseparable.

4

Ecosystems, World Systems, and Environmental Justice

The environmental justice movement is an indication that we are beginning to appreciate the extent to which environmental problems are also problems of social *distribution*. It is elementary market logic, for instance, that causes the location of garbage dumps in the United States to be systematically oriented toward the poorest parts of the country. On December 12, 1991, World Bank chief economist Lawrence Summers was candid enough in an internal memorandum to advocate the same pattern on a global scale. Using impeccable economic arguments, he suggested that the World Bank should be encouraging a migration of "dirty" industries to less developed countries. His candidness was disturbing to everybody, yet he was only accounting for a reality that is already here.

PREAMBLE: POSTMODERN SOCIAL
SCIENCE AND THE CONCEPT OF JUSTICE

How can we relate to this reality? How can we argue for *environmental justice*? In *Justice, Nature and the Geography of Difference* (1996), David Harvey discusses the dilemmas faced by social scientists in the 1990s who wish to employ the concept of "justice." Postmodern social science, he observes, has entailed a celebration of *differences*. Researchers have focused on local narratives and specific interests. Instead of elucidating the

49

structures through which women of color in the United States tend to be allotted the poorest working conditions, for instance, they have devoted themselves to documenting these workers' *life-worlds*, not so much in order to criticize capitalism as to convey a sense of the diversity of identities. When Harvey himself became engaged in an Oxford car factory threatened with shutdown, he discovered that the struggle of the car workers' union was more geared to safeguarding traditional identities than to long-run improvements in working conditions. Postmodern social research, he seems to argue, joins the labor unions in reproducing class differences. A postmodern approach will not accept any hierarchical grading of life-worlds, which means that neither can it endorse any abstract definition of justice, because such a definition would imply a privileged perspective, a *grand narrative*. In this way, the denial of discursive privileges can contribute to the reproduction of economic and environmental privileges. Harvey talks about the postmodern death of justice. There is no doubt that, for a great many social scientists, the adoption of postmodern approaches has entailed a kind of moral-political paralysis.

Who are the targets of Harvey's criticism? Hardly politicians or that majority of their constituents who continue to believe in a rational social project guided by *some version* of justice. The criticism is aimed at those mainstream social scientists who in the 1980s and 1990s were overcome by human diversity and saw their engagement and ideals dissolve into a blasé rhetoric about cultural "constructions" of reality. Once it is established that people in different cultures, of different sex, or belonging to separate social classes literally *live in different worlds*, even the most benevolent attempts to apply universalizing perspectives are undermined. Every political program risks being perceived as biased toward some special interest group, and every description of reality is seen as a political act. To the postmodern skeptics, there is no longer any credible claim to speak for the common good. The problem is not that the postmodern approach is politically or morally unconscious, but that its intense reflexivity concerning the political dimensions of knowledge has led to political paralysis. Harvey seems to forget that leading postmodernists such as Jean Baudrillard have a Marxist past. It is consciousness of the "constructed" nature of all knowledge—and uncertainty about the responsibility that this implies—that is so paralyzing. Yet it is just as reasonable, in the long run, to expect this reflexivity to make researchers more morally focused (cf. chapter 8).

Harvey introduces his book with an anecdote from a conference on globalization in an American hotel, where he is so intrigued by the participants in a conference next door—a group of Evangelical Pentecostal preachers and their families—that he attends one of their sessions. He listens with amazement as they talk about their "foundational beliefs" and amuses himself by imagining what kinds of responses such expressions would elicit among the participants in his own conference across the hall: postmodernists whose only "foundational belief" is a deep skepticism toward all foundational beliefs and toward the "dinosaurs" who espouse them. Is Harvey a "dinosaur" for explicitly arguing that justice is a moral truth? Can concepts of "injustice" always be reduced to *local* values? Harvey's answer seems to be no. But if he is advocating some kind of universalism, it appears to be founded more on morals than on Marxist social theory.

After a critical review of the whole spectrum of environmental movements, Harvey reminds us that ecological arguments are always sociopolitical, and vice versa. Conditions of ecological scarcity are socially produced. Referring to Raymond Williams, he notes that economic theories—whether Marxist or bourgeois—tend to celebrate triumph over natural constraints whenever times are good, only to revert to Malthusian arguments in times of economic decline. Harvey concludes that the challenge is "to find a language to make radical ecology truly radical" (Harvey 1996:175). Perhaps he means that, ultimately, the only points of reference that can have some measure of permanence are our *values* (our "foundational beliefs"). This would be a perfectly legitimate standpoint. "Facts" and "theories" are generally negotiable, but explicitly affirmed values are not susceptible to deconstruction. At this point, Harvey could have referred to moral philosophers such as Emmanuel Lévinas, Hans Jonas, and Zygmunt Bauman. Attempts to legitimize political programs exclusively by reference to "objective" science are no longer credible (cf. Bauman 1993). There is finally nothing more credible than personal morals and the affirmation of deeply felt values.

The British geographic journal *Antipode* devoted a special issue (January 1998) to seven long reviews of Harvey's book. Several of the reviewers imply that his wish to resurrect a universalizing theory of justice is regressive. But it is precisely in its ambition to *transcend* the postmodern impasse that the book is of such great value. Harvey is not a relic of the 1970s stubbornly isolating himself from more recent, discursive currents. He is very well acquainted with phenomenological and constructivist objections to modernist science and politics. It is with sensitivity and sympathy, for instance, that he reads Raymond Williams's literary struggles with "the politics of abstraction." Harvey's ambition is to bridge the rifts between particularism and universalism, phenomenology and historical materialism, constructivism and objectivism. A fundamental point is that it is the same socio-ecological and political-economic structures that generate both social differences *and* the various understandings and experiences of them (including different concepts of justice.) New technologies of communication compress time and space and admit the radically *differ-*

ent into our living rooms. Ultimately, it is the objective flows of capital that create the "spatio-temporalities" within which human beings construct their experiences of place. The postmodern condition is itself a product of a disorienting "time-space compression" originating in the struggle of capital to increase velocities and reduce distances. It is these fetishized, historical-geographical processes and relations that Harvey wants to illuminate. Drawing on Nancy Munn's (1986) study of shell money in Melanesia, which like his own research seeks the very link between phenomenology and political economy, Harvey discusses the role of money in generating various kinds of spatio-temporal constructions. How do flows of money and commodities intervene in our experience *and* in ecosystems, and at which scales (place, bioregion, nation, world) is it possible to create moral communities? Along with Williams, Harvey believes that the various particular interests, adequately connected, can converge in a general interest. An example is the movement for environmental justice, which in the United States has largely succeeded in shifting the debate from NIMBYism ("not-in-my-backyard") to "not-in-anyone's-backyard."

Harvey explicitly rejects positivism and simple empiricism but is equally critical of incommunicable particularism. He refuses to accept the kind of phenomenology (e.g., Heidegger's) that ignores moral responsibilities beyond one's own place. In a globalized capitalism that is constantly forced to reduce distances, a crucial question must be our moral reach. How far does our consciousness extend? How far our solidarity? Does it include the people who "put breakfast on our table"? A chapter is devoted to the 1991 fire in a chicken-processing plant in Hamlet, North Carolina, in which twenty-five workers died and fifty-six were seriously injured. Harvey notes that the new, "special issue" social movements might have observed that eighteen of the twenty-five dead were women, or that twelve of them were people of color, while everyone continues to be conspicuously silent about the class dimension of the catastrophe. The fragmented, postmodern *resistance* denies itself the sort of "normative armament" (and the structural understandings) that are required for a successful struggle.

Harvey's argument leads in two apparently contradictory directions. On one hand, he clearly suggests that we have to abstract and generalize in order to understand what it is that unites various environmental justice movements around the globe. On the other hand, we must maintain our involvement in specific places and our personal roles as moral subjects in time and space. We must, in other words, both immerse ourselves in our life-worlds *and* see them from the outside. To avoid excessive emphasis on one or the other—that is, to avoid becoming an alienated, placeless theoretician or a selfish, local NIMBY—this would require developing our capacity to stand with one foot in the local and the other in the global. It is not a coincidence that the postmodern paralysis is a condition that mainly afflicts academics, for it is *at a distance* that human meanings assume the appearance of "constructions."

Justice, Nature and the Geography of Difference (Harvey 1996) accommodates almost everything that is relevant to the problem of environmental justice. Throughout its 468 pages runs the polarization between the particular and the universal in economics, politics, and science. The challenge for environmental justice movements, says Harvey, is to find ways of being as flexible—in theory and in political practice—as globalized capital. It is obvious that the "socialism" he espouses cannot emerge unmodified on the far side of postmodernism. In its theory it must learn to acknowledge the difficult relation between experience and language, lifeworld and system, the local and the abstract (cf. chapter 12). As we shall see in the remainder of this chapter, it must also learn to embrace environmental issues, both in its theory of exploitation and in its concept of social justice. I would add that it must develop an entirely new theoretical understanding of *technology*. Like other Marxists, Harvey can criticize capital accumulation without ever questioning the *machine*, its material form. Yet it is precisely through technology that money remolds the "spatio-temporalities" to which he refers. Time-space compression relies on global processes of *time-space appropriation*. A "truly radical" (Harvey 1996:175) theory of global environmental justice would recognize modern technology as a zero-sum game involving the spatial and temporal resources at human disposal worldwide. It would quite simply see the machine as an institution for redistributing time and space.

ECOSYSTEMS AND WORLD SYSTEMS IN HISTORICAL PERSPECTIVE

With exception for the anecdote about Lawrence Summers's infamous memorandum, Harvey's discussion of environmental justice is unduly focused on internal injustices in the modern United States. In a global perspective, the distributional aspects of environmental problems become even more apparent. It is somewhat peculiar that such a voluminous book concerned with structural injustices in the space of global society should be completely silent on world system theory (e.g., Frank 1978; Wallerstein 1974–1989). To the extent that we need a science of global injustice, world system theory is an essential point of departure. How has the distribution of natural resources afforded possibilities for technological intensification, urbanization, and capital accumulation in specific sectors of the world system? How is "development" in certain regions connected to environmental problems and ecological deterioration in others? *Whose* land-scapes and ecosystems are afflicted? Most generally, which are the forces in human society, economy, and culture that produce the accelerating bi-ospheric transformations that we are witnessing as we enter the third mil-lennium? The vast spatial scale addressed, I would add, requires a befitt-ing time scale. To achieve an appropriate perspective on global phenomena, we need a historical approach with a minimal time depth of several centuries.

Two bodies of data would need to be brought together if we are to get a fuller picture of the last few centuries of global environmental change. On one hand is the tangible evidence from paleobotany, geology, and other natural sciences of long-term changes in vegetation, soil quality, and other parameters. On the other hand is the record of economic his-tory, plotting the expansion and decline of centers of accumulation founded on various regimes of production and trade. Both types of data are easily and regularly represented in the form of *maps*. It would be most useful if maps and syntheses could be developed that highlighted the very *connections* between economic history and changes in land cover.

Three landmark books have prepared the ground for this discourse. The most recent of them is the monumental volume *The Earth As Trans-formed by Human Action*, edited by B. L. Turner II et al. (1990). The editors of this exceedingly valuable work recognize only two precursors in the genre of "long-term, global stocktaking" (*Ibid.*:3): George Perkins Marsh's *Man and Nature: The Earth As Modified by Human Action* (1864 [1965]) and the two volumes of *Man's Role in Changing the Face of the Earth*, edited by William L. Thomas, Jr. (1956). Together, these three books provide a trea-sure-house of information and insight. The primary challenge for re-search on the so-called human dimensions of global environmental change is not the continued, detailed monitoring of our species's disman-tling of its own life-support systems, but the bringing together of infor-mation and insights from different disciplines. Libraries are filled with different genres of empirical case studies, each couched in its own notions of relevance. What we now require more than anything else is synthesis. The field of environmental history has produced much of relevance for this kind of work (e.g., Cronon 1983, 1991; Crosby 1986; Worster 1988; Merchant 1989; Ponting 1991; Hughes 1994), but rarely with a theoretical concern for the political and distributional aspects of environmental dete-rioration reflected in concepts such as "accumulation" and "unequal ex-change." Studies in environmental history usually are good reading but generally suffer from lack of theoretical and political acumen.

World-systemic processes of capital accumulation are inextricably in-termeshed with ecology. Not only do they have obvious repercussions on landscapes and ecosystems (e.g., erosion, deforestation), but they are also fundamentally *dependent* on ecological assets such as topsoil, forests, or minerals. The analytical disjunction of ecology and economics is a persistent feature of modern science. The minority of researchers who have seriously tried to integrate them in a common theoretical framework (cf. Martinez-Alier 1987) have run into major conceptual difficulties. In what follows I will address some additional, analytical issues raised in an attempt to ground the notion of *capital accumulation* in the physical realities of ecology and thermodynamics. Making such connections clearer would be an important corrective to the illusion of a "disembodied" economy that seems to underlie mainstream economic thought. A "greening" of world system theory could thus serve as an empirical complement to the emerging field of ecological economics. It would also provide a deeper understanding of the complex relationship between issues of ecological sustainability, on one hand, and issues relating to the global distribution of resources, on the other. Although the connection between these two threats to human survival have been at the center of attention since the WCED conference in Rio de Janeiro in 1992, its fundamental logic continues to escape us as we reiterate the conventional rhetoric on "sustainable development."

In previous chapters, I have argued that the capacity of technological systems and other social institutions to *shift resource extraction to less empowered social categories* renders ecological and distributional issues inseparable. To restrict attention to either type of issues is to miss the complete picture. Ecological conditions are implicated in all processes of accumulation, and such processes of accumulation in turn tend to transform ecosystems. It would be impossible to understand the global polarization of rich and poor without reference to ecological factors (such as net energy transfer; cf. Bunker 1985), just as it would be impossible to understand the expansion of unsustainable technological systems without reference to unequal global exchange. Yet the hegemonic doctrines of economics remain impervious to *both* these issues—the *material* and the *moral* correlates of capital flows—the first by ignoring the laws of physics (Georgescu-Roegen 1971), the second by assuming, as an implicit axiom, that (noncoerced) market prices by definition are just and fair. It is no coincidence that these two seemingly unrelated aspects have been repressed by mainstream economics, for it is only by closing our eyes to the material dimensions of exchange that we can circumambulate its moral aspects, and only in opening them that a moral perspective becomes possible.

Challenging these dominant doctrines, I would advocate an ecologized version of dependency theory that recognizes the world market and modern technology as more of a zero-sum game than a cornucopia. What we have long perceived as "development" is basically a manifestation of capital accumulation, and capital accumulation has always been an uneven and inequitable process, generating an increasing polarization between "developed" centers and "underdeveloped" peripheries. Against this background, the faith of the Brundtland report in global economic growth as a road to equity and sustainability is not very persuasive. We need only recall Wackernagel et al.'s (1997) observation that global equity along Western standards of living would require three additional Earths.

How do we conceptualize the interface between ecosystems and world systems? It is my conviction that all the major issues of global survival (environmental destruction, resource depletion, world poverty, armament) ultimately can be traced to capital accumulation. The concept of "capital," however, continues to elude stringent analysis. To many authors (Marx included) it has an aspect that leads us to think of a material infrastructure of some kind. On the other hand, it suggests abstract wealth, or purchasing power. This is the dimension of capital emphasized, for instance, by Max Weber. It is also the perspective that has achieved hegemony both in standard economics and in world system theory (cf. Wallerstein 1974–1989; Frank 1978), suggesting a disembodied, immaterial force moving about the planet in pursuit of rewarding investment opportunities. In advocating a revival of Aristotle's distinction between *oikonomia* and "chrematistics" (Martinez-Alier 1987; Daly and Cobb 1989), the proponents of ecological economics in a sense join forces with Marx in trying to show how the symbolic and the material interact. As we saw in the previous chapter, however, there are many analytical obstacles on the way.

The absence of a common definition of capital has made it difficult for historians to date the origins of "capitalism." The orthodox, Marxist definition (involving industrial machinery and the commoditization of labor) would date capitalism no earlier than eighteenth-century England (cf. Wolf 1982). If the focus is shifted from industrial to merchant capital, and to production for the world market as the basic criterion, capitalism recedes backward in history. Wallerstein (1974–1989) traces it to the sixteenth century, and Braudel (1979) to the thirteenth. Frank (1995) collapses the concept entirely by identifying capital accumulation and a world system as far back as 3000 B.C.

The old debate between "productionists" and "circulationists" can be resolved by recognizing "industrial capitalism" and "merchant capitalism" not as different historical stages but as strategies for accumulation practiced by different agents in the same system. Industrial capitalism could thus be viewed as the latest in a series of local modes of production anchored in material infrastructures of different kinds, whereas supralocal strategies of merchant capitalism have always integrated such local production processes in larger reproductive totalities. It is the complex interdependency of local and supra-local strategies that tends to obscure this analytical distinction.

MODES OF ACCUMULATION AND "DEVELOPMENT" AS PRIVILEGE

Let us systematically consider the various strategies possible. We may speak of them as *modes of accumulation*, or simply *ways of increasing one's access to resources*. The strategies can be grouped into five main categories:

1. The first and simplest category is *plunder*. There are good reasons to believe that it is as old as the human species. To this category belong, for instance, the practice of bride capture, horse raids, slave raids, and colonial wars of conquest.

2. The second major category is *merchant capitalism*, or the exploitation of cultural differences in how goods are evaluated ("buying cheap and selling dear"). This strategy certainly can be traced back thousands of years, for example to the ancient tin-silver trade between Assyria and Anatolia in the second millenium B.C. (R. McC. Adams 1974; Yoffee 1988a). Merchant capitalism does not *in itself* imply any form of material (infrastructural) "capital," but historically it generally has required some form of transport apparatus—for example, ships, wagons, horses, camels, donkeys, or llamas—as well as a military apparatus to protect its interests.

3. The third category is *financial capitalism*, or the servicing of debts. Demanding interest on credit can be traced back to ancient Sumer in 3000 B.C. It was controversial in Europe prior to its explicit legitimization in the Reformation. Today it is one of the major institutional means by which resources from the "underdeveloped" South are transferred to the affluent North (Körner et al. 1984 [1986]; Altvater et al. 1987 [1991]). Financial capitalism does not *in itself* imply material capital but tends to require a voluminous financial bureaucracy, judicial apparatus, and police force, both nationally and internationally.

4. The fourth category is *undercompensation of labor*. I would specify "undercompensation" as referring to the relation between what the laborer produces and what he or she gets in return, in terms of either labor time, energy, resources, or money. Various cultural strategies are applied. (a) The most obvious form is coercion (i.e., *slavery*), known at least from the time of the earliest urban civilizations and particularly essential to the economies of ancient Greece and Rome. (b) The second, most ancient form is that which may occur in con-

junction with gift exchange or barter—transactions conforming to the principle that Karl Polanyi (1944) called *reciprocity*. It has been shown that even the direct exchange of simple manufactured items between tribal groups can entail an asymmetric transfer of labor time (Godelier 1969). (c) The third and classic form is associated with the principle that Polanyi called *redistribution*. It has been characteristic of chiefdoms, states, and empires, where it is usually quite easy to show that the grassroot producers deliver more tribute, taxes, and so forth to the centers of power than is returned to them, or those centers would not survive. (d) The fourth and most subtle form is wage labor, which belongs to Polanyi's third principle, the *market*. Marx showed that capitalist accumulation can be based on the difference between the value of what a laborer produces and the wages that he or she is paid, that is, the difference between the output and the cost of labor.

The first of these forms of the fourth type, coercion (4a), like those in the first category differs from all the rest in not involving some form of cultural persuasion—that is, in not requiring that the exploited party subscribe to some particular form of ideology that represents the exchange as reciprocal or at least legitimate. In all the other cases listed in this typology, there are fundamental, cultural concepts—vernacular representations of "tribute" or "corvée," "price," "interest," "wage," and so on—that have to be shared by both parties in order for the mode of accumulation to operate.

5. The fifth and final category is *underpayment for resources*, including raw materials and other forms of energy than labor. Again, by "underpayment" I refer to the relation between the quantity of finished goods or services that these resources can be converted into (their *productive potential*, so to speak) and the fraction of that quantity (or equivalent of it) that is obtained in exchange for them. The nature of the resources involved is geared to the technological mode of production and the kind of material infrastructure that needs to be reproduced. (a) For pre-industrial, urban manufacturing centers, mines, or specialized slave plantations, a major source of energy is the *foodstuffs* imported to maintain the labor force. (b) For the maintenance of draft animals, caravans, or cavalry, the major source of energy is *fodder*. (c) For most workshops or industries, finally, the primary energy resource is *fuels*. As mentioned, specific kinds of raw materials (e.g., ores or fibers) may also be required and underpaid in the process.

We could define "undercompensation" and "underpayment" as a condition in which the exchange rates allow the manufacturer to increase his or her relative share of the system's total purchasing power, at the expense of the groups delivering labor power, energy, or raw materials. By "purchasing power" I here mean something more general than money, namely the *symbolic capacity to make claims on other people's resources*. If the total purchasing power were constant, it would not be hard to conclude that any increase is unilateral and that the system is a zero-sum game. However, the total purchasing power in a system obviously can expand (e.g., by striking gold or printing more money), which gives the illusion of global "growth" and tends to obscure its zero-sum properties. Economists would object that the resource base can also be expanded, but to a very large extent this must be recognized as an illusion. First, transforming ecosystems to our immediate purposes, we may gain a specific kind of resource, but only *at the expense of others* (e.g., farmland at the expense of wetlands or forests), the value of which may not become apparent until later (cf. Jansson et al. 1994). Second, many resources are simply physically impossible to expand (e.g., fossil fuels, phosphates, or metal ores). Third and finally, what *locally* appears as an expansion of resources may conceal an asymmetric social transfer implying a loss of resources elsewhere.

The point I wish to make, here, however, is that any increment in one party's *relative* share of the total purchasing power will alter the exchange rates, or terms of trade. Such relative increments are often self-reinforcing because the altered terms of trade in material goods and resources may increase the aggrandized party's technology-mediated capacity to accumulate an even greater share of the purchasing power, and so on. In other words, even if the system as a whole gives the appearance of "growing," any increase in the *relative* share of total purchasing power will be at the long-run *expense* of another party, because it will aggravate unequal exchange and systematically drain the latter's labor (Emmanuel 1972) or other resources (Bunker 1985; Watts 1994).

Let us now apply these perspectives to a classic example of accumulation, the triangle trade between Europe, West Africa, and America, in order to consider how different modes of accumulation can be combined in the same system. Merchants carried manufactured goods such as rifles and textiles from England to Africa, where they were exchanged for slaves. The slaves were then transported to America and sold in exchange for cotton and other plantation produce. Finally, the cotton was brought back to England and exchanged for manufactured goods. The completed cycle involved several points of accumulation, enriching merchants, African chiefs, American plantation owners, and British industrialists. With reference to the typology offered above, we can detect, within this trading system, the occurrence of *all* the modes of accumulation mentioned:

1. European and African slave raiders pursuing their victims.
2. European merchants exploiting cultural differences between three continents.
3. Merchants, cotton growers, and industrialists servicing their debts to European bankers.
4a. American slave owners thrashing their African labor.
4b. African chiefs bartering slaves for rifles.
4c. African commoners paying tribute to their chiefs.
4d. British textile workers collecting their wages.
5a. Slave owners bargaining for cheap corn and wheat to feed their slaves.
5b. American grain merchants buying fodder for their horse-drawn transports to the eastern slave plantations.
5c. British industrialists haggling over the price of cotton and coal.

All in all, this combination of strategies within a larger reproductive totality provided the conditions for the Industrial Revolution. Marx's theoretical edifice on "capitalism" was built on the observation that the local mode of production in England combined strategies 4d and 5c—wage labor and mechanization. But rather than a historical stage, industrial capitalism should be understood as a functional specialization within a larger field of accumulative strategies. Rosa Luxemburg (1913 [1951]) was probably the first to see the full implications of this. Still today, industrial capitalism is very far from the universal condition of humankind, but rather a privileged activity, the existence of which would be unthinkable without various other modes of transferring surpluses of labor and resources from peripheral sectors to centers of accumulation at different spatial scales.

A WIDENED CONCEPT OF CAPITAL FOR A "GREEN" DEPENDENCY THEORY

The debate about whether to define "capitalism" in terms of merchant or industrial capital can thus be resolved only by recognizing that circulation and production are mutually interdependent. In relying on fossil fuels and combustion engines, industrialization was certainly revolutionary, but the growth of a material infrastructure through unequal exchange was not an innovation of eighteenth-century England. To trace such processes further back in history, as would Wallerstein, Braudel, and

Frank, we would need to widen Marx's concept of capital so as to make it more abstract and inclusive, both in its symbolic and in its material aspects. In the previous chapter, I argued that such an extended concept of "capital" could be defined as *a recursive (positive feedback) relationship between some kind of technological infrastructure and some kind of symbolic capacity to make claims on other people's resources*, and that such a definition would be as applicable to the agricultural terraces of the Inca emperor in ancient Peru as to the textile factories of industrial England. What the two examples have in common is the recursivity between the symbolic and the material. In both cases, the material infrastructure is used to produce an output that is culturally transformed (i.e., through the mediation of symbolic constructs) into more infrastructure. Industrial machinery is only the latest version of infrastructure, and wage labor only the latest version of cultural persuasion.

Marx was too focused on labor to see that exploitation could also take the form of draining another society's natural resources. Nor could he see Luxemburg's (1913 [1951]) crucial deduction that capitalism could never constitute its own, self-contained market. He, like his contemporaries, was thus able to put his faith in the global, emancipatory potential of the industrial machine. As the twentieth century drew to a close, however, mounting global inequities gave us reason to reexamine the promise of the machine. Could the industrial infrastructures of Europe, North America, and Japan *exist* without the abysmal gap between rich and poor? Or are they one and the same, inextricably linked, as the material and the social dimensions of a single global phenomenon?

The global gap is deepening (cf. N. A. Adams 1993). It has been calculated that the 225 richest individuals in the world own assets equal to the purchasing power of the 47 poorest percent of the planet's population (Hart 1999, ref. to UNDP 1998). Yet, ironically, dependency theory has been on the wane. A major problem for its opponents seems to be the difficulties that they are having in visualizing "metropolis-satellite" (Frank 1966) or "core-periphery" (Wallerstein 1974) relations, and notions of "surplus exploitation," as spatial, material realities (cf. Brewer 1990:168–169). There is often a tenuous congruity between the different spatial parameters that one can think of. Where are the investments made? Where do the capitalists live? Where are their bank accounts? Where is the infrastructure being accumulated? Where are the products consumed? These difficulties can be alleviated, I believe, by thinking less in terms of national trade statistics and more in terms of net flows of energy and materials, irrespective of political boundaries. Nightly satellite images of luminescent technomass in Europe, Japan, and eastern North America are convincing evidence of the material reality of center-periphery relations.

A "greening" of world system theory essentially means supplementing the labor-oriented, Marxist concept of exploitation (focused on category 4 above) with a resource-oriented one (category 5). A lot of analytical work remains to be done, however (cf. Bunker 1985; Martinez-Alier 1987). An important step is to see that human economies rely on two types of resources, *labor time* and *natural space*. These correspond to the two factors of production known as "labor" and "land." They can be variously combined and transformed into material infrastructure ("capital"), generally for purposes of saving time and/or space for somebody. This is the essence of human technology: the *use* of time and space to *save* time and/ or space for *some social category*. Technology or capital thus amounts to a way of *redistributing* temporal and spatial resources in global society. The time saved by nineteenth-century train passengers (relative to stagecoach) should be weighed against the time spent by steel and railway workers to make these train rides possible. Similarly, the space (land) saved by more "efficient" (intensive) forms of industrial agriculture in nineteenth-century England should be weighed against the space elsewhere devoted to making this local mode of production possible, for example, cotton plantations in America, sheep pastures in Australia, and mines and forests in Sweden (cf. Wilkinson 1973, 1988). More recently, we could add the land devoted to provisioning industrial farmers with fossil fuels, chemical fertilizers, pesticides, machinery, biotechnology, and so forth. The same kind of logic applies to the intensified use of space that we know as urbanization. High-rise buildings can be visualized as gigantic machines for accommodating a maximum volume of marketable services per unit of urban space, but elsewhere demanding vast spaces of natural resources. In becoming interfused with one another in "capital," moreover, the economies of time and space are rendered indistinguishable, so that time saved can represent space lost, and vice versa. Perhaps it is in the very nature of advanced technology that one party's gain of time or space is some other party's loss.

A major handicap in our pursuit of a clearer understanding of these relationships is the fact that most trade statistics are in monetary units, rather than invested labor time, energy, or hectares. Let me give an example of how this can lead us astray. Opponents of Emmanuel's (1972) argument that low-salary countries were victims of unequal exchange suggested that the import into developed countries of produce from the developing countries was too marginal (2.5% in 1965) to be of any significance to the condition of either category. Emmanuel replied, however, that if salaries had been the same as in the advanced countries, the cost of that import would have been ten times as high, or equivalent to 25% (Brewer 1990:208). Brewer (*Ibid.*) writes that one can "doubt whether anything like the same volume of trade would take place at these prices," but this, of course, is precisely the point. The entire rationale of the trade is the asymmetric transfer of labor time. Statistics in dollars obscure the real transfers in hours of labor. Similarly, if invested energy (Odum and Arding 1991) or hectares (Wackernagel and Rees 1996) were counted instead of dollars, the significance of imports from the South would be recognized as much greater than that suggested by monetary measures. Still, even the dollar-based statistics of the General Agreement on Tariffs and Trade (GATT) reflect a fundamental pattern in global, center-periphery relationships: in 1984, *fuels* accounted for 46.8% of exports from "developing areas" but only 7.8% of those from developed countries (cf. Chisholm 1990:96).

If, in this book, I am preoccupied more with the dynamic of world systems than with the transformations of ecosystems, it is because we are so much better acquainted with the latter. I need here only hint at the connections between the two types of systems. Let us return to the trans-Atlantic trade and briefly consider some of its ecological repercussions. Without this particular constellation of accumulative strategies, England would not have industrialized in the eighteenth century, and the environmental history of the past few centuries would have taken a different course (Worster 1988). The soils of the American South would not have been cultivated in such an unsustainable manner (cf. Earle 1988). The American wheat belt would not have been pushed as far into areas vulnerable to erosion. Australia and Argentina would not have been converted in such a wholesale fashion into pasture, nor the West Indies into sugar plantations. The deforestation of India probably would not have been as severe (Tucker 1988). The list can be extended indefinitely. These global environmental changes are tangible imprints of the world system of capital accumulation. The industrial infrastructure of eighteenth-century Lancashire grew not only from the sweat of the British proletariat and of African slaves but also from American soils, Australian pastures, and Swedish forests. Vast quantities of human time and natural space were exploited and intertwined in the process. After two hundred years, such concentrations of technomass in Europe, North America, and Japan are still expanding at the expense of their peripheries and of global life-support systems. Capital accumulation is a blind, self-reinforcing process. Instead of just continuing to monitor its ecological effects, we urgently need to grasp its fundamental dynamics. Recent concepts such as "political ecology" (Johnston 1994) and "environmental justice" (Harvey 1996) recognize that such an understanding can emerge only from a consideration of how ecological issues and distributional issues are interfused.

5

⌗

Conceptualizing Accumulation from *Spondylus* Shells to Fossil Fuels

I n this chapter I shall elaborate the comparisons made in previous chapters between ancient Andean mechanisms of accumulation and those prevalent in the modern world. As in the previous chapter, a basic question continues to be how to define "capital accumulation," a central concept in world systems discourse. Considering how liberally the concept of "accumulation" is applied in the literature on world systems history, it is surprising to find so little discussion of how it is to be defined. At times the impression is that it remains a matter of personal idiosyncrasy whether "capitalism" is traced to the eighteenth century (Wolf 1982), the sixteenth century (Wallerstein 1974–1989), or 3000 B.C. (Frank and Gills 1993). There is a wide consensus that the cycles and shifts of world system history can be best understood in terms of accumulation, but very little explicit agreement on what accumulation is, how it is achieved in different historical contexts, and whether historical discontinuities are at all significant. It is my belief that long-term continuities such as those proposed by Frank and Gills (1993) are easier to visualize once we are able to analytically clarify the discontinuities.

TOWARD A TRANSDISCIPLINARY UNDERSTANDING OF ACCUMULATION

The Concise Oxford Dictionary defines "accumulate" as to "acquire an increasing number or quantity of; heap up" or "grow numerous or considerable; form an increasing mass or quantity." When world systems theorists apply the concept, however, it is seldom clear *what* is being accumulated—whether purchasing power (abstract wealth), an infrastructure of some sort, or both. Some, for instance, would speak about infrastructure (e.g., technology) as a *means* of accumulation, as if there was a transcendent object of accumulation separate from the means. If accumulation is a self-reinforcing, positive feedback process, however, the object and the means of accumulation are, to some extent, one and the same.

Accumulation is the common denominator underlying the major threats to global human survival, including resource depletion, environmental destruction, global inequality, and armament. Yet a general definition of accumulation applicable to world systems history is not immediately evident. It might appear that the common denominator of all accumulation is the growth of some kind of material infrastructure; yet Frank and Gills (1993:7) include investments in such nonmaterial assets as education and ideological legitimacy. So as not to risk committing it to the historical specificities of any single kind of material logic, the concept might be defined in a deliberately vacuous manner, such as by equating it with any strategy, material or other, yielding an increment in abstract purchasing power. Cumulative infrastructural growth (of, for example, irrigation systems, armies, or industrial technology) could then be viewed as a manifestation of, and/or a particular strategy for, growth in purchasing power. It is conceivable, however, for purchasing power to increase with but a minimal mediation of infrastructure (e.g., on the stock exchange) and for material infrastructure to be accumulated with but a minimal mediation of abstract wealth (e.g., through plunder). Though closely connected to both, then, the concept of accumulation does not seem to be completely congruent either with growth in purchasing power or with growth in material infrastructure. We seem to be left with a residual and even more abstract formulation: capital accumulation as a self-reinforcing, symbolic, and/or material expansion of the capacity to command various kinds of resources. Both "capacity" and "resources" would here have to encompass the symbolic and social as well as material dimensions, and the concept of capital would be very close to collapsing into the concept of power.

While recognizing its political implications, I think it is essential that capital accumulation continues to be understood and analyzed as a phenomenon of human *exchange*. This is not the same, however, as saying that it can be understood and analyzed within the conceptual framework of current economic theory. The sciences of economics and economic history have not been able to clarify the nature of either the continuities or the discontinuities between pre-industrial and industrial accumulation. The reason seems to be that accumulation is a phenomenon at the interface of the social sciences, the humanities, and the natural sciences. As we saw in chapter 3, any account of accumulation will need to consider (1) the social institutions that regulate exchange, (2) the symbolic systems that ultimately define exchange values and exchange rates, and (3) the thermodynamic and other physical circumstances that allow us to determine the direction of net flows of energy and materials. Only by juxtaposing the operation of these different factors can we come to a full understanding of the continuities and discontinuities represented by modern industrial capitalism.

Such a transdisciplinary understanding of accumulation is obviously beyond the conceptual grasp of conventional economic theory. It requires broadening the horizons of economic thought in three separate directions. First, and probably least problematic, it implies familiarity with the relativization of market institutions accomplished long ago in economic anthropology (Polanyi 1957). Second, it means acknowledging the cultural dimension underlying any definition of value or rationality (Sahlins 1976). Third, and undoubtedly most difficult to assimilate, it requires consideration of how physical factors such as thermodynamics impinge on the development and maintenance of socially constituted infrastructures (Georgescu-Roegen 1971; Martinez-Alier 1987). Unfortunately, the people who read Polanyi or Sahlins generally are not the same as those who read Georgescu-Roegen. It is toward a confluence of these separate sets of considerations that this argument is directed.

There have been attempts to include "nature" in the world system model (cf. Chew 1997), and it is indeed imperative that ecological considerations are incorporated into theories accounting for the spatial dynamics of accumulation over time. I would add that if we are going to include nature, we shall need some conceptual tools from the natural sciences. Civilizations are "dissipative structures" in the sense defined by Prigogine. They are structures that can be maintained only through the continuous degradation of imported exergy. If market-organized center-periphery structures are typically founded on the exchange of manufactured goods for the resources required for their production (including fuels and food for laborers), the general implication, as we have seen in previous chapters, is that price and exergy content are inversely related.

Social transfers of exergy, though generally invisible to economists, are in fact fundamental to capital accumulation. To conceptualize the successive modes of accumulation in world history, a crucial question is the *scale* of exergy appropriation. Whose exergy resources are being exploited by whom? This is the question that will illuminate both the significant discontinuities and the role of technology in the history of accumulation. To clarify these issues, we will have to pay more attention to the specific properties of key trade goods. It will not be enough to consider relative prices and the monetary rates of profit accruing to various kinds of trade; we shall also have to consider the exergy content of the traded products and the concomitant net transfer of exergy between different zones of the world system. Only then can we appreciate the extent to which the feasibility of infrastructural accumulation at any point in time is confined to a restricted social space.

MODES OF CONVERSION AND
MODES OF ACCUMULATION

Human economies rely on three distinct kinds of socially organized conversion that generally are confused in the conventional terminology of "investments," "returns," "production," and so forth. The first type of conversion is the application of labor, draft animals, tools, and machines to the *appropriation* of crops and natural resources. Second, there is the *transformation* of food into labor, of fodder into draft animals, and of labor, fuels, and materials into tools, machines, and finished consumption goods. Finally, there is the *social* conversion of any of these things into any other through exchange.

The first and second modes of conversion (let us call them *appropriative* and *transformative*) are conventionally subsumed under the concept of "production" and are not generally distinguished. The third mode of conversion (exchange) is unique among the three in being completely social in nature and obeying no immediate material constraints. Precisely because they are not subject to any immediate physical constraints, commercial or other social modes of conversion introduce an illusion of reversibility into a system of conversions, the material aspects of which are irreversible (figure 1). The first two types of conversion jointly constitute an asymmetric, linear process: fuels are burned, materials are transformed, exergy is degraded, labor is expended, technology is worn out. Yet, though epitomizing this linear conversion, consumption goods can be commercially reconverted into the very same kind of resources from which they were made, and in fact into more of them than were required for their own production. In those conventional images of the economy that determine its operation, no distinction is made between what is physically convertible (through production) and what is socially convertible (through exchange). Consequently, irreversible conversions are constructed as reversible, and cycles of production and exchange generate linear processes of accumulation (in the center) and impoverishment (in the periphery). It would seem important to develop a more differentiated approach to what we in varying contexts recognize as "production" or "accumulation," with particular attention paid to the kinds of goods

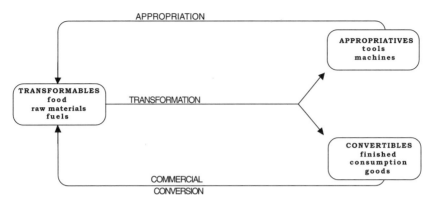

Fig. 1   Modes of conversion in human economies

traded and the relationship between their exchange value and their physical, productive potential.

The different modes of economic conversion allow us to construct a simple typology of goods according to the uses to which they may be put. We may speak of *transformable* goods such as food, raw materials, and fuels; *appropriative* goods such as tools and machines; and items that are simply *convertible*, such as valuables and consumption goods. We might note that labor can serve as a transformable good (e.g., in relation to tools or machines), as an appropriative good (e.g., in relation to crops or minerals), and as a socially convertible good (e.g., in relation to products bought with wages). Because accumulation is always founded on some kind of conversion, these categories are fundamental to the typology, presented in the previous chapter, of different *modes of accumulation*. To reiterate, the basic conceivable strategies are as follow:

1. Plunder.
2. Merchant capitalism.
3. Financial capitalism.
4. Undercompensation of labor in relation to its products, either through
   a. slavery,
   b. barter implying an unequal exchange of labor time,
   c. redistribution, or
   d. market wages.
5. Underpayment for the productive potential of energy and raw materials in relation to the products into which they are transformed, either for

a. food in relation to labor and/or the products of labor,
b. fodder in relation to draft animals and/or their contribution to transports or agriculture, or
c. fuels and raw materials in relation to manufactured products.

Which of these modes are to be characterized as "capital accumulation" or "capitalism"? Strategies 2 and 3 are founded on social convertibility, symbolic exchange value, and the appropriation of abstract purchasing power, whereas strategies 4 and 5 are founded on physical convertibility, productive potential, and the concrete logic of material transfers. Although more or less "pure" forms are conceivable, most processes of accumulation will tend to involve both kinds of strategies. Though analytically distinguishable, in practice they will tend to be inextricably intertwined. Because food and fuels usually have exchange values as well as productive potential, they can be exploited for purely mercantile as well as thermodynamic, "productive" profit by different parties in the same system. As we saw, there are several different modes of accumulation that may be employed by different actors and gain predominance in successive historical systems. As long as it remains useful to retain the generic term "accumulation" through all this variety, the discontinuities will not obscure but in fact enhance our view of the fundamental continuity. This will be more apparent as we employ the analytical distinctions introduced here to reconceptualize the phenomenon of industrial technology.

In what sense, then, does industrial technology represent a discontinuity? To have something to compare with, I will first offer a condensed interpretation of accumulative processes in a pre-industrial context. The context I have chosen, because it is the region I happen to be most familiar with, is the sequence of prehistoric civilizations in the Andes. Pre-Columbian Nuclear America is especially interesting to world system theory for several reasons. First, if the Afro-Eurasian world system was basically one single system (Frank and Gills 1993), then the New World system (and there are reasons to believe that it, too, should be phrased in the singular) is the only other one we will ever have for comparison. Second, it has often been suggested that it was precisely the historical articulation of the Afro-Eurasian with the American system in the sixteenth century that, through the injection of bullion, created the preconditions for the new modes of accumulation that were to spark the Industrial Revolution. The Andean part of the American world system, although linked to Mesoamerica by long-distance exchange for at least three millennia, can be characterized as a relatively autonomous subsystem. Against this background, it was indeed one of those momentous occasions in world history when in 1525 Pizarro's pilot, Bartolomé Ruiz, heading south from Panama in pursuit of gold and silver, encountered Peruvian merchants heading north for *Spondylus* shells.

Some readers may find the following section somewhat too specialized to warrant detailed attention. It is intended in part as an example of how we might apply perspectives from world system theory to the pervasive theme of civilizations that "rise and fall" (cf. Sabloff and Lamberg-Karlovsky 1974; Yoffee and Cowgill 1988; Sanderson 1995). As such it is very much an experiment, because Andean culture history is a field that so far has seen very little theoretical interpretation of this kind. The main purpose of this discussion in the present context, however, is to facilitate analytical distinctions between industrial and pre-industrial modes of accumulation.

A PRE-COLUMBIAN CASE STUDY:
MODES OF ACCUMULATION IN
THE ANCIENT ANDES

A growing body of data is beginning to suggest a framework for interpreting Andean culture history that focuses on the struggles of local elites to control long-distance trade in items essential to their redistributive political economy. If such an interpretation is justified, our understanding of the ancient Andean system will not have to be as different from our understanding of the Mesoamerican or Old World systems as some Andeanists have suggested. Both in Mesoamerica and in various regions of the Old World, the control of access to rare and valuable goods has long been recognized as a basis for social stratification. Not least in Mesoamerican studies, long-distance exchange has figured prominently in explanations of the emergence and collapse of local hierarchies and the spatial expansion and decline of specific cultures over time (cf. Flannery 1968; Rathje 1973; Webb 1973; Jones 1979; Millon 1988).

Archaeologists working in the Andes have been more hesitant to use long-distance exchange to account for early stratification. Very rarely do we hear them addressing standard Mesoamericanist topics such as the localization of ancient sites on strategic trade routes, urbanism as a reflection of specialized export production, and other subsystem responses to the articulation (or disarticulation) of wider spheres of interaction. The models traditionally employed by Andeanists generally have been concerned with cooperation or conflict relating to local subsistence. This may be due in part to the conspicuous role of hydraulic agriculture and topographical circumscription imposed by Andean geography, and in part to our relatively spotty view of Andean culture history, particularly in the highlands and the *montaña*. Even now, as new indications of long-distance contacts are accumulating, a reluctance to treat these contacts as crucial to local developments often lingers.

This is a paradox, considering that few regions in the world seem more naturally conducive to trade than the Andes. We would expect the extreme diversity of ecological zones across the Andean profile, from coastal desert to Amazonian rain forest, to have generated bilateral demands for trans-Andean products and facilitated strategic control of supplies by "middlemen." However, ethnohistory and ethnography jointly suggest that the flow of goods up and down the Andean slopes was traditionally regulated by institutions granting each local group direct access to several zones (Murra 1972 [1975]). The documentation of these "vertical" economic systems has dominated Andean studies to a point at which at least one leading Andeanist would deny, for instance, that there was any actual "trade between the highlands and the forest" whatsoever (Murra, personal communication 1981). The projection of Murra's concept of "vertical archipelagos" onto the extent of Andean culture history has generated a rather parochial discourse that tends to subsume any new evidence of exchange under the functionalist category of "ecological complementarity" (cf. Masuda, Shimada, and Morris 1985).

"Trade," when opposed to such "verticality," is probably best defined as a relation of indirect access, based on the mediation of specialized middlemen pursuing goals of their own. In periods of political fragmentation (e.g., the so-called Intermediate Periods, 200 B.C.-A.D. 600 and A.D. 1000–1476), evidence of long-distance exchange undoubtedly reflects mercantile trade (thus defined) to an extent improbable in the empires of the Middle and Late Horizons (namely Huari A.D. 600–1000 and Inca 1476–1532). Though always more or less embedded in social ties and obligations to local elites, Andean traders were not always as "administered" as the Inca officials (camayoc) delivering their various goods to Cuzco. This seems also to have been the point of departure for Murra's early discussion of trade and merchants in the Inca empire (Murra 1956 [1980], chap. 7), which remains an essential source for the historical evidence of indigenous Andean commerce.

The evidence for "vertical archipelago" economies certainly abounds as far back as ethnohistorical sources go. The question is whether direct access has always been the Andean rule or whether its pervasive distribution derives largely from the impact of large-scale political schemes to convert trade into tribute. In areas such as the Titicaca Basin (Pease 1982; Wachtel 1982), "vertical archipelagos" and strategic allocation of assigned colonists (mitimas) predate Inca expansion, but even in these areas they did not preclude specialized, trans-Andean exchange activities. Wassén (1972) has shown that Callahuaya herbalists traded their tropical plants in the southern highlands at least as early as the Middle Horizon (cf. also

Isbell 1988). Rostworowski (1977) has adduced documentary evidence for the existence, in the southern Peruvian valley of Chincha, of specialized merchants dealing in copper, Ecuadorian *Spondylus* shells, and other items along the coast at the time of the Spanish conquest and suggests that their activity would have been even more intensive prior to the Incas. Similarly, Salomon's (1986) archival research on the archaic highlands of Ecuador reveals that specialized, long-distance merchants (*mindalá*), by providing their highland allies with exotic goods for strategic, local redistribution, were of key political importance prior to Inca dominance. These goods included *Spondylus* shell beads (*mullu*), gold nuggets, copper hatchets, coca, salt, red pepper, and cotton cloth. Salomon shows that the advantage in procuring such wealth objects "amounted to leverage on the reproduction of society itself" and specifically mentions that copper hatchets and "hatchet-coins" served as bride-wealth and grave goods in Pre-Columbian Ecuador (*Ibid.*:92–94, 141, 214). Shimada (1985, 1987) has found that hatchet-shaped copper currency was produced in large quantities on the North Coast of Peru in the Middle Horizon, presumably as a means of obtaining *Spondylus*, gold, and other valuables from Ecuador. It has been suggested that the trade in *Spondylus* was the basis of a maritime exchange system stretching from southernmost Peru to the west coast of Mexico (Murra 1971 [1975]; Paulsen 1974, 1977; Lathrap, Collier, and Chandra 1975; Marcos 1977/78; Salomon 1986:92). Some of the more striking similarities between Mesoamerican and Andean cultures—for example, ceramic jars with stirrup spouts (Paulsen 1977:146) or shaped like acrobats (Lathrap et al. 1975:60)—suggest that the two areas were already integrated into a common "world system" by about 1000 B.C.

Long-distance exchange in so-called primitive valuables can be fully understood only when its local, cultural incentives are accounted for. Unfortunately, the symbolic schemes underlying such cultural incentives are generally lost irretrievably to archaeology. In the Andes, however, the prospects of a more profound understanding are unusually bright, thanks to the rich ethnohistoric record. Ethnohistoric studies summarized by Murra (1971 [1975]), Paulsen (1974), and Marcos (1977/78) reveal some of the symbolic significance of the *Spondylus* shell, already a major trading commodity in the Early Horizon Chavín culture, 900–200 B.C. (Keatinge 1981:183–184). In the Inca empire, *Spondylus*, known as *mullu*, represented rain and fertility and was considered the principal food of the gods. Besides being used for ritual offerings, ornaments made from *Spondylus* shell have been found in elite burials in various parts of Peru from around 1000 B.C. and later. Access to *Spondylus* shell for ritual and redistribution appears to have been a major basis of political power in the agricultural theocracies of Peruvian prehistory. Consequently, we may suspect that it was one of the crucial factors determining the shifting course of political evolution in the pre-Hispanic Andes.

Sallnow (1989:226) suggests that gold and silver in the pre-Hispanic Andes constituted a restricted sphere of exchange distinct from the circulation of food or cloth. His reference to "a common cultural fixation in both the Old World and the New on gold and silver as *the* supreme forms of value" (*Ibid.*:209; emphasis added) is debatable, however, as it disregards the pivotal role, in the New World, of other elite goods, such as cloth or *Spondylus*. Gold and silver were, of course, also highly valued in pre-Hispanic Peru, but, like *Spondylus*, more in terms of their culturally specific symbolism than in terms of abstract exchange value (Helms 1981; Lechtman 1984; Sallnow 1989). In Inca Peru, gold represented the sweat of the Sun and silver the tears of the Moon, both signalling the celestial qualities of state power.

The Inca based their power on the strategic deployment of valuables such as *mullu*, cloth (Murra 1962), and other goods. Inca administration was embedded in deeply rooted, cultural contexts of kinship, reciprocity, and ritual. Morris (1978, 1979, 1982) has brought archaeology closer to Andean cultural realities by demonstrating that impressive "administrative" centers such as Huánuco Pampa were primarily designed for hosting the large-scale, ceremonial consumption of maize beer (*chicha*). It is also noteworthy how concepts and institutions such as *mitimas* (relocated ethnic groups), *yanacona* (loyal followers), *aclla* ("chosen women"), and *capacocha* (human sacrifices) all reflect the fundamental Inca strategy of redistributing people as readily as goods (Julien 1982; Murra 1982; Pease 1982; Rowe 1982; Wachtel 1982). Many of these relationships seem to have been based on traditional aspects of kinship and affinity (cf. Carrasco 1982:30–31). *Yanacona* (traditionally translated as "servants") appear often to have been actual or adopted kinsmen of their masters (Salomon 1986:171–172). The accumulation of "chosen women" conceived of as the property of the Inca king and their use as labor or items of redistribution in alliance-making appear to be a permutation of the widespread practice of privileged polygyny (cf. *Ibid.*:129–130). To the extent that his *yanacona* received *aclla* from the hands of the king and resided in the vicinity of the royal court (cf. *Ibid.*:132–133, 169), their status may even have had an ingredient of bride-service.

Inca domination was achieved by establishing an atmosphere of reciprocity between Cuzco and the various local elites that reproduced local, pre-Incaic structures on a vaster scale (cf. Morris 1978). But the rationale of Inca expansion was Cuzco's unwillingness to let its position as "middleman" between the four divisions (*suyu*) of the empire depend on the vicissitudes of market exchange. Products from coast, highland, and jungle were redistributed within *Tahuantinsuyu* ("The Four Divisions") according to patterns that probably reflected pre-Incaic demand, but within its limits trade was replaced by other institutions, primarily various forms of labor service (Rowe 1982; Murra 1982), designed to maintain the metabolic flows of the empire. The South Andean "vertical archipelago" model was used as the blueprint for a successful imperial institution, whereby Cuzco everywhere could lay claims to lands of its own and set up colonies to supervise their management. Mercantile activities survived on the fringes only, as Cuzco's only link with not yet conquered territories. The Callahuaya, the *mindalá*, and the maritime merchants of Chincha thus represent the expanding frontier of *Tahuantinsuyu*, but they undoubtedly had plenty of predecessors throughout the pre-Incaic Andes (cf. Carrasco 1982:38; Shimada 1987). This pattern agrees with Sahlins's (1972) structural account of the relegation of balanced reciprocity, money, and market exchange to peripheral social sectors. (For one of many similar observations on the historically marginal and extracultural status of mercantile activity, cf. Berdan 1989:99–102.)

The Middle Horizon expansion of Huari and the Late Intermediate Period expansion of the Chimú capital of Chan Chan appear to have been based on strategies of institutionalized generosity to which Cuzco was merely an heir. Sites designed for *chicha* consumption and other redistributive activities seem diagnostic of all three periods (Morris 1982; Isbell 1987; Klymyshyn 1987; Mackey 1987), and the rationale for expansion was probably similar. The Huari, Chimú, and Inca empires represent attempts to consolidate preexisting interaction spheres into corporate polities, in order to guarantee the supply of exotic goods crucial to the redistributive maintenance of power. The allocation of valuables provided access to the labor of dependent subsystems, a part of which was invested in infrastructures for agriculture and manufacture (for example, maize, textiles, metallurgy, and shell ornaments), thus further enhancing the elite redistributive potential.

The long-term continuities in Andean culture are striking. Colonies of *mitimas*, redistributive *chicha*-drinking bouts, elite accumulation of cloth, and specialized trade in tropical plants and *Spondylus* can all be traced at least to the Middle Horizon. On the northern coast of Peru, the same system of fortifications was used repeatedly in the Early Intermediate, Middle Horizon, and Late Intermediate Periods (Topic and Topic 1987:55). Similarly, the Inca road network was built on the main arteries of Andean exchange established much earlier (cf. Salomon 1986:151, 158; Schreiber 1987:92; Shimada 1987:132; Raymond 1988:297–298). Traditional Late Intermediate ethnic boundaries, conspicuously manifested in costume, were kept largely intact throughout the Late Horizon (Rowe 1982:110; Hastings 1987). Cosmology seems similarly timeless. Symbols and iconographic patterns, such as the "staff" motif (cf. Isbell 1988:180) and the connection between *Spondylus* and fertility, can be traced from the Early Horizon Chavín culture through two and a half millennia to the Spanish conquest.

Together, such disparate kinds of continuities suggest that, while the fortunes of imperial politics were fluctuating in the Pre-Columbian Andes, the local building blocks (ethnic groups, cultural traditions, communication routes) were surprisingly constant (Carrasco 1982:34–35; Pease 1982). In the light of this, a summary of Andean prehistory could show the various regional populations as nodes in a network more permanent than the recurrent political attempts to encompass it. The dynamic of expansion and decline in space and time should then lend itself to topological approaches, such as tracing the "implosion" of peripheries into centers (Gills and Frank 1993:96) in ways similar to those identified in Mesoamerica (e.g., Rathje 1973; Jones 1979; Millon 1988) and the Old World. The various archaeological indications of Andean trade and accumulation certainly deserve such a systematically synthetic treatment. This is obviously beyond the scope of this chapter, but a tentative outline may be offered. Though the interpretative framework of the following account remains speculative, the archaeological data on which it rests have been published in recent anthologies (Haas, Pozorski, and Pozorski 1987; Keatinge 1988).

ANDEAN CULTURE HISTORY AS SHIFTS IN CENTER-PERIPHERY RELATIONSHIPS: OUTLINES OF A TOPOLOGICAL INTERPRETATION

By the late Pre-Ceramic Period (ending 1800 B.C.), a number of small, intercommunicating chiefdoms along the northern and central coasts of Peru (figure 2) were linked to a second interaction sphere in the north-central highlands and adjacent *montaña* (Callejón de Huaylas, Upper Huallaga). Finds of *Spondylus* at Aspero also suggest maritime trade with coastal Ecuador. Both these long-distance connections may have provided coastal elites with valuables crucial to the redistributive political economy.

The Initial Period (1800–900 B.C.) saw the unprecedented expansion of a powerful coastal polity based in the Casma Valley and the intensification of trans-Andean exchange, linking the coast with the north-central highlands and tropical-forest areas, such as the Middle Ucayali. Toward the end of the Initial Period, there was a major shift in dominance as the Casma polity collapsed and the valley was invaded by its former trading partners in the highlands. The invaders introduced camelids, guinea pigs, and redistributive *chicha*-drinking on the north coast. Meanwhile, in southern Peru, trans-Andean trade networks were already conveying obsidian from Huancavelica, copper from Chiripa in the Titicaca Basin, and tropical plants from the Bolivian *montaña*.

Having engulfed the Casma area, the north-central-highland Chavín polity in the Early Horizon (900–200 B.C.) continued to threaten neighboring polities on the north coast, who responded by fortifying their settlements. Conflicts seem to have focused on the access of coastal polities to the coca-producing *chaupiyunga* zone (between coast and sierra) and to

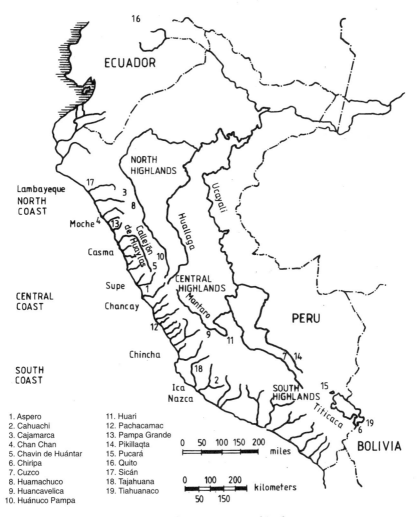

1. Aspero
2. Cahuachi
3. Cajamarca
4. Chan Chan
5. Chavin de Huántar
6. Chiripa
7. Cuzco
8. Huamachuco
9. Huancavelica
10. Huánuco Pampa
11. Huari
12. Pachacamac
13. Pampa Grande
14. Pikillaqta
15. Pucará
16. Quito
17. Sicán
18. Tajahuana
19. Tiahuanaco

Fig. 2   Map of the central Andes with sites mentioned in the text

trade routes leading to the highlands. The Chavín elite may also have sought to control the import of gold work from the Lambayeque Valley in the far north and of *Spondylus* from Ecuador. Chavín was also connected, probably through maritime trade, with the Paracas area on the southern coast of Peru, where access would have been gained to obsidian and cinnabar from Huancavelica, copper from the Titicaca area, and locally produced cotton cloth. In exchange, Paracas may have been offered gold work and *Spondylus* from the north. Toward the end of the Early Horizon, the entire exchange network was rearranged. The south coast's connections with the Casma area seem to have been broken, whereas its contacts with the south-central highlands and the Titicaca Basin were intensified. Also toward the end of the Early Horizon, the expansive north-coast Moche polity, which had escaped Chavín dominance, established direct, llama-caravan trade with the northern highlands and the *montaña* beyond. This may have undermined Chavín's "middleman" position between *montaña* and coast. Of even greater significance in undermining Chavín's hegemony, however, may have been Moche's ability to control the import of gold work and *Spondylus* from the north.

These two shifts encouraged an unprecedented colonization of the *montaña* in both areas in the Early Intermediate Period (200 B.C. to A.D. 600), a major focus of which may have been the cultivation of coca and other tropical plants for purposes of trans-Andean trade. Moche developed an intensive production of cloth and metals and seems to have founded colonies for controlling metal production on the far northern coast, textile production on the central coast, and guano exploitation off the south coast. The voluminous production of *Spondylus* artifacts at the last Moche capital, Pampa Grande, indicates intensive maritime connections with Ecuador. In exchange for *Spondylus*, Moche may have offered copper and cotton cloth. The threat of an expanding Cajamarca polity in the northern highlands prompted heavy Moche fortification and may, perhaps by impeding access to the *chaupiyunga* or trade routes to the *montaña*, have been partly responsible for its eventual demise and eclipse by the Sicán polity, based in the Lambayeque Valley further north. Meanwhile, the south-central-highland Huari polity in the Mantaro Basin established colonies in the Nazca Valley on the southern coast, and Nazca textile production relied increasingly on alpaca wool from the adjacent highlands. In the Titicaca Basin, emerging urban centers like Tiahuanaco and Pucará intensified the production of metal objects used in trade with the Bolivian *montaña*, the Mantaro Basin, and the south coast. Direct maritime contact between the northern and southern coasts seems to have been reestablished toward the end of the period.

In the Middle Horizon (A.D. 600–1000), the Titicaca metal industry began producing bronze, which should have been in high demand throughout this trade network. Tiahuanacoid iconography was diffused by means of woolen textiles and the paraphernalia associated with narcotic and medicinal plants conveyed by *montaña*-oriented herbalists. These traveling herbalists stimulated the demand for tropical plants in the Mantaro Basin, and Huari intensified the colonization of its adjacent *montaña*. Huari's manipulation of local labor was based on the redistribution of valuables and *chicha* beer, which stimulated trade, craft production, and maize agriculture. In addition to trade goods from Titicaca and the *montaña*, Huari would have obtained *Spondylus* and cotton cloth via the Nazca capital of Cahuachi (only ten days distant on foot) and also the important center of Pachacamac on the central coast. Obsidian and turquoise were also widely exchanged. In struggling to control these vital flows, the expanding Huari polity finally embraced the entire southern and central coasts and the highlands from Pikillaqta in the south almost as far north as Cajamarca. Urbanism in the incorporated, central-coast polities of Supe and Chancay-Pachacamac reflects intensive craft production, probably with an emphasis on ceramics and cloth. Unconquered by Huari, the urbanized, north-coast, Sicán polity imported copper ore from the northern highlands in order to produce hatchet-shaped copper currency (today referred to as *naipes*) for importing *Spondylus*, gold nuggets, and gems from Ecuador. Sicán also maintained contact with the emerging center of Chan Chan in the Moche Valley, Pachacamac on the central coast, and Huari itself. The expansion of Chan Chan seems to have been correlated with the demise of Huari at the close of the Middle Horizon, perhaps by undermining its access to copper and *Spondylus*.

In the Late Intermediate Period (A.D. 1000–1476), a reincarnated Moche (i.e., Chimú) polity based at Chan Chan reconquered the adjacent Sicán and Casma polities and also came to dominate the central coast, where only Pachacamac was able to preserve its identity. An alliance with the urbanized, northern-highland, Cajamarca polity was probably crucial to the Chimú expansion. Like Huari, Chimú control was based on the redistribution of valuables and *chicha* beer, and the metal industry of Sicán was the main target of conquest. Control over the massive trade in *Spondylus* was probably also a major incentive. Compared with Sicán, the Casma polity maintained a relatively autonomous status within the Chimú kingdom. Chimú agriculture was largely devoted to the production of cotton fiber for the textile industry. There is some documentary evidence of conflict with a northern-highland, Huamachuco polity over coca-producing *chaupiyunga* lands. The same type of coast-highland conflict is documented on the central coast. Throughout southern and central Peru, the collapse of Huari left fragmented, local polities warring against their neighbors. The urban craft centers of the southern coast and the Titicaca Basin were abandoned, but a trade-oriented Chincha polity on the south coast continued to convey *Spondylus* into the southern highlands. One of Chincha's primary trade connections in the southern highlands was a small kingdom centered on the town of Cuzco, only kilometers away from the ruined Huari outpost of Pikillaqta on the southern border of the former empire, where it controlled trade routes into the *montaña* and the Titicaca Basin. Predictably, Cuzco's first step toward the Late Horizon empire of *Tahuantinsuyu* was to subdue the neighboring Chanca, heirs of the Huari heartland, who blocked what was to become the Inca highway to Chinchasuyu. The rest is history.

This admittedly speculative and sketchy interpretation of the dynamics of Andean accumulation points to some possible ways in which political consolidation into states and empires would tend to leave traces in the archaeological record. An obvious difference between politically unified regions and nonpolitical interaction spheres is the capacity of corporate polities for militarism (Webb 1987). Second, previously united regions are more easily annexed to other, expanding polities (Pease 1982; Rosaldo 1982:463; Salomon 1986:134). On the other hand, like those ethnic groups that allied themselves with the Spaniards against Cuzco, they may also have been more easily lost in times of crisis. A third aspect, then, is the tendency of long-standing political unification to produce ethnicity and regional resiliency. Fourth, there is a difference in the scale of vulnerability. Even if empires are designed to prevent them, the impact of inevitable disturbances in crucial exchange flows will have repercussions over a wider area if what is threatened is not a few local elites but the entire imperial superstructure. The abruptly truncated "horizons" testify to this. Finally, as indicated, for example, by Gills and Frank (1993:96), the emergence of new centers of accumulation will tend to occur on trade routes just beyond the established political reach of antecedent polities. This pattern seems to be applicable to a long series of Andean centers, including Chavín de Huántar, Moche, Nazca, Huari, Cajamarca, Chan Chan, and Cuzco, each of which emerged on the periphery of earlier centers. Significantly, the Inca civil war that met the Spaniards (cf. Hemming 1970) suggests that Quito was about to be added to this list.

I foresee, of course, the possible objection that this way of accounting for the general dynamics of Andean culture history is monocausal in its emphasis on long-distance exchange. It may be useful to recall, however, that to recognize how "primitive valuables" may have guided the political and economic history of the Pre-Columbian Andes is simply to acknowledge that *Spondylus* shell ornaments may be no less desirable than the yellow and gray metals that lured the Spaniards and transformed two worlds.

ACCUMULATION BASED ON SYMBOLIC
VERSUS INTRINSIC "PRODUCTIVITY"

Several interrelated modes of accumulation appear to have been in operation in the Pre-Columbian civilizations of the Andes. With reference to the typology I have suggested in this and the previous chapter, long-distance exchange in items such as *Spondylus* shell and copper would have provided opportunities for strategy 2: the exploitation by merchant groups (such as the Chincha traders or the *mindalá*) of intercultural discrepancies in evaluation. Locally, however, such items were used at various levels of leadership according to mode 4c: the strategic deployment of valuables in redistribution and ritual so as to gain access to corvée labor. Much of the labor thus appropriated was invested in infrastructure (e.g., terraces) and the production of other goods destined for redistribution such as maize beer, cloth, and metalwork. It is no doubt fair to say that the rationale of such redistributive cycles required that labor was continuously "undercompensated" in relation to its products. By way of a simplified example, mentioned in earlier chapters, the *chicha* with which to appease laborers on the maize fields could only have represented a fraction of the harvest.

If accumulation in the Inca empire relied primarily on the exploitation of local labor, the access to long-distance imports such as *Spondylus* shell would have been a crucial element in maintaining the "fictive reciprocities" to local leaders and priming "the pump of the state economy" (Morris 1978:325). The local, evaluative mechanisms that determined the "productive potential" of the redistributed products hinged on symbolic systems and social conventions of reciprocity. In addition to such local standards for conversion, which organized the exchange between elites and their subordinate populations, the rates organizing long-distance exchange (e.g., of copper for *Spondylus*) represent another evaluative mechanism, partially geared to local evaluations but subject to its own, supralocal logic. It represents the supra-cultural and socially disembedded sphere of conversion that we have come to know as the world market. Schematically, the total conjuncture of prerequisites for ancient Peruvian accumulation thus included, for example, (1) the rate at which *Spondylus* could be locally converted into corvée labor, (2) the rate at which copper could be converted into affinal obligations in coastal Ecuador, and (3) the rate at which long-distance merchants could convert copper into *Spondylus* (figure 3).

It should be observed, at this point, that all these three points of conversion, though ultimately subject to material constraints, are significantly dependent on value systems and social negotiations. To the extent that we can speak of the ancient Peruvian civilizations as "centers" in relation to

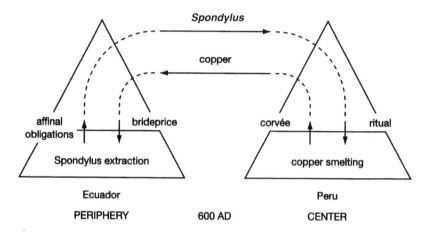

Fig. 3   Evaluative mechanisms in the exchange of copper for *Spondylus* shells in the ancient Andes

an Ecuadorian "periphery," this is a consequence of differences in local, *symbolic* determinations of the productive potential of the items traded, rather than of differences in "intrinsic" potential. In relation to the ratio at which copper was exchanged for *Spondylus*, the capacity of *Spondylus* to mobilize Peruvian labor obviously was vastly greater than the capacity of copper to mobilize the ancient Ecuadorians.

Turning now, with an equally schematic model (figure 4), to the salient characteristics of Peruvian trade in the modern world system, we may begin with the observation that Peru as a whole has been transformed into a peripheral sector in relation to a world economy dominated by the United States. A major export to the United States is oil, while a major import from the United States is arms. Which, then, are the local evaluative mechanisms that determine the "productive potential" of these products? In Peru, investment in arms is an effective elite strategy for guaranteeing a continued extraction of natural resources at minimum labor cost. In other words, the military government represents a mechanism for converting arms into oil. In the United States, the productive potential of oil (including the rate at which it can be converted into arms) is determined by its access to industrial technology. This technology, in other words, represents an evaluative mechanism analytically comparable to the various theocratic-redistributive, kinship-organized, and politico-military structures we have identified as elsewhere serving such functions of conversion. In analogy with the previous case, the conjuncture of prerequisites for accumulation in the United States includes (1) its technological

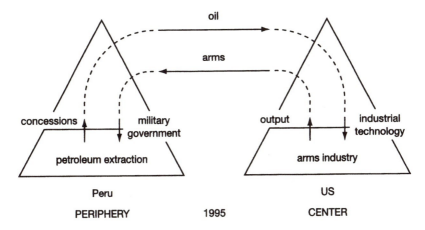

Fig. 4 Evaluative mechanisms in the exchange of arms for oil in the modern world system

infrastructure, (2) the capacity of peripheral governments such as the one in Peru to guarantee the extraction of natural resources, and (3) world market prices of oil vis-à-vis arms.

An implication of this analysis is that industrial technology represents an *objectification* of the local determination of an item's productive potential. We have seen that in societies where production is based exclusively on human labor, as in Pre-Columbian Peru, the productive potential of an item of exchange is defined by the local, symbolic context. The ratio by which labor was exchanged for maize beer or *Spondylus*, for instance, was defined by local cosmology and social institutions. In the case of industrial technology, on the other hand, the productive potential of its various imported components (such as oil) is locally objectified so as to *seem* independent of human evaluation, relying instead on the thermodynamic properties of the articulated substances. The conventional, objectifying view of technology, however, neglects the fact that this articulation itself relies on the supra-local evaluative mechanism we know as the world market (e.g., oil prices). The technological infrastructure of industrial sectors of the world system is not as much an index of Western genius as a sedimentation of the prevailing exchange rates of the past two centuries.

The appearance of noncontingent and extrasocial "materiality" that envelops industrial technology is achieved by objectifying its local, functional aspects, as if its efficacy were exhaustively accounted for in terms of a set of technical propositions concerning the articulation of variously derived components and substances. The structure of the social processes

by which these components and substances are being *supplied* is conceptualized as external to the definition of technology. This is what I refer to
as "machine fetishism." Following Marx, we can discover how relations
between people masquerade as relations between things. We shall return
to the Marxian concept of fetishism in chapter 8.

A significant difference between the two modes of accumulation we
have considered here is that the roles of "center" versus "periphery" in
the former instance hinge primarily on the relative potential for conversion inherent in the local value systems, whereas in the latter they hinge
on the intrinsic, thermodynamic properties of the traded items themselves. In the former case, imports to the center operate as catalysts un-
leashing the productivity of local labor, while in the latter case it is the
productive potential itself that is imported. In terms of our typology of
modes of accumulation, the former belongs to category 4c, the latter to 5c.
The large-scale import of food, fodder, draft animals, and wood fuels to
early centers of civilization all represent strategy 5: the underpayment for
the intrinsic productive potential of energy and raw materials in relation
to the products into which they are transformed. An intermediate instance is the slave trade, which, in its ambiguous position somewhere between strategies 4 and 5, illustrates the continuity between the two modes
of exploitation. Labor, of course, is also a potentially underpaid source of
energy, but a very special one because with exception for the case of slavery, it requires some form of symbolically mediated coaxing of the labor
force. Strategies 4b, 4c, and 4d represent three major forms of such cultural persuasion, corresponding, it will be noted, to Polanyi's categories
of reciprocity, redistribution, and market.

The point I wish to underscore is that the social element is as essential
whether we are addressing *ritual* or *kinematic* machinations (a pair of
terms introduced in a somewhat different argument by Pfaffenberger
[1988b]). The difference is in the *locus* of the evaluative act (whether local
or global). The dictionary definition of a "machination" (as "plot") highlights the social intrigue underlying the industrial machine. Both kinematic and ritual machinations are institutions for controlling human
labor and orchestrating the asymmetric exchange of its products, and
both tend to be very successful in obscuring these functions (cf. chap. 8).
A difference between the two kinds of social "plots" is the relative *inexo-
rability* of the kinematic variant, because of the relegation of local, evaluative functions to nonhuman (technical) agents. Whereas the amount of
work stimulated by a liter of maize beer is subject to negotiation, once
profits have congealed into a cultivator, the amount of work stimulated
by a liter of gasoline is fixed (until a more efficient cultivator is procured).
Another, related difference is that industrial food production may (and
indeed tends to) imply an energy input/output ratio that would not be

feasible in production based on human energy, where there is not much point in stimulating labor with energy inputs (e.g., maize beer) exceeding the energy content of the output. In any large-scale way, this is possible only within an industrial sector, but it relies on unequal exchange with other world sectors. Its prerequisite is a radical discrepancy between exchange value and intrinsic productive potential, to a degree feasible only where work is delegated from human bodies to mechanical structures animated by a continuous input of extra-somatic energy. As we shall see in the next chapter, the discussion of "energy budgets" has necessitated a distinction between thermodynamic *efficiency* and thermodynamic *achievement* (Sahlins and Service 1960:20–21). There has been no systematic attempt, however, to consider the various ways in which an expanded level of "achievement" (technological "development") may be dependent on unequal exchange.

Is "capitalism" or "capital accumulation" to be equated with modern industrialism and dated to the eighteenth century? A conventional Marxist answer is yes, because this was the point at which "the rate of profit was no longer determined solely by regional discrepancies in price (which allowed merchants to buy cheap and sell dear), but by the process of production itself" (Wolf 1982:353). This distinction between two analytically separate principles of accumulation is commendable (and would correspond to my distinction between modes 2 and 4/5), but in suggesting that the latter mode appears for the first time in eighteenth-century England, Wolf ignores all those earlier social systems in which mercantile profits were interwoven with systematic undercompensation of labor and underpayment for energy and materials. These latter versions of unequal exchange, in which the rate of profit and capital accumulation is partly determined by "the process of production itself," have in one form or another been a part of human history for thousands of years. The specific and novel form this mode of accumulation assumed in eighteenth-century England was primarily a matter of adopting a technology based on fossil fuels (initially the coal-fired steam engine). It can usefully be said to represent the advent of "industrial capitalism," but not the advent of "capital accumulation." Industrial technomass is only the latest in a series of socially constituted infrastructures, in which productive capacity is accumulated through unequal exchange.

Wolf rightly observes, however, that industrial capitalism also represents something new in terms of the degree to which commodities and labor were becoming commercially interchangeable. The phenomenon of wage labor (mode 4d) should be recognized as a historically specific construct. If only because of the constraints of transport technology, most earlier civilizations also seem to have maintained fairly distinct spheres of exchange for foodstuffs versus valuables, respectively. As illustrated by the redistribution of *mullu*, cloth, and maize beer in Inca Peru, however, there were also culturally specific modes of conversion between such spheres.

Modern industrialism based on fossil fuels introduces a historically new possibility for unequal exchange and accumulation, but with antecedents in earlier civilizations founded on large-scale imports of energy in the form of food, fodder, draft animals, wood fuels, or slaves. This mode of accumulation (strategy 5) can be contrasted with other strategies such as the mercantile exploitation of intercultural discrepancies in the evaluation of goods and the undercompensation of labor relative to its products, whether through barter, redistribution, or wages. Whereas unequal exchange founded on strategy 2 theoretically could be checked by an implementation of the neoclassical idea of the perfect market, that founded on strategy 5 could *not* be checked in this way, for its inequality is not geared primarily to the conjunctures of human demand but rather to the thermodynamic properties of the traded products and the concomitant, inexorable underpayment for energy and raw materials. Here, the productive potential of traded materials is not determined by their symbolic value (i.e., by the ratio according to which they can be converted into human labor) but, in the case of industrialism, by their functions within mechanical structures substituting for human labor. In this system, where the discrepancy between exchange value (price) and intrinsic productive potential is absolutely crucial, the neoclassical conflation of exchange value and use value, which we shall discuss in the next chapter, is obviously of supreme ideological significance. It leaves no room for the *idea* of unequal exchange. What could be more ideologically instrumental than to equate all forms of "utility" and to declare that the value of a product basically corresponds to its price? As in the case of the Inca laborer praising the hospitality of his host, this is another illustration of how unequal relations will "in one way or other—by means of some mysterious process that we must analyze—present themselves as a *reciprocal exchange* of services" (Godelier 1994:105).

I began by arguing that problems of human ecology such as environmental degradation, resource depletion, and world poverty can all be attributed to processes of accumulation, and that accumulation itself is a problem at the very interface of natural and social science. For instance, if industrial technomass is a dissipative structure in the thermodynamic sense, but the logic of its operation largely rests on specific cultural categories and social institutions, then neither natural nor social scientists can by themselves hope to grasp its total conditions of existence. I have been trying to advance an alternative understanding of economic "growth" and technological "development" that demonstrates the logic by which historically specific, sociocultural concepts and institutions interact with natural law (thermodynamics) in generating an inequitable world order. A crucial element in this understanding is the relativization or defamiliarization of cultural categories (e.g., "market" and "prices") that to most of us are as natural and unquestionable as water is to fish. Achieving epistemological distance vis-à-vis such categories is essential to any prospects for transcending them in the future. The transdisciplinary challenge is to develop a perspective on industrial technomass as a dissipative structure that also accounts for the specific sociocultural conditions for its reproduction.

My main point in this chapter was that both industrial technology and theocratic ritual are "machinations" dependent on evaluative mechanisms. The difference is that, in industrialism, the evaluative mechanism has been locally objectified (into technology) so as to seem entirely "material" and nonsocial. But what actually has happened is that the most significant evaluative moment has been shifted from the local to the global level. Locally, it has been delegated to the nonnegotiable, kinematic logic of machines, but these are in themselves manifestations of global exchange rates.

In ancient Peru, what were imported over longer distances were primarily symbols, which were *socially* convertible into work in the form of manual labor. The productive potential in the system was still local labor, and the rate at which prestige goods were converted into labor was to some extent negotiable. But in modern industrial centers, it is increasingly the *productive potential itself* that is imported, which means (1) that the imports are *physically* convertible into work, (2) that it is the global rather than the local conversion rates that ultimately determine the feasibility of accumulation, and (3) that asymmetric social transfers of exergy are increasingly global in scale. Increasingly, the productive potential that is being underpaid is resources in the periphery rather than labor in the center. Nor can the machines be negotiated with. No less than ritual, they mystify us, now by pretending to be productive independently of global exchange rates. Apparently, it will take more than something like the so-called oil crises of the 1970s to shake us out of that illusion.

6

Use Value, Energy, and the Image of Unlimited Good

I have argued in previous chapters that we cannot understand or hope to solve global problems of solidarity and survival unless we are prepared to experience a radical "defamiliarization" (Marcus and Fischer 1986) vis-à-vis conventional categories of economics and technology. What is required is a major epistemological or paradigmatic shift. The outlines of such a necessary shift are difficult to convey within the confines of our conventional vocabulary. The logical trajectory of economic anthropology must be to deconstruct our concepts of "production" and "technology" in order to grasp the full extent of what I refer to as "machine fetishism." At stake are fundamental assumptions about the material aspects of the productive process. Paradoxically, to accomplish this deconstruction, we have had to begin by going back on the steps of Baudrillard (1973 [1975], 1972 [1981]) and Sahlins (1976) to retrieve a notion akin to the concept of "use value."

THE CONFLATION OF USE VALUE
AND EXCHANGE VALUE

The distinction between use value and exchange value goes back to Aristotle:

> Every article or property has a double use; both uses are uses of the thing itself, but they are not similar uses; for one is the proper use of the article in

question, the other is not. For example, a shoe may be used either to put on
your foot or to offer in exchange. (1962:41)

To Adam Smith, trying to maintain the distinction between use value
and exchange value proved a daunting intellectual struggle (Blaug
1985:38), and David Ricardo subsequently paved the way for a conflation
of the two concepts in the neoclassical notion of "utility." Briefly, Ricardo
argued that an object must possess some measure of use value in order to
have an exchange value (cf. White 1959:338–340). The concept of "use"
was widened from the concerns of immediate consumption (as in Aristotle's version) to any mode of "gratification" (Blaug 1985:109). The neoclassical economic doctrine, which has since dominated Western thought,
equates utility and value. There is only one measure of value, and it is
determined by the market. In other words, value corresponds to price, the
amount of money that market actors are willing to pay. Thus utility
equals value equals price.

Neoclassical economic thought entered anthropology in the guise of
formalist theory through the work of Melville Herskovits, Raymond Firth,
and their followers. In reaction to formalist attempts to account for all
systems of human exchange in terms of a universalist model, the substan-
tivist school, founded by Karl Polanyi and George Dalton, argued that
there is not much point in reducing the great variety of local meaning
systems to a single formula. In trying to say everything, they argued, the
formalists say nothing that is not tautological. Reducing specific human
meanings and motives to abstract tautologies is not "theory" in any
meaningful sense.

Sahlins (1976) brought substantivism to its logical conclusion by showing that not even our Western economy can define utility without recourse to cultural context. Defining cultural context in terms of symbolic
schemes, Sahlins demonstrated how specific meaning systems determine
the objectives of production. Acknowledging inspiration from Baudrillard (1972 [1981]), he views consumption as a mode of symbolic communication. Ironically, however, it could perhaps be argued that Sahlins's
important contribution merely added a qualification to the abstract, tautological scheme of the neoclassicists, thus: symbolic meaning equals utility equals value (equals price?).

There are two major and interrelated problems left untouched by Sahlins. First, there remains a strong, intuitive suspicion that there is some
kind of "value" with which price is not automatically synonymous. The
problem, of course, is how to conceptualize the use value of a product if
not in terms of what people are prepared to pay for it. The second problem is that although Sahlins relativizes the *output* of Western production,
he does not address our cultural models of "production" itself. In the

final instance, he not only halts at the boundary of the "material" as if it were a level of reality somehow detachable from culture, but even reduces technology to this unquestionably and inherently "real" domain:

> Decompose the productive forces to their material specifications alone; suppose an industrial technology, a population of men, and an environment. Nothing is thereby said about the specific properties of the goods that will be produced, or about the rate of production or the relations under which the process shall proceed. (Sahlins 1976:207–208)

Industrial technology is treated as given; only its *use* is symbolically constituted. Against this view, I will argue that an industrial technology is much more than a set of "material specifications" and that in fact it says so much about the social relations of production that the two are inseparable.

Gudeman (1986) has explicitly addressed the cultural construction of "production." He has set himself the task of relativizing Western models of livelihood, of the productive activity itself, or what Polanyi called the substantive definition of "economy." He shows that various local, non-Western models all tend to employ metaphor to convey a sense of meaning to the activity of gaining a livelihood. By relating livelihood to other domains, such as social relations (e.g., by conceiving of production as the work of the ancestors), local models tend to *position* human subjects in relation to what is construed as a highly meaningful activity. The universalist, Ricardian model, on the other hand, is uniquely self-referential (derivational) in that it is stripped of metaphorical meaning. It relates to nothing but itself and is formulated as a self-contained set of propositions. Whereas the local models are charged with meaning and necessarily imply a positioning of the subject, the Ricardian model is decontextualized and objectifying, reflecting, we might add, an approach characteristic of Western science. The contrast could be represented thus:

Local model	*Ricardian model*
Metaphorical	Self-referential
Conveys meaning	Conveys no meaning
Culturally contextualized	Culturally decontextualized
Positions the subject	Objectifies

Whereas Sahlins relativizes the rationality of American production by revealing its "arbitrary" goals, Gudeman seems to accomplish the opposite by defining the Western constitution of livelihood in terms of its noncultural (i.e., nonmeaningful) premises. Paradoxically, however, it is Gudeman (1986:viii, 154–157) who ends on a relativistic note, whereas Sahlins

(1976:205–221) concludes by discussing the distinctiveness of Western culture. To neutralize the paradox, this is where they meet. Gudeman's observations imply that the universalist rationality of the Western model is, by virtue of its very *unspecificity* (its etic, imperialist aspirations), itself an expression of the culture with which it is associated. Similarly, Sahlins emphasizes how money fetishism, through the abstract notion of a growing GNP, disguises the fact that production is the creation of symbolic value. Western theories of human behavior based on pragmatic interests, utility, and objective conditions are vacuous illusions, but this very vacuity turns them into tools for comprehending all human activity. In his final sentences, Gudeman suggests that we should rethink "imperialism" in terms of "who gets to model whom." The ideology of abstract utility emerges as the legitimation of Western market expansion. Parallel to the social process whereby the market conspires to subsume all local cultures, its own tautological, peculiarly nonmetaphorical cosmology aspires to engulf all local systems of meaning.

Taussig (1980) has approached the same problem from the perspective of a uniquely "symbolic" brand of Marxism. He demonstrates how the way in which rural Latin American peasants perceive encroaching capitalism in terms of meaningful metaphors reflects a distinct anticapitalist positioning. Employing religious fetishism in an attempt to control the forces that regulate their lives, their way of construing the workings of capitalism poses a challenge to our objectifying, Western model. In an illuminating discussion of the Marxian concept of commodity fetishism, Taussig dislocates the Western observer by relativizing his own everyday experience of the market so as to reveal a fetishism no less mystifying than the peasant metaphors. It is as if the workings of world capitalism protrude with greatest clarity in its confrontation with peripheral populations actively trying to grasp its seemingly evil and unnatural forces. Until they submit to the objectifying stance of the market mentality, such populations will employ the religious or other metaphors that served to organize meaning in their precapitalist economies. As in other forms of fetishism, the Western perception of "money" and "commodities" involves the decontextualization, animation, and empowerment of human representations (Ellen 1988).

Sahlins, Gudeman, and Taussig jointly open our minds to a deconstruction of our Western concept of "production" and suggest a lever with which to communicate the scope of our misunderstanding of the role of industrialism in the world. In order to rethink "production" in any profound sense, we have had to begin by (provisionally) reintroducing the distinction between use and exchange value. I should immediately add, however, that the purpose of this move is merely to retrace a crucial moment in the history of economic ideas, so as to demonstrate the ideological significance of the conflation of the two concepts of value. As was made abundantly clear in chapter 3, it is finally only confusing to use the word "value" for the material properties of traded goods.

Largely stimulated by Baudrillard, the recent anthropological preoccupation with the cultural and symbolic aspects of consumption (e.g., Sahlins 1976; Douglas and Isherwood 1978; Appadurai 1986; Löfgren, Harbsmeier, and Trolle Larsen 1990) is certainly an important line of inquiry, but it entirely skirts the crucial economic questions of growth versus exploitation. To answer these questions, we are not helped by the insight that people will pay for whatever their cultural contexts prompt them to desire, implying that value is created in the process of consumption. If anthropology stopped here, it would merely contribute to the hegemonic, neoclassical consensus. In the context of the present discussion, the specific *content* of consumption (i.e., the *output* of production) is irrelevant. My concern is rather with how our specific, cultural construction of "production" systematically obscures relations of exploitation and unequal exchange.

THERMODYNAMICS AND THE
ECONOMY OF "ORDER"

In a monetarized market economy, unequal exchange can be *conceived* of only if we maintain the analytical distinction between exchange value and some other quality, such as "use value" or the thermodynamic concept of exergy introduced in chapter 3. To use a thermodynamic concept to approximate the ancient notion of use value is perhaps to concede that the satisfaction of *human* needs has ceased to be the fundamental problem of economics. The essential measure of "usefulness" I suggest is being obscured by money prices is defined by the metabolism not of human bodies but of industrial technology. Viewed as in some respects analogous to living biomass, the suprahuman "technomass" of industrial society must be fed specific kinds of substances in order to grow. Whatever form its excretions assume is irrelevant; what matters is the process of production itself. If I may be excused for the metaphor, imports and exports are to the industrial infrastructure what eating and discharging are to organic life. In both cases, structure can be maintained only as long as there is a net gain in *order* drawn from the environment (Schrödinger 1944 [1967]; Georgescu-Roegen 1971). Whereas Schrödinger and Georgescu-Roegen consistently speak of "negative entropy" or "negentropy," much recent literature (e.g., Gaggioli 1980; Wall 1986) employs the similar concept of "exergy," introduced in chapter 3. Both denote a measure of order or nonrandomness. Although the term "exergy" was not coined until

1953, the precise quality it stands for was visualized by Carnot in 1824 and elaborated by Gibbs in 1873. It is a crucial concept for understanding the relationship between energy, information, and material structure, because structures such as living organisms do not really consume "energy," which can neither be created nor destroyed, but instead consume the *order* they can derive from energy. Exergy is a quality of energy, indicating the degree of order, or information, it contains. This order in energy can be "embodied" in the order of material structures or reconverted into radiation, but always with a resulting loss in total order.

The Second Law of Thermodynamics states that all processes of energy conversion must entail a net reduction of order in the universe. For the Earth's biomass, this simply means that, in reproducing the structure of living things, high-quality (highly ordered) solar energy is degraded into heat. For the industrial technomass, on the other hand, it means that the Earth's limited stocks of mineral energy are disordered into waste and pollution. Moreover, it implies that industrial technology and its products, though suggesting local accumulations of order, *entail* an overall decrease of order in the biosphere. In other words, industrial goods *represent* less order than the energy and raw materials that went into their production. The same, of course, is true for living things, but the implications are entirely different. In subsisting on an extraterrestrial source of order, organic structures—or economists concerned exclusively with pre-industrial societies—need not worry about the Second Law. By comparison, technomass ultimately derives its order from within a finite, inorganic realm, and the economists of industrialism have every reason to be concerned with thermodynamics.

Benton (1982) has suggested that a significant rethinking of economic problems may occur in the wake of an ongoing, radical transformation of the Western worldview. I suggest that the key issue is to modernize the underlying biological metaphor of economic "growth" so as to make it an explicit and useful tool for economic thought. The neoclassical concept of growth was borrowed from a natural science founded on the mechanical world view of Isaac Newton, to whom it would simply have meant a process of aggregation. Whereas natural science has moved on to a more organic or systemic perception of growth, that is, as *appropriation* of order (cf. Schrödinger 1944 [1967]), mainstream economists remain confined within the old, mechanical version.

It is essential to recall that the Ricardian image of economics emerged in connection with a specific *form* of production, namely, industrialism. Whereas Ricardo was initially preoccupied with agriculture and highly influenced by the Physiocratic image of limited good (cf. Gudeman 1986:65–66), his attempt to grasp the essence of industrialism led him to formulate his labor theory of value, which paved the way for what we might refer to as the Western "image of unlimited good." The key issue here is to which factor of production the essential "productive" capacity is assigned. Whereas the Physiocrats embraced a widespread, pre-industrial concept of land fertility (Gudeman and Rivera 1989), the Ricardian theory of labor value came hand in hand with other ingredients of the neoclassical ideology: the skirting of the whole issue of what industrial "production" represents, the conflation of use value and exchange value, and the implication that consumption itself generates value. "Labor" became the magic wand that could summon limitless growth and prosperity from raw nature. Industrial production was not to be radically reconceptualized until Georgescu-Roegen (1971) clarified its thermodynamic constraints. He observed that industry is "completely tributary" to agriculture and mining, that "it is the pace at which low entropy is pumped from the environment into the economic process that limits the pace of this process," and that, in the end, "the issue of returns boils down to that of returns in mining and in agriculture" (*Ibid.*:292, 294). When juxtaposed with a theory of imperialism, this perspective allows us to defamiliarize the very concept of industrial production. Industrial "refinement" is conventionally represented as the creation of higher order out of "crude" or "raw" materials, but Georgescu-Roegen demonstrated that order is in fact wasted in the process.

The 1970s saw several attempts at rethinking human societies and exchange in terms of thermodynamics, from the vantage points of both ecology (Odum 1971) and anthropology (e.g., Ruyle 1973, 1977; R. N. Adams 1975, 1978; Gall and Saxe 1977). The contributions from anthropology often echoed the pioneering approach of Leslie White (1959) and his students (Sahlins and Service 1960), but did not pursue the implications of the Second Law for industrialism in the direction indicated by Georgescu-Roegen. Let us briefly review a few of these contributions in order to assess some of their merits and shortcomings.

ENERGY, VALUE, AND SOCIETY: SOME PERVASIVE PROBLEMS IN EARLIER THEORY

To White (1959:344–345), the possession of wealth (including money) is equivalent to power over the labor energy of other people, whereas debt is equivalent to slavery. Odum (1971) similarly observes that money and energy flow in opposite directions at some average but changing ratio, and that the ratio of money to energy increases "downstream" along the energy flow (pp. 174, 182, 185, 189). He also suggests that the uneven distribution of wealth in the world "is really an uneven distribution in the application of fossil fuels" (*Ibid.*:132, 183–184). R. N. Adams (1975:121) shows how "social power" is based on the "control over energetic processes" but finds that there are serious problems in using money as a measure in discussing energetic phenomena, because monetary units "vary in both price and value" from time to time and from one society to another (*Ibid.*:112, 196). In a rather careless formulation, Ruyle (1973:606) suggests that labor, value, money, and capital are all "forms of ethnoenergy," where ethnoenergy is defined as "somatic energy . . . expended by the members of the population" (Ruyle 1977:213). He characterizes property as an "ethnoenergetic field" and money as "a symbol for energy, a claim on the energy of other people" (*Ibid.*:227, 212).

White suggested that money-based, commercial, market exchange originated in intersocietal relations but became established as an intrasocietal process with the advent of "civil" society (1959:334, 338, 345), where, however, it is still typically "impersonal, inhumane, and unethical": "Lying, cheating, misrepresentation, and stealing are natural and normal features of the commercial process" (*Ibid.*:346–347). This perspective, emphasizing the peripheral and socially uncommitted relationships associated with money and market exchange, is reiterated by Sahlins (1972:228–229). Its thermodynamic aspects have been pursued by Ruyle (1977):

> Exchange is a form of ethnoenergetic flow characterized by higgle-haggling, with each party consciously attempting to maximize his inflow and minimize his outflow. . . . Money . . . has a thermodynamic aspect as a symbol facilitating ethnoenergetic exchange. . . . Where there is unequal ethnoenergetic flow . . . we may speak of exploitation. . . . [T]he flow of capital, a form of ethnoenergy, has always been from the now underdeveloped world to the developed world. (Pp. 228, 224, 233)

R. N. Adams shows how products are valued higher the further they are removed from their "pristine source" and the closer they are to being consumed (1975:139–140). In his figure 10, the two opposite ends of the production process, namely raw materials and waste, are contiguous in value terms, and the process itself is visualized as a cycle beginning and ending at the low end of the scale. Adams notes that "at every turn in the system there is loss of part of the original energy input to waste and entropy." The addition of value is "equated with loss of energy," but

> it is not yet clear what kind of consistent relationships we may eventually find through the history of human culture between ranking, energy cost of production, high entropy build-up, and other facets of this entire process of man's ecology of energy. . . . Odum (1971) touches on this area in a number

of places . . . but does not approach the problem of how cultural systems actually do evaluate energy forms. (Adams 1975:195–196)

Ruyle (1977:212) defines use value or utility as "the ability to satisfy some human need or desire" and "value," in Marxian fashion, as the amount of socially necessary labor energy, usually measured in hours, required to produce the commodity. He suggests that the appeal of Marx's labor theory of value is that it is "thermodynamic in nature" (*Ibid.*:213, 232). White (1959:335–336, 338, 350) and Odum (1971:181–182, 189) make similar connections between Marxian theory and thermodynamics. As we saw in chapter 3, there is indeed an analogy between labor and energy theories of value. In chapter 4, however, we showed that the Marxian focus on labor tends to obscure the role of other sources of energy in accumulative economic processes.

It is noteworthy that R. N. Adams (1975:109) finds it difficult to incorporate the Second Law of Thermodynamics into the context of his own discussion. Although he quotes Schrödinger's account of living organisms as "sucking orderliness" (negative entropy) from their environment, he elsewhere suggests that "order" or "organization" is "a thing of zero dimensions" that "can hardly be accumulated, added, or built up" (*Ibid.*:116, 122–123). He is aware that, in energetic terms, a system will receive "more from other systems than it returns in usable form to them" (*Ibid.*:137) but does not seem to recognize that this "usable form" so unevenly traded is another word for "order" or "negative entropy." Adams (*Ibid.*:140) notes that at every turn in the production process "there is loss of part of the original energy input to waste and entropy" but does not recognize that which is lost as a quantity in its own right. The First Law of Thermodynamics tells us that it is not energy itself that is being lost, but, as stated in the Second Law, its quality or "orderliness." The widespread refusal to recognize "order" in another sense than the negative— that is, its absence (referred to as entropy)—has constrained most attempts to describe social processes in terms of thermodynamics.

In an ironic misunderstanding of Georgescu-Roegen, Adams (*Ibid.*:124–125) sets out to correct him as to the relative order embodied in copper sheeting vis-à-vis copper ore. Georgescu-Roegen had mentioned that a copper sheet represents lower entropy (more order) than the copper ore from which it was produced. Adams objects that this higher orderliness is merely cultural, lying "wholly in our mind's eye," and that the copper sheet "is clearly of a less highly complex matter than is represented by the original ore." Adams's objections, however, merely confuse the issue. It is surprising to find Adams, having just asserted that "there is only one order, and that is nature's" (*Ibid.*:98), thus confusing cultural and thermodynamic notions of order. By implication, do we refine oil into gasoline in order to please "our mind's eye"? Refined copper does have objective qualities that make it suitable for various material purposes and that require an ordering process. Georgescu-Roegen's whole point was that the act of producing as nonrandom an order as copper sheeting requires an input of order greater than that incorporated in the product. The misunderstanding boils down to whether we focus on the transformation of the copper ore in isolation or take the total process of energy expenditures into account. Industrial products do represent a high measure of order, yet signify a decrease of order in the total system.

This is related to what was visualized by Sahlins and Service (1960:20–21) as the difference between thermodynamic *achievement* and thermodynamic *efficiency*. White (1959:37, 47) duplicated Alfred Lotka's failure to be very concerned with this distinction. He was not concerned with specifying what R. N. Adams (1975:136) would call the "focal unit," the energy expenditures of which determine whether production is to be judged as "efficient" or "economical." Clearly, the judgment would differ depending on whether the focal unit was the U.S. farm laborer, the United States as a nation, or the world system. White (1959:55) quotes Ostwald's suggestion that "we call every machine and every process better which yields a larger amount of useful energy for an equal amount of raw energy, that is, which works with less waste," but does not recognize that this definition of efficiency is irreconcilable with the rest of his discussion, which emphasizes total *achievement*. Thus he tries to articulate the two approaches in a confusing and contradictory summary:

> Culture advances as the amount of energy harnessed per capita per year increases, or as the efficiency or economy of the means of controlling energy is increased, or both. (*Ibid.*:56)

Odum (1971:119–120), on the other hand, emphasizes how industrial agriculture yields only about 10% of the total technological energy costs, and R. N. Adams (1975:118) notes that the ratio between the amount of energy expended and the amount of energy gained is "an extremely important one." Adams recognizes that "human labour provides the cheapest input in terms of energy; as other energy sources are tapped, the energy cost of production must necessarily increase" (*Ibid.*:194; cf. also 121, 152). The implication is that thermodynamic achievement and thermodynamic efficiency are, on the whole, inversely related to each other in "cultural evolution." White's attempt to straddle the issue (in his definition of cultural "advance") mystifies the distributional aspects of technological growth. In classical Marxist fashion, Ruyle (1977:215) similarly speaks of the "progressive development" and "cultural evolutionary advances" of technology, which "renders human labour more efficient." In not perceiving the exploitative dimension of modern technology, it is ironic that he should congratulate his own version of Marxist economics for "its ability to cut through the fetishism . . . and reveal the hidden ethnoenergetic structure upon which bourgeois society rests" (*Ibid*.:232). On the whole, White and his followers have paid too little attention to technology itself as a "dissipative structure" (Glansdorff and Prigogine 1971; R. N. Adams 1978), approaching it simply and anthropocentrically as an increasingly useful "tool" for serving human needs.

Somehow, Adams (1975:301) reaches the remarkable conclusion that "man's particular relation to the environment is fundamentally similar to that of any other species" and that "he is not doing anything particularly 'unnatural.'" White (1959:46), on the other hand, shows how production, or "harnessing" (as opposed to "appropriation and consumption," e.g., hunting, fishing, and gathering), was an innovation of "tremendous significance." Odum (1971:39) refers to such harnessing as the operation of "work gates," where one flow of energy (ultimately human) makes another flow of energy possible. I would emphasize that such energy conversions are fundamentally different from those involved in eating—that is, conversions along natural food chains. The energy spent in capturing a fish is not incorporated in the fish itself, but when the fish is eaten, its energy will be incorporated in the fisherman. As we saw in the previous chapter, the failure to distinguish between these two types of energy conversion often results in illusory, circular models of "production." Odum (*Ibid*.:121), for instance, suggests that "by substituting for system work, oil is energetically converted to food." Martinez-Alier (1987:28, 36–37) uses the same expression, but it is as misleading as the notion that a farmer's labor energy is converted into food. Whether industrial or non-industrial, farmers harness linear energy flows deriving from the sun. They will spend various amounts of energy doing so, but that energy is *lost in exchange for* the crops, rather than "converted into" them.

Odum's book contains a number of figures illustrating his contention that fossil fuel energy is "put back" into the environment (1971:6). Although mentioning that "money circulates whereas energy flows are unidirectional" (*Ibid*.:174), he presents several diagrams designed to represent "circular stimulation" (*Ibid*.:19) but propagating the illusion of circulating energy (figures 1–2b, 2–3b, 4–3, 4–7, 6–2, 6–4, and 6–8). He speaks of "pathways that become circular with further use" (*Ibid*.:150) and of "measuring the ratio of the loopback to forward flow when both are in calories" (*Ibid*.:190). In the same vein, Ruyle (1977:217, 220) depicts the "flow of productive ethnoenergy (labour)" as circulating between population and environment, and the relationship between capitalist and worker is described as an unequal exchange of "hours of energy" (*Ibid*.: 231). These are illusions stemming from economics (ultimately the agriculturally biased Physiocrats, for whom they might at least have *worked*, even though they were illusions). The work capacity of energy cannot circulate, and human food is not human labor or mineral energy in converted form.

Adams (1975:115, 117–120) correctly distinguishes between energy flow as conversion from one state to another and as an "energy cost of triggering energy release," and he identifies Odum's "work gates" as such trigger mechanisms. It is not clear what Ruyle (1977:217) means, however, when he speaks of "ethnoenergetic flow between individuals." Economic exploitation, defined as "differential ethnoenergetic flow," is said to be analogous to predator-prey relations between animal species, except that "the stakes involved are not the food energy locked up in animal flesh but instead the labour energy the human animal can expend in production" (*Ibid.*:224). This brings us to the question of "consumption":

> When material use-values are consumed by an individual, the individual is consuming not only the object itself, but also the ethnoenergy expended in the production of the use-value. . . . If the amount of ethnoenergy consumed by an individual is greater than the amount of ethnoenergy he expends in production, . . . then this individual, or group, is a predator, living, in part at least, on surplus exploited from the rest of the population. . . . Just as predation in the animal world requires the expenditure of ethnoenergy in hunting, so predation among men requires the expenditure of ethnoenergy into an exploitation system. . . . The subsistence technology of ruling-class populations is exploitation, and the econiche of the ruling class is different from anything existing in the animal world. (*Ibid.*:223–225)

Ruyle's intuitions about intraspecific energy exploitation among humans are relevant to the argument in this book but remain analytically crude and misleading. He does not distinguish, for instance, between the consumption of food and the consumption of other "material use-values," only the former of which is actually *consumed* in the sense of being incorporated in the body of the consumer, but only the latter of which (i.e., manufactures) are *produced* in the sense of incorporating energy expended by the producer.

These are some of the recurrent problems with previous thermodynamic approaches to society. Theoretical discussions of energy and society have also been burdened by the assumptions of functionalism, evolutionism, and determinism. The "purpose" of culture is to "serve" the needs of man (White 1959:9), and money "serves" as "a kind of lubricant," "to stimulate energy flow," and "as an automatic regulating and equalizing device" (Odum 1971:194–195, 203). Mankind would have "remained in a condition of savagery indefinitely had not an increase of his available energy resources been made possible" (White 1959:43), and "for the rich countries to give up their present power control to a system of untried capabilities may be very risky for the whole world's progress" (Odum 1971:203). What is theoretically even more of a burden, White not only makes a clear-cut distinction between social organization and technology (1959:8, 55) but also frequently represents the relationship between them as one of simple causality (*Ibid.*:18–20, 24, 26–28, 32, 369).

The 1980s and 1990s shifted the attention of anthropology away from prosaic problems of matter and energy. Might we still hope for a nonevolutionist, nonfunctionalist, and nondeterminist reconciliation of symbolic and material perspectives, one that addresses the thermodynamic conditions and consequences of symbolically orchestrated human behavior without a priori assumptions of "progress," "adaptation," or "determination"?

CIRCULATION VERSUS LINEAR FLOW

The basic problem with conventional economic thought is the notion that value *circulates*. Though it may apply to money (symbolic exchange values), the Second Law of Thermodynamics says that it can only to a limited extent apply to resources. The matter that living structures organize does circulate, but this organization in itself is reproduced by a linear (irreversible) breaking down or consumption of order. I suggest that a useful metaphor for organisms and societies (as for the biosphere as a whole) is that of "eddies" or "loops" in the unilateral conversion of concentrated solar energy to heat. A society of hunter-gatherers could thus be represented as in figure 5. The tapering-off loop conveys some of the basic conditions of living systems. (1) The input of order is always greater than the order embodied in a system's structure and thus available for future conversions. (2) Structure is process: the process of gaining access to order—often described as "serving" to maintain structure—*is* the structure itself. (3) Self-organization or self-reproduction thus means that order appropriated from the environment is directed toward continued appropriation of order. (4) The order expended can never re-enter the loop, only facilitate access to new order.

In figure 5, the point where the linear flow of exergy is—for want of a better mode of exposition—depicted as "crossing" itself represents the conversion of wild food to human life, that is, to physiological and social processes directed toward gaining access to the new plant and animal exergy that continually reproduces human society. As the solar exergy stored in wild biomass is consumed, what remains is organic refuse, which soon finds other uses in the natural food chains, and heat. Societies such as this, like societies based on certain kinds of pastoralism or agricul-

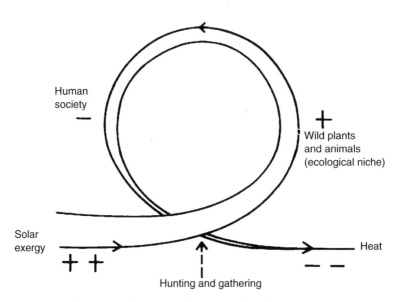

Fig. 5   The transformation of exergy in a hunting-and-gathering society

ture, theoretically could live in balance with their environments (i.e., in a "steady state") for as long as the sun shines on Earth. For this reason, they are able to visualize the process of social reproduction as circular, as if work spent on procuring food was "exchanged" for their harvests of organic exergy. (In reality, this circularity must always remain an illusion, because work merely gives *access* to food exergy but is not *incorporated* in food in the sense that prey are incorporated in predators; cf. Ingold 1979:276.)

Modern industrial society, on the other hand, is based on a different "loop" (figure 6). In addition to renewable, solar-propelled flows and funds, limited *stocks* of order are converted, by way of labor and raw materials, to industrial products. In two different ways, these products can be employed to gain access to new exergy so as to reproduce industry. (1) On one hand, (a) foodstuffs produced in industrial agriculture, by being converted into labor, and (b) technology can be used to gain access to local sources of exergy. (2) On the other hand, and more crucially, industrial products are *exchanged* for new raw materials. Industrial production and world trade are thus mutually reinforcing modes of exergy appropriation. To export industrial goods would be meaningless if the money gained could not be used to purchase new resources with *higher exergy content*. The "net order" thus appropriated by industry is as fundamental

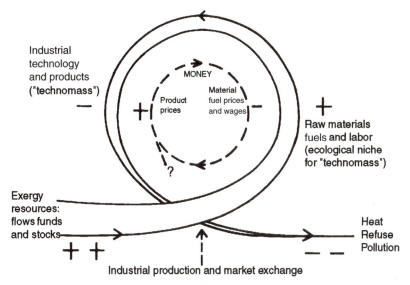

Fig. 6   The transformation of exergy in industrial society

to its reproduction (as a synthetic "biomass") as food is to an organism. Again, we should be careful not to reify the distinction between "structure" and "process." Rather than concluding that we need increasing amounts of high-quality energy to provide for human life, we may recognize that it is *industrial* structure that is being provided for, and that industry and trade *constitute* that process of provisionment.

Note that human work here assumes a different position than in figure 5; here labor is an exergy niche for a suprahuman "technomass." We have argued that the concept of "use value" could be reconsidered in terms of the kind of structure that is the primary objective of reproduction: human or industrial "biomass." The relationship between human labor and technology is clearly ambiguous in terms of which serves which. In figure 6, human labor is depicted alongside raw materials as an exergy resource for the industrial technomass. Because the actual products of human labor (as distinct from food) cannot be eaten by other humans, it is misleading to describe exploitation of labor as predation among men (cf. Ruyle 1973:607; Gall and Saxe 1977:264), but artifacts embodying human energy can indeed be incorporated in the technomass. Industry itself, then, is the metaphorical predator to which humans fall prey. *What* is produced is uninteresting as long as labor and materials can be had in exchange, because human needs are not the issue. "Production" is the goal in itself, answering to the needs of the technomass.

The flow of money can be drawn as a circle within the industrial "loop" but running in the opposite direction (cf. Odum 1971:174). Money is the symbolic, social operator orchestrating the industrial flow of exergy. However, it is the incapacity of the money circle to measure linear flows of real productive potential that is the fundamental flaw of economic theory and a fundamental problem confronting human society as a whole. Thermodynamic theory asserts that energy quality and order are *consumed* in maintaining a structure, whereas economics is founded on the idea that value is *generated* in production. Merely to manage maintenance, industry must be paid *more* for its products than it spends on fuels and raw materials, even though it has achieved a *decrease* in the overall sum of order. This is indicated by the plus and minus signs in figure 6. Industry must see to it that the sum of product prices is higher than the sum of expenditures on wages, fuels, and materials. This seemingly legitimate demand not only has the questionable effect of rewarding an accelerating degradation of order but also, as indicated by the question mark in figure 6, raises the question of from where the extra money is to be derived. As Rosa Luxemburg long ago observed (cf. Fieldhouse 1967:85–91), industrial capitalism cannot subsist by itself, because the money spent by industry cannot constitute a sufficient market for its products. This perennial predicament is the motor behind (1) the imperative, continuous expansion of production ("growth"), primarily through increased mechanization ("technological development"), (2) the pursuit of new markets (imperialism), and (3) the pervasive process of inflation, stemming from the struggle to keep the sum of sales always one step ahead of the sum of costs.

The declining *net* productivity of a growing structure (resulting from rising energy requirements for maintenance) is as inexorable for the technomass of late capitalism as it is for the biomass of a climax rain forest. Industry's demand for profit is not, as Marx saw it, a specifically "capitalist" problem that can be neutralized by altering the system of ownership and distribution, but a symptom of the thermodynamic *inefficiency* of industrial production. Whereas hunter-gatherers even in areas such as the Kalahari Desert may retrieve 9.6 times the energy they spend on hunting and gathering, industrial agriculture generally yields only a fraction of the total, human-orchestrated energy input (cf. Ellen 1982:123–153). Such a wasteful form of production can continue only as long as it is "subsidized" by an asymmetric world trade in energy. Only from a *local* perspective can it appear "productive" or "efficient." The enormous thermodynamic losses can be compensated for only by a continuous expansion. If industry actually *were* to generate order, rather than extract it from elsewhere, it should be possible for money to circulate without chronic deficits: the sum spent on wages, fuels, and raw materials could be equal to the sum gained from sales, yet growth would be feasible. Because this is not the case, growth, imperialism, and inflation are all symptoms of the accelerating thermodynamic waste of industrial production. To the extent that manual labor (biological process) is replaced by machines, the efficiency of this conversion is drastically reduced (cf. R. N. Adams 1975:194; Martinez-Alier 1987:34–35; Debeir, Deléage, and Hémery 1986 [1991]:101–102).

Figure 6 indicates how the ecological and socioeconomic problems of industrial society are two aspects of the same basic structure. The depletion of limited stocks of mineral exergy and the unevenly distributed deterioration of the biosphere that follows in its wake (cf. Watts 1994; Rival 1997) constitute a socially mediated process. It is based on a social *exchange* of substances with different exergy content, presupposing and reproducing local accumulations of exergy to the detriment of increasingly impoverished peripheries.

ECONOMIES AND TECHNOLOGIES AS CULTURAL CONSTRUCTIONS

Economists continue to ponder the impossible task of matching the money circle to a thermodynamic reality that is linear. In the rare instances when they visualize measures of value other than money, they tend to assume that there is some kind of natural correspondence between the two. It is no coincidence that David Ricardo undermined the distinction between "use value" and "exchange value." What could be more ideologically instrumental, we asked in the previous chapter, than to equate all forms of "utility" and to declare that the value of a product basically corresponds to its price? In the same way that we intuitively sense that the "utility" of food really cannot be compared to the "utility" of electrical toys (whether for children or adults), we should hesitate to compare the value of rain forests to that of the trivial merchandise for which they are exchanged. Westerners might have a lot to learn from the "multicentric," non-Western economies they have been so busily breaking down. General-purpose money was the universal solvent that gave Western industry access to the resources of its global periphery. The abstract, neoclassical notion of "utility" thus emptied human livelihood of specific and intrinsic meaning in order to render it subservient to the industrial world organism. As the ancient "loop" by which living-time was exchanged for food came to be mediated by industry, life had to be redefined as "labor" (cf. Baudrillard 1973 [1975]).

Gudeman (1986:65–66) argues that in shifting his emphasis from land fertility to labor as the generator of value, Ricardo adopted a more optimistic view of growth. The same applies, of course, to modern economics as a whole compared to the eighteenth-century Physiocrats. The shift in relative importance of nature versus labor in these different outlooks is important and interesting because, from an anthropological perspective, the attribution of generative qualities to labor is not a universal. Gudeman and Rivera (1989) have shown how Colombian peasants view the earth and its products as the only source of *fuerza* ("force"), whereas neither tools nor work are productive. This pre-industrial cosmology, which they share with the Physiocrats, is closer than conventional economics to a formulation that would be acceptable in terms of thermodynamics. Based on various versions of the labor theory of value, the ideology of "growth" is a local, industrial perspective that excludes the reduction of order in non-industrial sectors from its field of vision.

In retrospect, we might say that the pre-industrial Physiocratic model failed because it was so strongly contradicted by world trade. The metaphor of restricted "circulation," however workable it may have been in a pre-industrial context, seemed obsolete when the horizons of economic thought were no longer restricted to a more or less autonomous bioregion, but merely embraced the limb of an emergent, global supersystem. Ricardian theory was born at a moment when Western Europe was experiencing the transformation of colonialism into the inexorable, kinematic logic of industrialism. As industrial accumulation progressed, and so long as the colonial basis of affluence was obscured, no one could possibly believe that the land was the ultimate source of affluence. The result was an image of unlimited good based on a labor theory of value and the illusions of machine fetishism.

Anthropology is in a unique position to pursue Mumford's (1934) project of deconstructing the machine. I can think of plenty of reasons why this should be an important undertaking, and like Pfaffenberger (1988a:237), I am baffled by the relative lack of anthropological interest in discussing or even defining the concept of "technology," a term that stands "at the very centre of what Westerners (and Westernised people) tend to celebrate about themselves." Pfaffenberger (*Ibid.*:250) observes that technology is "a mystifying force of the first order, . . . rivalled only by language in its potential (to paraphrase Geertz) for suspending us in webs of significance that we ourselves create." In the same vein, Ellen (1988:232) concludes that "material culture can no longer be treated as though it were, somehow, outside culture."

Although there is a growing awareness of the need to reconceptualize technology by identifying its social and ideological contexts, our commitment to the "case study" approach may prevent us from gaining a truly holistic perspective on industrial technology as a global phenomenon and a specific social form. Recent attempts at subjecting technology to cultural analysis tend to concentrate on the peculiarities of *specific* technological systems in fairly restricted social contexts. In all this work, we are witnessing a laudable dissolution of the distinction between technology and society (Bijker et al. 1987; Pfaffenberger 1988a), but the horizon rarely extends beyond identifiable social categories such as inventors, users, or victims. From another point of view, it has been suggested that the "complete machine" includes both the work-piece and the worker (Ingold 1988, citing Reuleaux 1876), but why stop there? If we focus on material and thermodynamic prerequisites rather than specific technological forms, we can only conclude that the flows that sustain industrial production are nothing less than global in scale. It is at this level that technology *as a whole* is "socially constructed." If specific technologies require and reproduce specific forms of social organization, it is no less true that industrial technology as a general phenomenon requires and reproduces a specific world order. Our celebrated Western, technological knowledge is "true" (i.e., "works") only within a restricted social space. The social definition of what is technologically feasible is not external to technology but so intrinsic to it that it should be inscribed in any representation of it. Machines are not "productive"—they do not "produce," other than from a socially restricted perspective. To visualize the machine as a productive force *in itself* is to submit to a misleading distinction between technology and economy, the material and the social.

Industrial machines *are* social phenomena. These inorganic structures propelled by mineral fuels and substituting for human work *could not be maintained* but for a specific structure of human exchange. We might agree with the mercantilists that *world trade* is what is "productive," but then only from a Western point of view. The profit, in terms of order, that we make on the world market is transformed in our consciousness into an inherent, generative, and self-aggrandizing capacity within those fetishized metal and plastic contraptions. If industrial technology ultimately rests on a systematic appropriation and accumulation of exergy rather than on a decontextualized, socially innocent, and intrinsically potent body of knowledge, the science of technology itself is founded on some basic socioeconomic premises. (Thus, to tell the whole story, technological textbooks should always begin with the qualification, "If world market prices can guarantee access to sufficiently cheap forms of exergy, then. . . .") The notion of intrinsic machine fertility seems to be another instance of the deluding, culture-specific "air of simple wisdom" that Geertz (1983) identifies as "common sense."

Industrialization no longer suggests a temporal development progressively emancipating the human species from ecological constraints, but a spatially restricted emancipation that is *illusory* precisely because it is local and dependent on the exploitation of other sectors of global society. To a certain extent, the use of industrial technology to extract and harness various forms of order *within* its own boundaries will give the "developed" sector the appearance of thermodynamic self-sufficiency, but the imperative of external realization (keeping sales higher than costs) expresses the ultimate thermodynamic dependency of industrial on non-industrial space. Increasing output and domestic consumption ("growth"), underpinned by inflation, are marginal, day-to-day solutions that can never eclipse the basic structure by which the total, global technomass subsists on exchange rates directing net flows of negative entropy from non-industrial to industrial sectors of world society. Any attempt to visualize industrial technology as a material reality independent of monetary flows is illusory, for its materiality makes it no less social in constitution, that is, no less dependent on a continuing process of expanding reproduction.

The imperative of external input visualized by Luxemburg ("realization" over and beyond domestic consumption) has haunted industrialism from the start. In the long run, industrialism is faced with the same problem whether restricted to eighteenth-century England or having engulfed the global niche to which it aspires. In the latter case, however, it will have reached the critical point at which expansion is no longer possible.

I have argued, first, that economic growth is *appropriation*, not mere aggregation, of order, and second, that this appropriation is *social*. This could have amounted merely to another formulation of "imperialism" or "dependency" or "world system" theory if I had not also drawn out its epistemological implications for our everyday conception of industrial technology. Even the Marxist recognition of the exploitative, imperialist foundation of capital remained confined within the industrial, Ricardian paradigm. Once "capital" was converted into the "productive forces" of industrialism, it became miraculously exempt from criticism. The machines that in late eighteenth century and early nineteenth century England congealed from the global flows that constituted the British empire, in assuming this objectified, material form, were automatically granted the innocence of a *natural*, self-evident feature of existence. Conjured as a developmental "level," harmless in itself, industrial technology is represented in Marxist thought as separable from the capitalist "relations of production" that spawned it, and not only adoptable by, but even historically conducive to, an egalitarian future world.

The role of money and machine fetishism is as crucial to the operation of industrial capitalism as beliefs in the divinity of sovereigns in tribute-organized, agricultural polities such as that of the Inca. The epistemological implications are that knowledge is true if it *works*. Technology thus serves as the verification of science in the same way that pre-Columbian Andean harvests verified the divine ancestry of the Inca emperor and the efficacy of his ritual communication with the Sun. Science relates to technology as Ricardo's economic theory to his own success on the stock exchange: it works, therefore it is true. People who readily concede that industrial technology is generated in a process of global exploitation will still find an engineer's account exhaustive. I am arguing, however, that it is deluding to separate the "social" from the "material" existence of technology. Like an organism, the machine cannot be understood or explained, other than in a medical/technical repairman's sense, if decontextualized from the flows of exergy that sustain it. Though we know quite well how rising oil prices or shrinking markets will affect "economic growth," it is remarkable how we fail to allow these insights to contaminate our image of what technology really *is*.

If the veracity of knowledge tends to be judged by its instrumentality, the final question must be to which ends knowledge is produced. An engineer's account of industrial technology is obviously sufficient for an engineer. He does not need to ask the question why industrial machinery is so unevenly distributed over the face of the earth. But to anthropologists and others concerned with the Sisyphean task of "development aid," it is increasingly obvious that the truths of engineering work only within a restricted social space. Increasingly, we are probably going to see economics—the repairman's view of industrialism—not "working" even within that space. Following Marx, I would suggest that such contradictions are conducive to paradigmatic change. Having rethought some basic, Western concepts such as "production," "growth," "development," "labor," and "technology," we can only conclude that the first step toward a sustainable society must be to reform our vocabulary.

7

Language and the Material: Probing Our Categories

In 1981, I visited an agricultural cooperative in the Andean highlands near Huancayo, Peru. In various parts of the Andes I had previously seen agriculture practiced in much the same way as it had been for centuries: groups of people working the soil of narrow terraces or small plots with shovels and hoes, or resorting to the trampling of animals to separate grain from straw. But in the center of this little community of adobe houses, subsidized by federal grants and intent on gearing itself to the world market, was parked a huge and shining red Massey Ferguson tractor. It seemed conspicuously out of place, and when someone remarked that it had been inoperative for some time, this merely confirmed a suspicion. To me, the unlikely setting in combination with its ardently polished finish charged that striking contrivance with a symbolic dimension I had not previously recognized in tractors.

A similar sensation struck me as I interviewed the villagers of a small community about six hours' drive from Ayacucho, as well as their relatives in the *barriadas* of Lima. When asked by a Swedish solidarity group what kind of support they would most appreciate, they spoke with an unmistakable reverence about the semi-industrial Singer sewing machines they had seen in shop windows in downtown Lima. The idea was to establish a small textile industry geared to the market for traditional-style Andean garments. A year later, when the solidarity group had raised enough money for them to purchase their first machines, the Lima colony arranged an impressive ceremony in which their new possessions were solemnly decorated with colored ribbons and baptized after their Swedish benefactors. Since then, their aspirations have been tragically eroded, but with all the scapegoats provided by the official discourse on "inflation," "unemployment," and "national debt," their sewing machines still maintain their luster.

In both cases, the disillusionment is represented as having nothing to do with the intrinsic properties of industrial technology, but with the allegedly mutable socioeconomic setting into which it was introduced. In the course of the following argument, I will continue to focus on the illusions produced by the distinction between "technological" and "socioeconomic" phenomena. Ultimately, the subtly non-Western reverence conferred on the tractor and the sewing machines prompts us to ask questions about the meaning of machines in our own construction of reality.

CRITICISM AND LANGUAGE

The ultimate justification for anthropology is not the comprehension of others as an end in itself, but the possibilities of converting experiences of cultural multiplicity into a critical scrutiny of our own, Western habits of thought (Marcus and Fischer 1986). The many pledges that have been made to this creed have given it a ring of triviality, as if defamiliarizing domestic systems of meaning is what most of us are already doing anyway. However, the gap between rhetoric and practice is noteworthy, and most of us tend to keep immersing ourselves in exotic hermeneutics, savoring the "subtleties of distinction and discretion such discourse demands and renders possible" and taking the very disinterestedness of our pursuits "for the sign of their supreme value" (Bauman 1988:230). This is understandable, for if distant fieldwork is a jarring experience, the anthropologist returning from the field may be more hesitant about deconstructing his own familiar domains of reality than is generally appreciated. Where anthropologists have tried to bring anthropology home, there has been a tendency to address relatively harmless issues such as the symbolism of food, clothing, or family pets. This conspicuously uncontroversial nature of much anthropology "at home" is undoubtedly linked to the day-to-day conditions of anthropological activity as such. Though anthropologists may like to think of themselves as "respectable anti-establishment eccentrics" (Rayner 1989), in their consumption of airline tickets and personal computers, and in their constant eagerness to qualify, they remain very much a part of the establishment.

A recurrent anthropological critique of Western civilization is the idea—which goes back to the notion of a Golden Age or a biblical Eden—that we in the West have lost what "primitive man" still has, in terms of ecological, social, and spiritual values (Marcus and Fischer 1986:129). Though widespread and convincing, this critique of civilization as a kind of transgression rarely amounts to more than a mood of bitterness or nostalgia. Traditionally, in most of these formulations, there is an implicit inevitability about our industrial development, and insofar as we ourselves in some respects are represented as the losers, an air of lament and resignation. In subscribing to the conventional image of "development," much anthropological critique seems to have been unable to escape from the confines of a Western vocabulary.

To anthropologists "at home," it could be argued that the dictionary is the foremost cultural text. This agrees with what Marcus and Fischer (*Ibid.*:137–157) have called "defamiliarization by epistemological critique." Such a strategy rests on the recognition that we Westerners live in "as culturally constructed and non-'natural' a reality" as any others. But how do we discover the cultural lenses and linguistic grids through which we construct reality? There is a growing awareness that attention should be focused on "the materialist or utilitarian bias of Western thought" (*Ibid.*:141), but there have been several different approaches to this key issue, for materialism can be confronted at various levels. *Webster*'s dictionary renders "materialism" as "the theory that matter, and matter only, exists in the universe" but also as "an attitude which ignores spiritual values." The former definition refers to a philosophical position assuming that the ultimate essence of reality is material ("corporeal," "occupying space"), whereas the latter suggests an ideology of pragmatism or even avarice.

The allegedly materialist foundations of Western reality construction do seem to pervade our language. Dictionary synonyms for "material" include "essential," "appreciable," and "worthy of consideration." The hegemony of philosophical materialism is equaled only by the unanimity with which we deplore too overtly materialistic pursuits in everyday life. The two seemingly disparate senses of materialism thus form inverted and complementary aspects of a cultural configuration that lies at the heart of Western civilization. Although codified as standard usage, a consistent equation of things material with things "worthy of consideration" would strike us as vulgar, and in some quarters still as blasphemous. When we find blasphemy thus encoded in our unconscious categories, we may suspect that we are addressing something significant. On one hand, it suggests that "materiality" as a category, and by definition its otherworldly, "idealist" antithesis, deserves further scrutiny. On the other, it suggests that a critique of materialism (whatever that is), though an established ingredient of Western discourse, is but a ripple on our well of basic categories.

MATERIALITY AND CULTURE

Confronted with entirely different schemes for classifying reality, anthropologists have tried in various ways to transcend the idealist-materialist dichotomy in Western thought. Sahlins (1976) has argued that material conditions never directly determine human behavior, for humans can relate to those conditions only through a specific system of meanings. There are no unmediated, exclusively practical or utilitarian motives or activities; cognition and behavior are always rooted in culture. Sahlins exemplifies this by showing how the modern, American production of food and clothing is geared to the symbolic status, in American culture, of various animals (and parts of animals) and textiles. As noted in the previous chapter, however, he does not defamiliarize the concept of production as such, only its orientation, or output. Gudeman (1986), on the other hand, investigates how production ("livelihood") is culturally constituted in various societies, but without hesitating to single out recent, Western conceptions as uniquely "logical" and "rational" in their refusal to endow production with metaphorical meaning. Stripped of the culturally defined meanings and motives that propel real human actors, the positing of a universal "rationality" and its derivational "logic" approaches tautology. Sahlins (1976:210) suggests that this formalist illusion—"that the economy and society are pragmatically constructed"—may be unique to Western civilization.

On this last point, I believe Sahlins is slightly beside the mark, for it implies that traditional, non-Western cultures would perceive their own behavior as somehow nonpragmatic or non-utilitarian. The dictionary defines "pragmatic" as "concerned with practical consequences" and "utilitarian" as "of practical use"; surely this is not an exclusively Western concern. If asked about the general purpose of production, I am sure people universally refer to the use they have for its output, and in elaborating the usefulness of each specific product, they will reveal the fabric of meaning out of which the economy is constituted. Even where production is constituted in ways which to Westerners seem mysterious (e.g., as the work of the ancestors; cf. Gudeman [1986] on the Bemba and Bisa), the various ways of appeasing these ancestors are no less pragmatic than Western technology. Among the Azande, it is common sense that abstention from sexual intercourse is prerequisite to success in pot making. Is not abstention from sexual intercourse prior to pot making, then, a pragmatic precaution? Referring to Evans-Pritchard's discussion of Azande witchcraft, Geertz (1983:78–80) concludes that even these seemingly "magical" or "mystical" assertions do not transcend commonsense thought but reinforce it by reassuring the Zande that "their fund of commonplaces is, momentary appearances to the contrary notwithstanding, dependable and adequate." Pfaffenberger (1988b:8) similarly argues that the purpose of Hindu temples in Sri Lanka is "frankly utilitarian." To understand this, "we need only to concede that Hindus really believe this is so" (*Ibid.*:12). The representation of human behavior as pragmatic or rational is not unique to Westerners, for both concepts apply to formal features of human motivation, regardless of its substance or content. If we want to discuss the uniqueness of Western civilization, we must address its *specific* version of utilitarian and pragmatic beliefs and considerations. This is where our task of defamiliarization becomes particularly demanding, for we immediately find that we can no longer use familiar words in the way we are used to. To begin with, we can no longer speak with the same certitude of "objective" or "material" conditions.

Sahlins's attempt to bridge the "antique dualism" (1976:ix) of mind and matter is highly successful, but there are a few additional steps to be taken. His basic point is that "there is no material logic apart from the practical interest, and the practical interest of men in production is symbolically constituted" (*Ibid.*:207). He cannot refrain, however, from speaking of "material" things as if he himself had access to their ultimate, "objective" identity. He challenges the *implications* of the view that material processes are "factual," "independent of man's will," and "fixed by nature," but ultimately not *that view itself*. He himself seems to submit to the conclusion that "thought can only kneel before the absolute sovereignty of the physical world" (*Ibid.*). Sahlins finally treats "material" things in themselves as given; it is only their use that is symbolically constituted:

> An industrial technology in itself does not dictate whether it will be run by men or by women, in the day or at night, by wage laborers or by collective owners, on Tuesday or on Sunday, for a profit or for a livelihood; in the service of national security or private gluttony; to produce hand-fed dogs or stall-fed cattle, blue collars or white dresses; to pollute the rivers and infect the atmosphere or to itself slowly rust away like the Singer sewing machine posed majestically in front of the house of an African chief. (*Ibid.*:208)

The machine is represented as standing there, aloof and innocent, intrinsically void of significance. Why? Because it is material. But what, then, do we mean by "material"? According to the dictionary, "material" means "essential," and "to materialize" is "to become fact." To say that something is material seems to be the Western way of saying that it is real. The concept of materialism thus takes on a new shade of meaning: it no longer only means saying that the material is real but also prescriptively defines our culturally posited reality as material. Apparently, we use the appellation "material" for those aspects of our Western reality construction that we posit as unquestionable. Here, in the culturally defined realm of unquestionable assumptions, is where we would expect to find the distinctive and pivotal aspects of Western constructions of the world. I will argue that the hidden agenda of this usage is precisely that thought should "only kneel" before the machine. And thought "kneeling" before its own objectified categories is a good definition of fetishism (cf. Ellen 1988).

To posit a material realm distinct from signification is to evoke a specifically Western version of the culturally axiomatic body of propositions that Geertz (1983) would identify as "common sense." The material is that which simply *is*, as if regardless of the perceiver. But the dictionary also suggests that "to matter" is "to signify." There is no uncategorized perception. Wittgenstein's (1921 [1971]:115) observation that "the limits of my language mean the limits of my world," although profoundly influential in the ethnography of other cultures, is inherently difficult to apply to our struggles with anthropology at home. Ardener (1989:173) remarks that "our worlds are inescapably contaminated with language." His own examples include the cultural constitution of the human body.

> It is an important advance to learn that the contamination extends into materiality, for that has long been for some the last refuge from language. Conversely, for others language has been a refuge from materiality. (*Ibid.*)

For Ardener, the familiar opposition category/object (*Ibid.*:172) must yield to what he calls "language-category-object simultaneities" (*Ibid.*:169). We can no longer accept references to objects as such (i.e., as objective phenomena), for in the same instant that we refer to them, we conjure a meaningful category. In this sense, I would argue, concepts like "machine" and "technology" are not as neutral and innocent as we think.

Ardener writes that language is "a hybrid medium, its map being partly interior, subjective, and rooted in regularities of the 'human mind,' and partly exterior, objective, and rooted in materiality" (*Ibid.*:171). Yet by the very act of submitting to the dualism he wishes to cross—by conjuring images of the "objective" and of "materiality"—he inadvertently illustrates the problem of which he is generally so acutely aware, namely "how anthropology can ever be 'logically' possible within the vocabulary provided by the present age" (*Ibid.*:210). Linguistic and symbolic representation introduces "arbitrary fixings" into depictions of a "neither-idealist-nor-materialist" social space, "which then develop automatisms of their own" (*Ibid.*:184). Ardener explores the prescriptive quality of concepts denoting phenomena ranging from ethnic populations to calendrical seasons and body parts, but in introducing the concept of *density* (*Ibid.*:169), he is careful not to use language as a "refuge from materiality":

The "density" gradients of categories must be related to frequency in some ways—perhaps we may put it as frequency of association or interaction with reality. Categories thus contain or coexist with a statistical feature—it is part of their materiality.

The problem of defining categories is thus transformed into one of trying to approximate their "densities." This seems a useful approach to adopt for those of us who have struggled, for instance, with the anthropological debate on prescriptive marriage categories (cf. Hornborg 1988, 1993, 1998b). It would help us handle the problematic (but inevitable) role of multiple genealogical specifications of kinship terms, not as exhaustively definitional sets or as lists of cognitive "extensions" of a focal definition (cf. Ardener 1989:169), but as provisional attempts to represent elementary structures of social reproduction in terms suggesting statistical "curves" (Lévi-Strauss 1969:xxxiii) in the flows of genes and prestations. Language must somehow be anchored in an assumed, if ultimately unnamed, reality. Conventional attempts at "definition" tend to ignore the problem of trying to establish a correspondence between bounded categories and a reality that appears to be continuous. In adopting Ardener's notion of "density," we remain anchored in reality while recognizing that language is always provisional.

But if the density of categories in Ardener's sense is "part of their materiality," the problem here is how to approximate the density of our conception of "materiality" itself. The dictionary tells us that "material" means "consisting of matter corporeal," and that "matter" in turn means "that which occupies space and is the object of the senses." "Corporeal" means "having a body" but also "physical," which in turn is rendered as "pertaining to physics" or to "nature." Now, "physics" are the "sciences which deal with natural phenomena, e.g. motion, force, light, sound, electricity, etc.," and "nature" is nothing less than "the world, the universe, known and unknown; the power underlying all phenomena in the material world; the innate or essential qualities of a thing; the environment of man." This chain of definitions creates a self-referential web of meanings that features tautologies as well as ambiguities and contradictions. If "material" is transitively synonymous to corporeal, physical, and natural, we might object that the natural phenomena addressed by physics are rarely corporeal or even "the object of the senses," and that "nature," in addition to admitting "unknown" (i.e., unsensed) aspects of the universe, signifies the "power underlying" the material world, rather than restricting itself to materiality itself. Although all these concepts connote a reality defined by its externality to the human mind, the circular cross-references by which their overlapping shades of meaning assert themselves ultimately provide no definition of the "material." If "matter" consists of bodies occupying space, what do we make of the vast, empty spaces within the atom? Organisms are literally corporeal, but what about corporate social groups? What about the sunlight that sustains those organisms, or the most elementary of "particles" organized by their metabolism?

Our commonsense definition of the "material" appears to cluster around a segment of reality defined by our own vantage point as organisms equipped with a specific array of sensory organs tuned to some evolutionary, ecological niche. Organisms seem more "corporeal" to us than societies because we can view the former from without, while being confined to conceptualizing the latter from within. But living systems at all levels of integration consist primarily of organization (structure, arrangement, orderliness, information), and the "material" parts that are thus organized upon closer scrutiny also dissolve into organization. With Eastern philosophy as a foil, it could even be argued that "matter," "energy," and "information" are culture-specific "arbitrary fixings" focusing on three different aspects or manifestations of a single existence, and physicists have indeed demonstrated how closely interrelated they are. One way of expressing this "simultaneity" might be to say that "information" (from Latin *informare*, "to give form to") is the way energy relates to matter: energy informs matter, and matter is informed energy. And "form," of course, does not restrict itself to "bodies," but denotes any "shape," "appearance," "configuration," "arrangement," or even "model." As modern physicists penetrate ever lower, subatomic levels of integration, the question of where to draw the line between matter and energy becomes increasingly irrelevant. Similarly, the "force" or "activity" of energy (from Greek *energeia*, activity)—its ability to do work—depends on how organized it is, which is a measure of information. Such a collapse of categories into one another, Ardener has taught us, is best met by devising new ones. This is precisely what has happened in physics: the energy-information-matter continuum has been conflated into concepts such as negative entropy or *negentropy* (Schrödinger 1944 [1967]; Georgescu-Roegen 1971) and the cognate form *exergy* (e.g., Evans 1969). The imperviousness of established Western thought vis-à-vis such crucial concepts may in fact be linked to our notions of "technology" and the "machine," for our fetishized way of thinking about these pivotal Western phenomena relies precisely on a compartmentalization into structure and process, corporeal and fluid, technology and society.

In his epistemological critique of the environmental movement, Evernden (1985) notes how the Western preoccupation with material forms is an expression of the sovereignty assigned to the sense of sight. Organisms, for instance, are visualized as bounded phenomena, confined within their skins, rather than as overlapping fields (cf. chapter 11). The continuous but invisible flows of energy, oxygen, information, and so on that sustain and in fact constitute a human being are not the primary way in which she presents herself to the senses. The isolation of form from process and of part from whole is an aspect of the proclivity to objectify that has been so characteristic of Western thought. It produces an atomistic, reductionist worldview supremely adequate for technical manipulation but hardly for holistic understanding.

EXISTENTIAL FOUNDATIONS: LANGUAGE AND TECHNOLOGY

Any analysis of discourse must be concerned with the constraints and possibilities of language. Structuralist and post-structuralist anthropology has its roots in linguistics, and its major concern is how to conceptualize the role of language in human behavior. Rejecting Cartesian models of language *versus* reality, Ardener consistently argues that the two are inseparable. From the classical, anthropological study of prescriptive relationship terminologies to myriad other domains of language, he demonstrates how words are generative of reality. Language generates "definition-spaces" or "world-structures," the boundaries of which define the limits of understanding and social behavior. It follows that the recognition and delineation of a definition-space can be pursued only from a more or less external vantage point. Whereas the externality of Foucault and the "historians of mentality" is a temporal one, the distance cultivated by anthropologists is one of cultural space. The specificity of Western concepts protrudes most clearly in the difficulties of translating them to the idioms of other cultures (cf. Taussig 1980).

Humans everywhere subscribe to some version of cosmology in the sense of a corpus of congealed and unquestionable meanings. Such a core of concepts and propositions is geared to social praxis and is a prerequisite for social interaction. In the case of the modern world market, for instance, it is evident that all participants must agree on the significance of a basic set of concepts such as "wage," "commodity," and "price." Such instrumental knowledge can be analytically distinguished from value judgments of a moral or affective nature (e.g., perceiving wage labor as evil; cf. Taussig 1980), but the former is of no less ideological import than the latter. The neoclassical economic vocabulary and the tenets of technical engineering resemble each other in this respect: both convey the impression of fundamental and self-evident "truths," yet both fields of discourse systematically omit the social foundations of the phenomena they pretend to represent. Economic "growth" and technological "develop-

ment" are thus represented as local, nonsocial, more or less physical processes generated in the interaction between labor, know-how, and natural
resources—that is, in the relationship between humans and nature rather
than in global relations of exchange.

Many have recognized that technology has a symbolic dimension, but
they differ as to exactly how (e.g., Mumford 1934; Ellul 1964; Winner
1977; Bijker et al. 1987; Pfaffenberger 1988a, 1988b). Several authors converge on the topic of control. Culture process—the construction of meaning—is propelled by a fear of chaos. Control is thus an important aspect
of meaning. "Ritual" can be defined as that meta-communicative, repeti-
tive aspect of social behavior (speaking, working, etc.) that serves to convey the message of nonrandomness, predictability, and control. Ritual aspects are integral to technology. The instrumentality of a productive act
(whether "magical" or "scientific") cannot be neatly divided into pragmatic versus expressive aspects (cf. Leach 1976).

A faith in technology seems to be synonymous with a faith in "progress" and civilization. It appears to be part of the platform of unquestionable meaning in which we all have a stake and without which modern
identity would be in jeopardy. Part of the cultural inertia of these hegemonic concepts ("progress," "development," "technological solutions"),
which continue to define the boundaries of our discourse, may thus be
fundamentally an existential problem. It would be superfluous to exemplify the matter-of-fact way in which we use the idea of "technological
inventions" to explain our own history and the present state of the world,
and to suggest brighter (or gloomier) scenarios for the future of humankind. But in representing machines as if their presence or absence in a
specific society hinges on its level of technological know-how, or as if
technology could be available to everyone, if only the socioeconomic conditions were different, we are the victims of a delusion. For an unevenly
distributed industrial technology and its setting of global socioeconomic
conditions are not separable circumstances but aspects of the same phenomenon: the former is rather an embodiment of the latter.

In being taught to talk about "technology" and "society" or "economy" as if they represented distinct phenomena, we have been introduced into a confined cosmological space with invisible boundaries, such
as Ardener called a "world-structure." Within that space, we have continued to talk about Western "progress" and "development" as if it were
merely a matter of being "ahead" of the "underdeveloped" or still "developing" countries in the adoption of industrial technology. Even the
most revolutionary of critical analyses, by reproducing the fetishized discourse on technology, was to find itself subsumed and disarmed within
the confines of the industrial worldview. It is to a closer scrutiny of the
vocabulary of this discourse that we now turn.

"Technology," the dictionary tells us, is the "science of mechanical and industrial arts." As a "science," it is a "systematic knowledge of natural or physical phenomena; truth ascertained by observation, experiment, and induction." "Mechanical" pertains to "machines, mechanism, or mechanics." A "mechanism" is "the structure of a machine," and "mechanics" is "the science of machines," dealing with "force and motion." A "machine" is "any contrivance for the conversion and direction of motion; an apparatus for doing some kind of work." But it can also mean "a person who acts like an automaton" or "a politically controlled organization," and "machinery" can denote "any combination of means to an end." The Latin noun *machina* corresponds to the verb *machinari*, "to plot," and "to machinate" is "to contrive, usually with evil or ulterior motive" or "to conspire." "Industrial," finally, pertains to "industry"— that is, a "steady application to work" or a "habitual diligence in any employment, bodily or mental."

It is noteworthy that "technology" does not refer to the machines themselves but to the "systematic knowledge" and ascertained "truths" that go into their construction. In everyday usage, in celebrating their "progress" Westerners tend to refer to their "technology" rather than to their "machines," which implies that they are celebrating their "knowledge" and skills for making these material contrivances available to them, rather than the contrivances themselves. The natural and physical phenomena thus "ascertained" are those of "force and motion," and to "contrive" an apparatus for a "steady application to work" is to "plot" the "conversion and direction" of such natural forces. "Work," like "machinery," can denote an "effort directed to an end" but also "production" (i.e., "the act of producing"), and "to produce" means "to bring forth; to give birth to; to yield; to make; to cause." The noun "produce" (i.e., "that which is produced") connotes "agricultural products; crops," whereas "productive" (i.e., "having the power to produce") also means "creative; fertile; efficient."

These references to crops and fertility suggest that the ancestral Latin word *producere*, "to lead forward" (cf. "to bring forth"), was an essentially agrarian concept. Indeed, Gudeman and Rivera (1989) indicate how modern, Western concepts such as "value," "fertility," and "power" may derive from a common root category approximated by the rural Colombian notion of *fuerza* ("strength"), which is applicable to the land, its products, and food, but not to manufacture, for it is held that "tools do not give at all" and "work itself is not productive" (*Ibid.*:272–273). In the view of these rural Colombians, strikingly reminiscent of the eighteenth-century Physiocrats, modern, Western economic notions endow "equipment and humans with qualities that pertain only to the earth." Gudeman and Rivera conclude that a European folk concept of "force" or "strength" may have been ancestral to both land and labor theories of "value." I would add that such a category is suggested by the semantic fields covered by the cognate concepts "power" (from Old French *poer*) and "potency" (from Latin *posse*, "to be able"), which range from "great authority or influence" through "capacity for action" and "procreative" ability to "motive force," "efficacy," and "energy." The modern extension of these concepts into the field of electricity (cf. "power station," "potential difference") is significant.

It is worth noting that "work" also can denote the "mechanism of a watch," for the clock has been advanced as the prototype for all machines (Mumford 1959:14). Originally developed as a simulator of celestial movements, its core idea is the retardation, or self-checking, of the energy of motion. Wagner (1986:93) doubts whether "the steam engine could have been conceived in effective form had the clock not preceded it." In being founded on negative feedback mechanisms regularizing the dissipation of negentropy, machines are analogous to living systems. Industrial technology is a fundamental "autocatalytic device" (R. N. Adams 1978:303–306) for maintaining the energy flows by which modern Western civilization reproduces itself as a "dissipative structure" (Glansdorff and Prigogine 1971). Itself inspired by natural systems, the idea of the machine has subsequently generated a web of cross-references by which nature and the machine are engaged in a reciprocal metaphor (Wagner 1986:94). Our review of some of the vocabulary suggests that the natural metaphors by which we represent industrial machinery may delude us in more ways than one. In Western symbolism, machines signify productivity and efficiency, but a global, thermodynamic perspective reveals the extent to which this signification is a misleading, cultural construct.

[margin note: clock 1st machine]

THE METAPHOR OF GROWTH

In previous chapters I have suggested that the accumulation of machinery at certain points or within certain sectors of the world system is in a sense analogous to the growth of organic biomass. Indeed, our talk of economic "growth" is a revealing metaphor, for the Old English *growan* referred to biological processes such as "to produce by cultivation; to raise; to develop naturally." To "accumulate" (from Latin *ad cumulus*, "to heap") means "to grow into a mass," and the word "mass" means "the quantity of matter in a body." Both biological and industrial "growth," it seems, are processes of accumulation. We are used to thinking of that which is accumulated as "mass" or "matter," but Schrödinger and Georgescu-Roegen have demonstrated that it is really a question of orderliness—that is, negative entropy.

[handwritten note: - technomass a cancerous growth]

To clarify how organic and economic growth differ, we must consider by which means these two kinds of "orderliness" (structure, organization) incorporate negentropy from their environments. For organic growth, the point of departure is the highly organized flow of energy that reaches Earth in the form of solar radiation. Life is the process by which the negentropy of sunlight further "informs" and animates Earth's thin surface layer of congealed matter-as-informed-energy. As the sun winds down by reconverting its own stock of matter-as-informed-energy into radiation, a very small fraction of this radiation transmitted in all directions is received by Earth and temporarily reconverted into structure before being refracted into space in the degraded form of heat. This structure is the biosphere, a momentary, whirlpool-like by-product of the irreversible dissipation of the sun. According to the Second Law of Thermodynamics (the "Entropy Law"), any such local accretion of order can occur only at the expense of the total sum of order in the universe. The quality of energy in the universe continually deteriorates, and local processes of growth or "refinement" always involve expenditures of negentropy in excess of that represented by the outcome of such processes. As far as terrestrial plant life is concerned, this simply means that the price for maintaining photosynthetic structure is that sunlight is degraded to heat in the process.

Because we can consider the input of sunlight available to the biosphere as a practically unlimited starting point, the closest thing to genuine "production" is photosynthesis, and plants are appropriately called "primary producers." From this point, each human act of energy conversion (from pasture and other crops through meat, human labor, and technology to manufactured products) entails a net degradation of negentropy. Thus it will be seen that any theories of economic value based on land or labor, for example (not to mention "utility" or "demand"), are cultural constructions, but that from the vantage point of human life in general, the assignment of generative properties to specific moments of the economic process has a relatively higher validity the closer they are to the input of solar radiation.

Refinement and degradation always go hand in hand, but biological and industrial growth differ in three important respects in terms of the implications of this thermodynamic regularity. Grasslands always risk being overgrazed by expanding populations of herbivores, but as long as a unit of biomass is directly dependent on its local niche for survival, there will tend to be constraints on overexploitation and a long-term (if oscillating) balance. Industrial growth, however, entails a *supra-local* appropriation of negentropy. The Western, industrial "technomass" feeds on distant ecosystems by means of world trade, and by shifting its tentacles, it can afford to remain insensitive to their degradation, leaving large surfaces of the earth increasingly degraded. Second, in order to reproduce this technomass, industry subsists on depletable stocks of mineral negentropy, which means that whichever time perspective we choose, it is not a sustainable structure. Finally, and this is the main point I have been trying to make in this book so far, industry is not only circumstantially but also inherently parasitic on other, non-industrial sectors of world society.

Marxist theories of imperialism, although acutely aware of global exploitation, have strangely circumambulated its own implications for our understanding of industrial technology itself. A factory does not grow out of subterranean ore deposits like a mushroom; it can reproduce itself only by exchanging its output of products for a continuous input of specific substances like fuels and raw materials. If this structure is generalized on a global scale, the secret of industrialism can be seen not so much as a matter of applying an increasingly intensive technology to a certain piece of land, as of "realizing" the industrial products on a global market at exchange rates that guarantee the industrialized sectors a continuous negentropic buildup. The industrial technomass cannot subsist by itself, drawing negentropy directly from nature, but depends on the existence of non-industrial sectors, where the price of negentropy (fuels, raw materials, and the labor to extract them) is so much lower that such exchange rates can be maintained. As Rosa Luxemburg long ago observed, the industrial sector cannot by itself swallow all its products but is dependent on the external realization of exchange values to achieve the exchange rates requisite for the reproduction of capital. This is another way of expressing the necessity, as compelling for industry as it is for organisms, to import order and export disorder. "Realization" means converting the "bound energy" of industrial products into the fresh, "free energy" (negentropy) of fuels and human labor continuously pumped into the industrial sector.

No economic theory aspiring to legitimate world market prices by means of the vocabulary of "utility" and "demand" can alter the condition that industrial growth is founded on an asymmetric, social exchange of negentropy. Like certain phases of organic growth, economic growth is a self-reinforcing, positive feedback process: each increment in structural volume in turn increases the capacity of the industrial technomass to appropriate more negentropy from its surroundings. The growing technological infrastructure continually augments the capacity of the industrial worker to convert negentropy (his "productivity" per hour); this in turn implies that exchange with non- or low-industrialized sectors (expressed as the relative market price of labor time) will tend to become increasingly asymmetrical.

A local accretion of industrial technology can be reproduced only by accelerating the pace of dissipation elsewhere. This is becoming increas-

ingly obvious in the degradation of the natural environment, the depletion of nonrenewable resources, and the impoverishment of populations
in the periphery. The collapse of the U.S.S.R. can be interpreted as a spec-
tacular illustration of the limitations of industrialism. The Soviet attempt
to confine a complete industrial metabolism (resource base, "realization,"
and all) within a single political boundary destined it to be the first industrialized nation to run into seriously crippling ecological and social disor-
ders. Yet our conventional understanding of industrial technology leads
us to visualize its drawbacks as circumstantial rather than intrinsic. The
alleviation of its problems is represented as an essentially technological
task, and if technological solutions are not effective, this is not recognized
as symptomatic of the industrial world order but of local, "socioeconomic" or "cultural" constraints.

Industrialization is crucial to the idea of Western progress and development, and recipes for alleviating world poverty are generally phrased in
terms of the transfer of technological "know-how" to the Third World.
But the notion of a transmissible technological capacity is founded on the
fetishized view of machines as decontextualized from the flows that reproduce them. Machines are not detachable entities but nodes within
structures of exchange; like living organisms, they are negentropic whirl-
pools. The introduction of industrial machines into Third World settings
may be as infertile as planting a fruit tree in the desert or a dairy cow on
a rock island, and the simile is not too farfetched: the flows of negentropy
to support them are simply not there. Industrial technology depends for
its existence on not being accessible to everyone; it presupposes non-industrial sectors. The idea of distributing it evenly among all the peoples
of the world would be as contradictory as trying to keep a beef cow alive
while restoring its molecules to all the tufts of grass from which it has
sprung.

This interpretation also casts a shadow of doubt over the prospect of a
miraculously sustainable, new technology that will render all the drawbacks of industrialism obsolete. Industrialism is an inherently supra-local
process of reproduction that relies on asymmetric resource flows. Technological inventions that claim to be locally and indefinitely "sustainable"
either rely on and serve the extant industrial infrastructure or are not
new. To believe that modern science can produce better versions of sustainable technology than the traditional, pre-industrial systems that it is
presently in the process of eclipsing is to disregard the exploitative foundation of technological science and represent it as a fund of pure knowledge emanating from a uniquely ingenious, Western civilization. If we
think we can outdo pre-industrial cultures in their own yard—that is,
without recourse to the exploitative structures of modern world trade—
this means that we continue to subscribe to the (officially obsolete) notion

that what distinguishes us from them is our enlightenment and their ignorance.

I have indicated how we are constrained by the vocabulary of conventional economics. To say that a machine is "productive" generally means that it is "profitable," which of course is contingent on prevailing exchange rates. Any manner of production for exchange can be rendered "profitable," given sufficiently advantageous prices. It is noteworthy that "to profit" derives from the Latin *proficere*, "to make progress." Usages such as these effectively obscure the requisite asymmetric exchange of negentropy on which all machines subsist, and in consideration of which our assessment of their productivity must be less self-congratulatory. We are used to thinking of machines simply as devices for achieving or producing more per unit of labor time, but a more complete view is to see them as contrivances for outworking other populations in order to outdistance them in trade. Some of this meaning is reflected in the verb "to machinate" (i.e., to "contrive" or "plot" with "evil intent"). Primarily, machines seem to be devices not for saving labor but for harnessing peripheral labor and resources into the service of the center. Like the world market prices that reproduce it, the machine represents an exploitative social relationship. It is a cultural (i.e., simultaneously material-social-symbolic) institution regulating the distribution of resources on a global scale. Without the world market on which it competes with manual labor in the periphery, the machine would be as sterile as the Physiocrats perceived it. In short, industrial machinery is in significant part a technology for exploitation.

THE EPISTEMOLOGY OF
CULTURAL CRITIQUE

It is ironic that in largely abandoning studies of material culture to concentrate on "social structure" and "symbolism," twentieth-century anthropology has to a large extent yielded to the mind/matter dichotomy that it frequently claims to transcend. Until rather recently, tools and machinery have been classified with "subsistence activities" and rarely represented as fundamental and active aspects of "society" or "cosmology." Once endowed with cultural meaning, however, artifacts have an undeniable inertia of their own that impinges on human thought and relations. The mediation of a cultural system of meaning implies a dialectical relationship between artifacts and human behavior (Hodder 1986:12). To archaeologists, for whom material culture is often all that remains, the way artifacts have appeared to and acted upon ancient human societies must generally remain a matter of speculation. For anthropologists reflecting on the modern world, a greater emphasis on material culture should not be confused with "materialism." In concluding his article on fetishism, Ellen (1988:230–232) observes:

> During the last fifty years anthropology has come to place less emphasis on the materiality of cultural phenomena and has become more interested— almost obsessively so—in intricate abstracted systems of belief and webs of significance. Material culture can no longer be treated as though it were, somehow, outside culture.

I have argued that a more profound understanding of the machine must rest on the recognition that "technology," "society," and "cosmology" are inseparable: as a socio-technical artifact, the machine simultaneously embodies and reproduces a specific configuration of cultural categories. With the aid of a dictionary, I have tried to show that these concepts form a web of meanings that represents itself as based on clear-cut definitions but is actually as arbitrary as any other system of cultural categories. To convey an alternative and more critical perspective on industrialism, I was compelled to resort to a thermodynamic vocabulary significantly alien to our everyday usage. If I am guilty of a number of "undisciplined" excursions into physics, ecology, economics, and philosophy, this is only because anthropology cannot afford to submit to the Western compartmentalization of knowledge whereby the sciences of "nature" and "culture" are represented as distinct and incommensurable enterprises.

To say that some familiar aspect of reality is something other than what we have generally considered it to be is a sign of our times. Postmodern deconstruction at times seems to serve no other purpose than to shock, but whenever basic concepts of social science are at stake, the argument is ideologically charged, and we are no longer in the realm of intellectual diversion. Such cultural critique necessarily embodies "an account of the positioning of the critic in relation to that which is critiqued" (Marcus and Fischer 1986:115). The necessity of "positioning" requires some further comments. When I struggled with ways of formulating "deep structures" of Amerindian social organization (Hornborg 1988), I arrived at the confounding, "postmodern" point where I realized that any attempt to *name* that underlying reality would be to simply add another representation to the spectrum of cultural representations that I was investigating (cf. Hornborg 1998b). We habitually distinguish between model and reality, or category and object, but "reality" and "object" are often spoken of as if ultimately accessible and nameable, beyond those idiosyncratic veils of culture. That which to us is "real" and "material" is visualized as elsewhere subject to various modes of cultural (mis)understanding (e.g.,

Sahlins's example of the African sewing machine), but it seems inconceivable to us that even our image of the tangibly and straightforwardly "real" (e.g., industrial machinery) is culturally constructed. As soon as we attempt to incorporate "reality" into our conceptual framework, however, it is endowed with meaning (cf. Wagner 1986). To fully grasp these implications and escape from the confines of our Western "world-structure" is an arduous mental undertaking. But it is what anthropology should be all about.

Here is a paradox, however. To allow our own cultural idiosyncrasies to protrude, we must have recourse to plausible, alternative images in the light of which our familiar models may attain that tinge of arbitrariness essential to defamiliarization. To traditional ethnography, the implicit world view of the anthropologist himself provides the foil against which the culture of the Other comes into view, but anthropology at home cannot simply invert the situation. Contrary to what is often implied, the exotic world views retrieved from traditional societies, though sometimes represented as more attractive, rarely impress Western anthropologists as more *valid* than their own (Crick 1982:302). I do not refer to social or ecological norms of conduct, but to basic categories of reality. To defamiliarize the Western image of "production," it will not do to simply compare it to that of the Bemba and Bisa, to whom it is the work of the ancestors (Gudeman 1986), because such a comparison is unlikely to prompt a Westerner to seriously reconsider his own version.

The paradox is this: to effectively challenge the cultural bias of Western conceptions, we would have to seriously champion alternative perspectives that we claim to be less culturally biased. An anthropology "at home" can thus not avoid entering the mainstream, ideologically tinted debates through which Western reality construction is continually being negotiated. Whereas a postmodern experience may serve as a crucial, dislocative jolt, the only way to critically apply our relativism is from a *position*. To transcend postmodernism is to concede that our choice of position represents a social act, even though in championing that position, we will employ that rationalist, objectivist style of discourse by which Westerners can hope to be persuaded.

The conception I have been trying to defamiliarize is the notion of the machine as a "productive" force, or of industrial "production" as such. To ascribe a generative force of its own to a specific moment in an economic process is an act of signification, one that renders the machine no less of a symbolic construct than any other aspect of culture. From a *local* vantage point, the machine may signify "productivity," "efficiency," and "progress," whereas from a *global* perspective it would be more appropriate to let it signify "destruction," "waste," and "exploitation." These propositions about the semiotics of machinery understandably raise the commonsensical objection that machines are not simply "symbolic": we cannot deny that they also exist, that they are real, that they are material! My use of an exclamation mark here is not fortuitous, for Geertz (1983:84–85) concludes that "it is precisely in its 'tonality'—the temper its observations convey, the turn of mind its conclusions reflect—that the differentiate of common sense are properly to be sought":

> It is only in isolating what might be called its stylistic features, the marks of attitude that give it its peculiar stamp, that common sense . . . can be transculturally characterized. Like the voice of piety, the voice of sanity sounds pretty much the same whatever it says; what simple wisdom has everywhere in common is the maddening air of simple wisdom with which it is uttered.

In referring to the tangible materiality of machines as evidence of their productivity, we are using the "material" as a prescriptive label for commonsensical, Western reality construction, that is, that which can be questioned only at the risk of sounding insane. But in employing an alternative vocabulary that has suggested itself to those who have probed the innermost recesses of that construction, we have found our way back to the etymological roots of the "machine": it emerges as a *machination*, a plot.

DISTINCTIONS THAT MYSTIFY

The Western mode of understanding reality is well summed up in the word "analysis"—the breaking up of something into its constituent elements. But the delineation of separate "elements" (such as "technology" and "economy," or "material" and "social") is a negotiable, cultural construction. The inadequacies of our conventional categories are continuously being exposed in a number of hyphenated or joined constructions such as "sociocultural," "socioeconomic," "socio-technical," and so on. Anthropologists often find distinctions between conventional categories arbitrary and try to dissolve the boundaries between them. One such distinction that has been challenged in recent years is between *science, ideology,* and *culture.* We still often implicitly distinguish between three such forms of cognition, as if science was *truth,* ideology was *lies,* and culture some kind of quaint, exotic *misunderstanding.* It has become increasingly evident, however, that they all belong to the same supercategory. They are *modes of representation,* modes of producing meaningful images of the world. Ultimately, the only way such images can be judged is by the ends they serve, for whom, and which kinds of social relations they reproduce.

This means that what we should be looking at is what images *do* (cf. Maturana and Varela 1987 [1992]).

We are living in an age of collapsing distinctions. After centuries of analytical fragmentation, our patterns of thought now increasingly tend to aspire to more holistic perspectives. The Western obsession with distanced dissection of reality has become a serious threat not only to our capacity to experience coherence and meaning but also to our capacity to understand the troubling social and ecological processes of our time. If technology is the verification of modern scientific thought, its social and ecological *failures* pose a challenge to that mode of thought. Though perhaps sufficient in a restricted context of engineering, analysis must be balanced with synthesis if we are to understand the conditions for its successes and failures.

As observed by Pfaffenberger (1988a), modern industrial technology is the major achievement that Westerners celebrate about themselves. It is, perhaps, what distinguishes us from the "Others." Paradoxically, it is also what we tend to be most self-critical about. Technology has been criticized for dehumanizing work and alienating workers, degrading and polluting the environment, being unaesthetic and artless, being risky and unhealthy, and even being inefficient and irrational. Much of the criticism of modern technology (Mumford 1934; Ellul 1964; Ingold 1988) focuses on the various ways in which it *dissociates* aspects of reality that were previously more integrated, namely tool/body, physical work/mental work, means/ends, work/agency, use/meaning, production/art, and work/life. Such processes of disembedding are very much a part of modernity. Technology and money are both the primary means and the primary expressions of decontextualization. In this book, I have been adding another kind of critique to this list, namely that industrial technology is inherently *exploitative*. It is apparent, however, that even its capacity to serve as a tool of exploitation hinges on the dissociative processes that are the hallmark of modernity.

All this is made more complicated by the fact that precisely this phenomenon which distinguishes us from the "Others"—the premodern—is construed as having little or nothing to do with culture. This is probably not a coincidence. We are willing to relativize almost everything else (including the designs of *specific* technologies), but not technology as a general phenomenon. Because it is, as we say, "material," it seems somehow out of reach for cultural analysis. But as a number of anthropologists have recently argued, culture does extend into—or "contaminate"—the material world. In this chapter we have turned the issue around and suggested that our concept of "material" is a cultural category. We use it *prescriptively* for those aspects of our life that we perceive as unquestionable.

8

꙲

Symbolic Technologies: Machines and the Marxian Notion of Fetishism

> No object, no thing, has being or movement in human society except by the significance men can give it. (Sahlins 1976:170)

My aims with this chapter are, first, to delineate a more precise definition of the Marxian concept of fetishism, and second, to consider whether this concept is applicable to machine technology. Machines occupy an ambiguous position in Marxist theory, both as manifestations of capitalist accumulation and as vehicles of proletarian emancipation. As I suggested in chapter 6, by extending the theory of fetishism from money and commodities to machines, we may achieve an epistemological shift in our understanding of the foundations of "technological development" and of the very ontology of mechanical work. It seems that the most central fetish of industrial capitalism has in fact escaped Marxist analysis. (I here use "Marxist" or "Marxian" in a very general sense to denote projects inspired by Karl Marx's ambition to uncover ideologically mystified, unequal relations of social exchange.)

There has been a lot of ambiguity about the concept of fetishism, to the point where some have even argued for its "abolition" (Pool 1990:126). I believe, however, that it will remain a useful tool in our struggles to understand the cognitive processes that produce various cultural perceptions of the relations between persons and things. The first part of this chapter discusses previous definitions of fetishism in order to distill some central themes that appear to be particularly significant to my argument on machine fetishism. I will be concerned primarily with narrowing down the Marxian definition, the core of which I understand to be *the mystification of unequal relations of social exchange through the attribution of autonomous agency or productivity to certain kinds of material objects.* To relate the Marxist definition to the wider discussion of fetishism from which it is rarely distinguished (cf. Apter and Pietz 1993; Spyer 1998), I suggest a taxonomic framework for the various definitions offered. In this framework, I briefly explore the usefulness of semiotic theory in understanding various versions of fetishism. I then discuss the role of symbols and "semiotic moments" in technological systems, finally returning to ecological economics and world system theory to elaborate the argument that machine technology can be understood as fetishized, social relations of unequal exchange.

EARLY HISTORY OF A CONCEPT:
A BRIEF SKETCH

The history of the concept of fetishism has been reviewed by, among others, Pietz (1985, 1987, 1988, 1993), Ellen (1988), and Pool (1990). Ellen traces its various uses through three distinct analytic traditions: the anthropology of religion, Marxism, and psychoanalysis. Only the former two will concern us here. By transferring the concept from the study of religion to the critique of political economy, Marx gave it a new and intriguing dimension that continues to pose a challenge to anthropological theory. I have here deliberately restricted my discussion to contributions that pursue, or are immediately relevant to, Marx's focus on collective representations as mystifications of unequal exchange. Recent studies of fetishism in, for example, art history and cultural studies have attempted to link Marxist and psychoanalytic approaches (cf. Apter and Pietz 1993; Spyer 1998), but the result is a more diffuse and aestheticized notion of fetishism than the one delineated here. (Symptomatic of this sensuous, postmodern trend is Taussig's [1993] shift toward exploring the idiosyncratic, sexual phenomenology of a policeman's badge in Genet's *The Thief's Journal.* Although they make intriguing reading, such contributions seem less immediately relevant to the analytical work attempted here.)

The fifteenth-century Portuguese had used the form *feitiço* for magical practice and witchcraft (Pietz 1985:5) and extended it to objects venerated among peoples whom they encountered along the western coast of Africa. In 1760, Charles DeBrosses used it for the worship of material objects such as stone figures, believing that it represented the point of origin of all religion. In 1830, Auguste Comte similarly viewed fetishism as the first stage in the development of religious thought, the defining feature of which was the attribution of human mental faculties to nonhuman objects. This wide and diffuse phenomenon was instead labeled "animism" by Tylor, who in 1871 restricted the term "fetishism" to beliefs in spirits working through inanimate objects. In 1921, A. C. Haddon similarly defined fetishism as the worship of "an intangible power or spirit incorporated in some visible form" (quoted in Ellen 1988:215). Ellen observes that the subsequently widespread avoidance of the term among anthropologists may be related to an "inner ambivalence" in the fetish phenomenon itself as to whether it is the objects *themselves* that have agency or a (separate) spiritual force that is represented by them.

Marx in 1842 borrowed the concept of fetishism from DeBrosses (Pietz 1993:134), but there are indications that his use of it was also inspired by Hegel (Ellen 1988:216, 232 n. 2). In the first volume of *Capital*, published in 1867, the fetishism of commodities is defined as

> nothing but the definite social relation between men themselves which assumes here, for them, the fantastic form of a relation between things. In order, therefore, to find an analogy we must take flight into the misty realm of religion. There the products of the human brain appear as autonomous figures endowed with a life of their own, which enter into relations both with each other and with the human race. So it is in the world of commodities with the products of men's hands. (Marx 1867 [1976]:165)

Alienated from their producers, commodities appear as autonomous sources of value rather than embodiments of the labor of human persons. Similarly, there is a fundamental propensity to see money (e.g., in the form of gold and silver) not

> as a social relation of production, but in the form of natural objects with peculiar social properties. And what of modern political economy . . . ? Does not its fetishism become quite palpable when it deals with capital? (*Ibid.*:176)

Parry and Bloch (1989:6) write that Marx saw the fetishism of money as "the pre-eminent example" of the fetishism of commodities. Money capital, however, is endowed with a special capacity for growth not attributed to commodities. In volume 3 of *Capital*, Marx observes that mainstream economists tend to view it as "a property of money to generate value and yield interest, much as it is an attribute of pear trees to bear pears" (Marx 1894 [1967]:392).

The application of the concept of fetishism to the everyday realities of European economic life was one of Marx's most remarkable achievements. It completes the peculiar trajectory of a concept that at one point may have implicated aspects of mainstream European religion (cf. saintly relics; Pietz 1987; Ellen 1988), then was exported and projected—condescendingly—onto the superstitions of primitive Africans, finally to be reflected back onto the presumptively secularized, economic world-view of modern Europeans. In repatriating the notion of fetishism so as to "defamiliarize" everyday, European categories, Marx was the first to apply an anthropologically informed, cultural critique (cf. Marcus and Fischer 1986) to Western power structures. As Bloch (1989:172) observes, what Marx did was to carry out a "symbolical analysis of capitalism." By suggesting that our own, commonsensical rationality could be as obfuscating as the darkest superstitions of tribal Africa, he managed to convey the unsettling suspicion that we are all the victims of some gigantic, ideological illusion.

AUTONOMOUS PRODUCTIVITY AS CORE THEME

Taussig (1980) completes this process of radical decentering by showing how rural Colombians, in struggling to control the exploitative and seemingly magical logic of money, engage in fetishistic practices (such as baptizing money or negotiating with the devil) that upon closer reflection appear no more fantastic than our own desire to have our money "grow." In a passage that deserves to be quoted at length, Taussig seems to capture the essence of the Marxist notion of fetishism:

> [T]hese apparently self-bounded and potent things are merely the embodiments and concretizations of relationships that bind them to a larger whole. Their identity, existence, and natural properties spring from their *position* in an all-encompassing organic *pattern* of organization in which things are understood as but partial expressions of a self-organizing totality. . . .
> [If] the atomistic view prevails, as it does in our culture, then the isolated thing in itself must inevitably tend to appear as animated because in reality it is part of an active process. If we "thingify" parts of a living system, ignore the context of which they are a part, and then observe that the things move, so to speak, it logically follows that the things may well be regarded or spoken of as though they were alive with their own autonomous powers. If regarded as mere things, they will therefore appear as though they were indeed *animate* things—fetishes. Capital, for instance, is often compared to a tree that bears fruit; the thing itself is the source of its own increase. Hence, reification leads to fetishism. (Taussig 1980:36)

The illusion of autonomous productivity—"the thing itself [as] the source of its own increase"—is an important aspect of the Marxist analysis. Within capitalism, writes Bloch (1989:171–172),

> commodities or money which are inanimate substances, and exchange which is a non-productive activity, appear to give forth life, as in the Voltair-

ian view of fetishes, where sticks and stones were worshipped because they were mistakenly believed to bring forth children, crops, wealth. In this way Marx showed that what had been represented by economists as merely technical devices were in fact ideological transformers which hid the true source of productivity and attributed productivity to things and activities which were not productive in themselves.

Against this background, Bloch (*Ibid.*:177) is able to conclude that, among the traditional Merina of Madagascar, the parallel to capital and money is the ancestral substance represented by the tomb and its content of human remains. Both kinds of objects, he argues, "symbolically appropriate the creativity of people and labour and attribute it to a fetish."

PERSONIFICATION, ALIENATION, AND OBJECTIFICATION: A SEMIOTIC APPROACH

Taussig (1980:36–38) suggests that premodern and modern versions of fetishism seem to be structural inversions of each other. As Marx showed, the perception of modern commodities as in some sense autonomous derives from the alienating split between persons and the products of their labor. Premodern fetishism, on the contrary, is based precisely on the perceived unity between persons and their products. The classical example is the spirit or life-force (*hau*) adhering to the Maori gift (Mauss 1923–24 [1967]). Evoking Frazer's concept of "contagious magic," goods exchanged in such contexts are perceived as metonymical extensions of the persons exchanging them. Taussig refers to Radin's (1957:273–274) conclusion that, in a premodern world, material forms are "mere symbols, *simulacra*, for the essential psychical-spiritual entity that lies behind them."

It does seem useful to consider the difference between modern and premodern fetishism in terms of semiotics. Mauss's and Radin's interpretations suggest that the difference between venerated gifts and coveted commodities is that there is a sense in which they constitute different species of signs. The gift signifies a specific social relationship, whereas the commodity at most signifies an abstract social value or quality, adhering to the item itself, that can be appropriated (and transformed) through purchase and use (cf. Baudrillard 1972 [1981]; Sahlins 1976). Whereas the gift retains its symbolic reference to the person of the giver, the commodity in the shop remains an anonymous embodiment of abstract value—a signifier without a signified—waiting to be afforded a referent in the form of the person of the consumer. Until it does become the attribute of a concrete person, there is a sense in which the commodity is a sign that stands only for itself.

The inversion identified by Taussig is closely related to the difference, recognized by Sahlins (1976:215) and Gudeman (1986:44), between the premodern personification of things and the modern objectification of persons. Sahlins notes that "Mauss wrote of the *hau* as if the exchange of things were by Maori conceptions the exchange of persons, even as Marx observed rather the opposite of our own thinking: the bond of persons is a relation between things." Parry and Bloch (1989:10–12) are probably right in criticizing such dichotomies for giving the impression of a simple divide between capitalist and precapitalist economies, arguing instead that they represent a polarity between two spheres of economic life that tend to recur in different proportions in most societies. This does not, however, detract from the relevance of Taussig's, Sahlins's, or Gudeman's analytical observations. Whether the two versions of fetishism succeed each other historically or exist contemporaneously in the same society, they seem to be generated within a single framework of semiotic possibilities, in which things may be treated as (signs or extensions of) persons, or persons may be treated as things.

It has been suggested that it is a specifically "Western" habit to conceptually distinguish between persons and things (Kopytoff 1986:84; Ingold 1996:129). Referring to Pietz (1985), MacGaffey (1990:45) observes that "the problem of the fetish, for the European mind, has been that it confounds the distinction, regarded as basic and natural, between objects and persons." Which, then, are the defining features of a "person" that Westerners are so reluctant to extend to things? Perhaps they emerge most clearly into view precisely where personhood *is* open to nonhuman entities, as in the assertion of the Waswanipi Cree that animals, the winds, and many other phenomena are regarded as being " 'like persons' in that they act intelligently and have wills and idiosyncrasies, and understand and are understood by men" (Feit 1973:116). Ingold (1996:134) characterizes personhood in terms of constituting "an undivided centre of awareness and agency," and Kopytoff (1986:84) similarly focuses on *individuality* as a distinguishing feature of persons. It is probably safe to suggest that the distinction between persons and things is more or less synonymous to the distinction between subjects and objects. Perhaps it is no coincidence, then, that a society that more than any other has been maligned for its tendencies to objectify people and treat persons as things should be so obsessed with discursively maintaining—as the last "cultural ramparts" against commoditization (Kopytoff 1986:85)—the boundary between them.

MacGaffey (1990:45) suggests that instead of asking "why Africans fail to distinguish adequately between people and objects, we might reverse the question and ask whence comes this dubious distinction in our own thought." The question inevitably brings us to the modern mind/matter dualism codified by Descartes. If the material objects through which a human mind engages itself in the world are conceived as radically divorced from that (alienated) mind, they are not likely to be experienced as extensions of persons. In fact, even the human body risks being treated, by the mind residing in it, as an external object. If, on the other hand, persons were perceived as "fields" of identification and agency extending outward from human brains and interfusing with their material surroundings (cf. Bateson 1979; Singer 1984; Evernden 1985; see chapter 11), it would be quite reasonable to experience their material traces as signs of human selves. In Cartesian modernity, however, the inclination to distinguish the self from its material surroundings is conducive to the inclination to treat *even people* as objects void of deeper significance. Other human beings risk appearing to us as primarily corporeal entities, rather than as signs of deeper essences inviting exploration. This semiotic transformation culminates in the postmodern preoccupation with surfaces identified, for instance, by Baudrillard. For present purposes, it will suffice to observe that modern, Cartesian objectification and premodern fetishism can be viewed as inversions of one another: the former denies agency and subjectivity even in living beings, whereas the latter attributes such qualities even to dead objects (cf. Hornborg 1999).

Appadurai (1986:48–54) offers yet another angle on different varieties of fetishism as expressions of alienation. His point of departure is how the perception of commodities relates to the positions and perspectives of different categories of producers and consumers. "Culturally constructed stories and ideologies about commodity flows," he notes, "acquire especially intense, new, and striking qualities when the spatial, cognitive, or institutional distances between production, distribution, and consumption are great" (*Ibid.*:48). This perspective immediately suggests that there are different varieties of alienation with respect to commodity flows and production processes, depending on the position of people in these global flows and processes. Appadurai gives examples of how the perspectives of traders, consumers, and producers can be distorted each in their own way, but how the common denominator of all such distortions is the incomplete view of the global system of which they are all a part. He is thus able to theoretically juxtapose such diverse instances as modern commodity futures markets, cargo cults in the Pacific, and Taussig's account of devil symbolism among Bolivian tin miners. The two latter examples illustrate very clearly how alienation and fetishism can appear at both ends of a production process, depending on whether it is a commodity's past or its future that is obscured from view.

THE FETISH AS INFRA- *AND*
SUPERSTRUCTURE, TRUE *AND* FALSE

Prior to the breakthrough of social constructivism in anthropology, a fundamental paradox of the Marxian notion of fetishism was its implication that a *misrepresentation* of social reality was simultaneously a condition for the reproduction of that reality. In one of the earliest anthropological discussions of Marxian fetishism, Friedman (1974b:56–57) defines fetishes as structures (of "the social mechanisms which distribute social labour") that do not contain "the *true* representation of their material effects" (italics added). Writing at a time when it was still fairly unproblematic to speak of "true" and "false" representations of social realities (or, in Marxist terms, "transparency" versus "opacity"), Friedman addressed the problem of how it is that "a fetish, which is supposedly a fantastic misconstrual or inversion of material reality . . . can simultaneously be that which determines that reality" (*Ibid.*:36). While anthropology was still anticipating constructivism, Friedman had to resort to convoluted theoretical acrobatics to account for his quite valid conviction that the place of fetishism is neither in the infra- nor the superstructure, but "in the center of the social formation" (*Ibid.*:60). He establishes that "money is not a mere mystified image of something more real" but "the operator of the system, determining the particular social form of exploitation as well as its misrepresentations" (*Ibid.*:35).

Friedman's modification of the conventional, Marxist model was timely but soon eclipsed, along with other versions of Marxism, by the symbolic turn in anthropology. Citing Bourdillon (1978), Crick (1982:304) some years later concludes that "cultural phenomena simply do not divide into informative and disguising systems." The new, discursive space of constructivism did not have truth versus falsity on its agenda. It has proven difficult in postmodern anthropology to juxtapose discourses about cultural representations of reality, on one hand, and about a material reality "transparent" only to researchers, on the other. The discipline has thus split along the same Cartesian line that divides the academic community as a whole into "objectivists" and "relativists" (Bernstein 1983), or "Scientists" and "Humanists" (Ingerson 1994). It is ironic that this split became more pronounced at a juncture when it was becoming increasingly apparent that it would have to be transcended. The structural-Marxist discussion of fetishism and Sahlins's *Culture and Practical Reason* (1976) were important elements in this revelation but seem to have provoked a regressive reaction diametrically opposite to their post-Cartesian, theoretical implications. Today, contributors to journals like *Cultural Anthropology* and *Human Ecology*, respectively, speak in different tongues, and it is rare to find studies seriously concerned with the interfusion of symbolic con-

structs and, for example, energy flows in human society. But the imperative of addressing such interfusion of participants' representations and
some less accessible level of "reality" is obvious once representations are
recognized as "real" not only in the sense of emerging from objective conditions (cf. Harvey 1989, 1996) but also—and more important—in the
sense of being active ingredients in those conditions.

In a recent reconsideration of his application of the concept of fetishism
to social processes among the Kachin, Friedman (1979 [1998]:17–25) contrasts the term both with Marxist notions of "ideology" as superstructure
and with Sahlins's (1976) use of the concept of "culture" as code (in the
tradition of Saussure and Baudrillard). Whereas ideology refers to "representations of lived reality" (with "no organizing power"), he says, fetishism refers to "the *very organization of that reality*, the fact that the real
is a lived fantasy" (*Ibid.*: 18). This would seem quite compatible with Sahlins's position, yet Friedman is determined to posit a theoretical difference between them. It is noteworthy that, in the course of trying to distance himself from Sahlins, he momentarily reverts to a rather obscure
distinction between "infrastructure" and "superstructure," a dichotomy
that he himself seemed to have transcended in his 1974 article on fetishism. "The difference between infrastructure and superstructure," he now
says, is the difference between those practices and representations that
are responsible for the "direct organization of social reproduction" and
those practices and representations that are merely "predicated on that
organization" (Friedman 1979 [1998]:20). While rejecting the classical contrast between the material and the conceptual as well as Sahlins's duality
of practices and representations, Friedman thus refurbishes the old Marxist dichotomy of base and superstructure in terms of organization and
"predication" (literally meaning to "be *based* on"). In the same vein, the
mystifying aspect of fetishism is no longer rendered in terms of true and
false, but as a condition in which its "representational properties are simply incommensurate with that to which they refer" (*Ibid.*:19).

Although far from clear, Friedman's struggle to maintain a duality of
infra- and superstructure can be read as an attempt to salvage the notion
of a social reality external to the representations of the participants. It expresses the dilemma of Marxist theory confronted with the hegemony of
constructivism. If the participants' models of reality are contingent constructions, how can the observers claim that theirs are *not*? However we
try to rephrase it, the Marxian concept of fetishism carries an inherent
assumption about an outside observer's privileged access to truth that has
been difficult for postmodern anthropology to digest, and that in part
may account for its declining use in recent years. Thoden van Velzen
(1990:78) writes that "fetishes tend to *conceal* rather than to elucidate." He
concludes that "a fetish reflects both the impotency and the reluctance of

humans to make progress towards the understanding of a hidden reality"
(*Ibid.*:78–79). Taussig (1980:31) similarly reminds us that the concept of
commodity fetishism is meant to indicate that "capitalist society presents
itself to consciousness as something *other than what it basically is*, even
though that consciousness does reflect the superficial and hypostatized
configuration of society" (emphasis added).

One way of reconciling such Marxist truth claims with the epistemological impasse of constructivism is to recognize "demystification" as a continuous process rather than a final moment of revelation. In such an approach, each attempt by a radical social scientist to increase
"transparency" should be understood as provisional and *situated* in time
and space, in the sense of aspiring, as far as is presently possible, to represent the perspectives of the most exploited social categories, as these
could be presumed to appear *if they had access to a more complete view of the
system*. Moreover, such advances in understanding should not be visualized as inherent in the syntagmatic properties of the representations
themselves, which will always retain a measure of arbitrariness (and the
apotheosis of which would itself be equivalent to a kind of fetishism, an
"autonomization of the signifier"), but in their paradigmatic reference to
actual structures of social relations, a relationship the adequacy of which
is finally assessable only in their potential as guides to social practice.
"Truth," in other words, is cumulative and performative rather than absolute and representational.

To posit social relations of unequal exchange necessarily implies invok-
ing a "grand narrative," even if it is admitted to be provisional. Such a
pursuit of historically situated, emancipatory "truths" in no way pre-
cludes recognition of the basic tenets of constructivism (cf. Harvey 1996).
Generations before the entry of postmodern constructivism, Marx's concept of fetishism recognized that human worlds are symbolically constituted. The notion implies that, to a certain extent, human beings are the
authors of their own realities. But Marxian theory also asks questions
about *uncognized* aspects of reality that are external and contradictory to
the symbolic representations of the participants. The notions of "infrastructure" and "superstructure" are not the most adequate of concepts to
capture this duality, but they at least express a tradition of concern with
such subjacent conditions and constraints that is entirely missing in mainstream constructivism. Moreover, Marxian theory recognizes that the
human authorship of society highlighted by constructivism should imply
responsibility rather than solipsist resignation. If our images of the world
take an active part in shaping it, we need to be more reflexive about the
potential impact of the images we produce (cf. chapter 4). Perhaps we
should understand the present impasse as hesitation at some kind of

threshold in the development of a morally more self-conscious social science.

ASSESSING THE USES OF FETISHISM

Daniel Miller (1990:98–99) suggests that the Marxist critique of capitalism has recently tended to move traditional, "tribal" societies "from being the place to find examples of fetishism to become the only place where fetishism is not to be found." His derisive conflation of the Marxist notion of fetishism with romantic images of a "pre-fetishistic" society should be understood against the backdrop of his wider concern with material culture, objectification, and the emancipatory potential of modern consumption. He concedes, in fact, that Marxists have been among those least prone to romanticize premodern societies. To show that modern society has its own mystifications is hardly to deny that premodern societies have theirs, particularly when the concept used to illuminate the former is borrowed from our representations of the latter. Miller distinguishes between three different uses of the term "fetishism" as a critique of modern consumption (D. Miller 1987:204–205). The first is as a diffuse discontent with consumer culture and "the general malaise of materialism." The second, "narrower and more reasonable accusation" argues that obsessive consumption is used as a substitute for social interaction. The third and "most precise" critique of fetishism is Marx's original argument outlined above. Miller discusses the concept only in relation to critiques of modern society. He is not at all concerned with the more original usage of the word, although this is still employed by some anthropologists, for example Mommersteeg:

> A fetish is a man-made object that is considered to contain certain magical powers and as such is supposed to protect its owner or render him successful in his pursuits. The crucial aspect, however, is that it is a human fabrication. (Mommersteeg 1990:64)

Reviewing several recent discussions of fetishism, Pool (1990:121) also distinguishes three applications. First, there is the "old and long discredited" notion of fetishism as a primitive stage in the evolution of religion. Second, the concept has been used for the belief that certain objects are invested with supernatural power. In the third and more recent application, finally, Pool finds that the term "has a much wider and more diffuse meaning" (*Ibid.*), noting, for instance, the discrepancy between Miller's and Ellen's approaches. Pool suggests that we can distinguish between fetishism as a "descriptive ethnographic term" and as an "abstract analytic concept" (*Ibid.*:122). In the former sense, he argues, it should be used only where it is part of the natives' own vernacular; in the latter, it has become "so indeterminate as to be practically useless" (*Ibid.*:122, 124). The first suggestion would amount to more or less abolishing the term, which is also Pool's explicit recommendation. It is difficult to see, however, why the concept of fetishism should have to be discarded any more than, say, "ritual" or "patrilineage," neither of which is a vernacular term. The latter statement, moreover, is contradicted by Pool himself, for in finally suggesting that "fetishism has itself become a fetish," he not only uses the term but even offers a definition, namely "an objectification, a cultural representation which we have created and over which we have now lost control" (*Ibid.*:125).

Is Pool justified in pleading for the abolition of the term, or is there a common foundation beneath all these uses of the concept of fetishism from amulets, relics of saints, idolatry, and tombs to cargo cults, consumer goods, and money bills? Ellen (1988) argues that the varieties of fetishism addressed by the analytic traditions that he reviews share four "underlying cognitive processes": (1) *concretization* (the reification of an abstraction and its representation in a material object), (2) *animation* (the attribution to such an object of qualities of living organisms), (3) *conflation of signifier and signified* (an ambiguity as to whether the object itself, or what it signifies, is the "active causative agent"), and (4) *ambiguous power relations* (an ambiguity as to whether the object is controlled by people or people by the object). Ellen adds that

> all lie on a processual continuum which begins with the identification of categories, relationships and phenomena, and proceeds—via reification and iconification—to their *personification*. In this sequence what we might loosely describe as "fetishisation" appears with a shift from the balanced simultaneity of signifier and signified towards "the thing in itself." (Ellen 1988:213, emphasis added).

Rather than follow Pool's example and throw the baby out with the bathwater, I completely agree with Ellen (*Ibid.*:232) that the concept of fetishism raises "issues far too important to be consigned to some cul-de-sac in the history of ideas." But instead of attempting to isolate a common denominator of all the phenomena that have been referred to as fetishism, I believe that it may be more useful to clarify their differences. It is possible to unravel, in the various definitions reviewed, a logical taxonomy of features beginning with the most general aspects and then bifurcating into more specific forms. In such a framework, moreover, it is rewarding to elaborate on the semiotic approach suggested by Ellen's notion of a conflation of signifier and signified. Whereas Ellen's concepts are derived

from the tradition of Ferdinand de Saussure, there are some dimensions
of fetishism that may be more usefully illuminated by the application of
basic concepts from the framework of Charles Sanders Peirce.

NARROWING THE MARXIAN
NOTION OF FETISHISM

The taxonomic framework I am suggesting is outlined in figure 7. A can-
didate for the most general definition of fetishism is Pool's phrasing, referred to above: *a cultural representation over which we have lost control.* Fetishes are symbols that have become masters of their authors. Thoden van
Velzen (1990:78) quotes David Simpson's observation that "fetishism occurs when the mind ceases to realize that it has itself created the outward
images or things to which it subsequently posits itself as in some sort of
subservient relation." A fundamental question is whether the fetish can
or cannot be said to *mystify* or *conceal* some aspect of social reality, as suggested by Friedman, Taussig, and Thoden van Velzen. This, as we have
seen, is a complex epistemological issue, because mystification may well
be an intrinsic aspect of the constitution of social reality. It is quite reasonable to argue that there is a sense in which we are never "in control" of
our symbolic representations, and that all symbols tend to mystify some
aspect of reality, which would imply that there is an aspect of fetishism
in all symbolism. To delineate a more precise definition of fetishism as a
particular variety of symbolism, we thus need to consider other, more
specific criteria.

The first real bifurcation is the issue of whether the representation is or
is not *material*. Pool suggests that even concepts (such as "fetishism") may
be fetishes. From now on, however, we shall be exclusively concerned
with fetishes in the original, fifteenth-century sense of material objects.
We then arrive at Ellen's first criterion: *concretization* or *reification*. The material object can be a reification in two rather different ways, however. On
one hand, following Ellen, it can be a concrete representation of an abstract idea or identity. On the other hand, following the Marxist notion
elaborated by Taussig, it can be a reification—in the form of a small part
of it—of a wider context of *real material relationships*, such as flows of
goods and services. As Pietz (1993:129) writes,

A factory machine, a wheat field, a pension fund, and other "things" reckoned as capital by accountants and political economists are fetishes, in
Marx's view, not in their physical existence or concrete functions per se but
in their reality as material forms ("part-objects") of a distinctive type of social system.

General definition of fetishism:

A cultural representation over which its authors have lost control, which at the same time mystifies and constitutes their social reality.

More specific considerations:

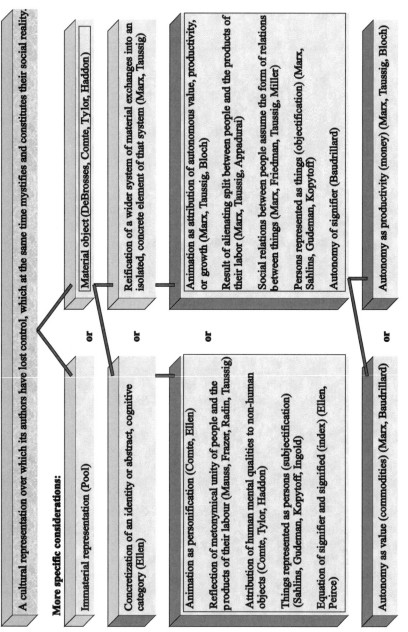

Immaterial representation (Pool)

or

Material object (DeBrosses, Comte, Tylor, Haddon)

Concretization of an identity or abstract, cognitive category (Ellen)

or

Reification of a wider system of material exchanges into an isolated, concrete element of that system (Marx, Taussig)

Animation as personification (Comte, Ellen)

Reflection of metonymical unity of people and the products of their labour (Mauss, Frazer, Radin, Taussig)

Attribution of human mental qualities to non-human objects (Comte, Tylor, Haddon)

Things represented as persons (subjectification) (Sahlins, Gudeman, Kopytoff, Ingold)

Equation of signifier and signified (index) (Ellen, Peirce)

or

Animation as attribution of autonomous value, productivity, or growth (Marx, Taussig, Bloch)

Result of alienating split between people and the products of their labor (Marx, Taussig, Appadurai)

Social relations between people assume the form of relations between things (Marx, Friedman, Taussig, Miller)

Persons represented as things (objectification) (Marx, Sahlins, Gudeman, Kopytoff)

Autonomy of signifier (Baudrillard)

Autonomy as value (commodities) (Marx, Baudrillard)

or

Autonomy as productivity (money) (Marx, Taussig, Bloch)

Fig. 7   A taxonomic framework of features associated with fetishism

There is thus an important difference between the material objectification of a cognitive category (e.g., "fertility") and the reification of a wider,
material system into an isolated, concrete element of that system. (It
should be noted, however, that Pietz's reference to the machine as a fetish
here merely serves to exemplify a general fetishism of capital. It does not
elaborate the specifics of machine fetishism as defined further on in the
current text.)

This difference is further reflected in a third bifurcation relating to Ellen's second criterion: *animation*. Fetishes are attributed with autonomous
agency, but there is a difference between perceiving them as having
"properties of living organisms" (Ellen 1988:223), such as autonomous
productivity (Taussig, Bloch), and perceiving them as *persons* (cf. Ellen on
"personification," *Ibid.*:213). This can be illustrated by the difference between perceiving money as a fruit tree (Marx) and perceiving gifts as persons (Mauss). As Taussig has shown, the former is the result of an alienating split between people and the products of their labor, whereas the
latter is a reflection of their metonymical unity. In one case, social relations between people assume the form of relations between things (Marx);
in the other, there is an attribution of human mental qualities to nonhuman objects (Comte). The former yields a representation of persons as
things, the latter a perception of things as persons (Sahlins, Gudeman). If
the former is an instance of objectification, the latter (personification)
must be understood as a "subjectification."

The polarity recurs with respect to Ellen's third criterion: the *conflation
of signifier and signified*. The shift from a "balanced simultaneity of signifier and signified towards 'the thing itself' " once again accommodates
two diametrically opposite phenomena. On one hand, we are left with a
signifier *without* a determinate signified (a material object alienated from
its human source), while on the other we are faced with a signifier *as* signified (an object *equated* with its human source). To conceptualize the first
condition, we may employ Baudrillard's Saussurean terminology and
speak of the "autonomization of the signifier," but to appreciate the second we are better served by Peirce's concept of *indexical* signs (as distinct
from icons or symbols). Peirce's triadic classification of indexical, iconic,
and symbolic signs has forerunners as far back as Plato and Aristotle
(Singer 1984:60). It recognizes the three major ways in which a sign can
relate to the object to which it refers: by being immediately contiguous
with it (index), by resembling it (icon), or by being associated with it by
cultural convention (symbol). In fact, the pervasive ambivalence as to
whether fetishism implies a veneration of material objects (DeBrosses) or
merely the forces or principles they *represent* (Tylor, Haddon) is precisely
an ambivalence as to whether to approach the fetish as an index, on one
hand, or an icon or symbol, on the other.

This finally brings us to Ellen's fourth criterion, which also brings us back to our point of departure in Pool's general definition: the ambiguity as to whether *the object is controlled by people or people by the object*. It would seem that the semiotic condition most conducive to such ambiguity is the collapse of a signifier/signified relation into an indexical sign. This apparently is as likely where the link between an object and its human source is recognized (Frazer's "contagious magic") as where it has been obscured. The difference lies in the *scope for creating new and imaginary signifieds*, which is obviously greater where the object has been decisively severed from its source. In the vein of Parry and Bloch (1989), however, we should recall that this is by no means a phenomenon unique to modern, capitalist society. Premodern, theocratic regimes such as that of the Inca consciously utilized such disjunctions to maintain popular respect for sacred symbols of power, frequently through the use of long-distance imports (see chapter 5 and below). We may conclude, however, that the disembedding tendencies in modern market capitalism are supremely efficient at generating such disjunctions, and thus supremely conducive to fetishism. Every commodity produced for the market at some point or points in its "biography" (cf. Kopytoff 1986) assumes the alienated, shopshelf condition we have referred to as "signifier without a signified." Precisely in having been stripped of its original social context, it is open to semiotic transformation. We have seen how the disembedding of commodities can generate fetishistic representations among consumers and producers alike (Appadurai).

But there is yet another bifurcation, which has to do with whether the autonomy of the fetishized object is perceived to reside in its value (commodities) or in its productivity (money capital). Unlike commodities, money is believed to possess an autonomous capacity for growth. In this sense, of the two forms of capitalist fetishism identified by Marx, it is only money that assumes the generative properties of a living organism. Money capital thus appears to be the most exact instantiation of the Marxian concept of fetishism—until we consider the machine.

MACHINE FETISHISM, OR THE POWER OF THE MACHINE

Against the background of our argument so far, it is not unreasonable to propose that the central and most "opaque" fetish of capitalism is nothing less than the *machine*. Money, after all, has been with us for millennia and repeatedly "deconstructed" at least since the days of Aristotle. But the special way in which machines conceal significant aspects of social reality, while at the same time constituting that reality, certainly deserves to be made more "transparent." Here are indeed material objects of our own making over which we seem to have lost control (cf. Winner 1977). As we saw in chapter 6, the ambiguous relation between people and their industrial technology raises questions concerning which kind of structure (human or mechanical) is the fundamental objective of reproduction, and which is the instrument toward this goal. Certainly machines are reifications of the wider social context of global flows of goods and services. It cannot be denied that in common discourse they tend to be animated and attributed with autonomous powers of productivity and growth.

The conventional view of technology ignores the real sources of productivity in *price relationships,* understood as an ideology of illusory reciprocity, permitting asymmetric flows of raw materials and human and mineral energy toward world centers of accumulation. I argue here for a worldview in which those asymmetric flows are recognized as the "signified" of the machine, rather than systematically obscured by the disembedding processes that are responsible for modern society's fragmentarized understanding of itself. As with commodities, it is the alienated, socially decontextualized condition of the machine that renders it susceptible to fetishization. The disembedded condition of the various artifacts of industrial technology has made it possible for people in the center of the system, such as David Ricardo and, significantly, Karl Marx, to equip them with quite other signifieds, such as "growth," "progress," and "development" (cf. Adas 1989). The fetish character of the machine resides in its ability to present itself to our consciousness as a local achievement rather than as a product of the confluence of global flows. It is high time to demystify the social forces that seem to literally animate our machines, beginning, perhaps, by asking why they continue to be so unevenly distributed over the face of the Earth.

The kind of unequal exchange, in material terms, that is a precondition for machine technology has never been a part of industrial society's self-understanding. Early British economists such as Ricardo chose to disregard the material properties of the traded goods in favor of a science that was exclusively concerned with exchange values and that, for this very reason, could not even raise the *question* of unequal exchange. The ostensibly free assignment of market prices axiomatically guaranteed justice, irrespective of the ungauged, net flows of material resources (energy, labor time, hectares of crops) that were thereby rendered either invisible or "natural" and legitimate. Nineteenth-century England required a practically *usable* theory of (and for) capital accumulation that attributed to industrial capital a generative force of its own and thus offered a morally acceptable explanation for why so much of the world's wealth was being accumulated in Britain. Yet, from the very start, there were marginalized dissenters who refused to be content with the hegemony of exchange value and instead struggled to make transparent what the price tags had concealed. To this category belong the Marxists, but also the tradition of "ecological economics" traced by Martinez-Alier (1987). They complement each other in the sense that the former have focused on the unequal exchange of labor time, whereas the latter have discussed the unequal exchange of natural space (resources).

To discover price relationships (terms of trade) as an opaque source of industrial productivity, obscured by machine fetishism, is basically to extend Marx's analysis of the exploitation of labor to the socially mediated exploitation of natural resources in the world system. If surplus and profit can be generated by the difference (in terms of exchange value) between the cost and the output of labor, it can also be generated by the difference between the cost and the output of (work conducted by) machines. Such calculations are possible precisely because of the hegemony of exchange value, an abstract measure that represents all things as commensurable and interchangeable. Many a critique of capitalism has denounced abstraction itself as the root of its evils, and rightly so. Paradoxically, however, the only analytical course open to those who seek to demonstrate the occurrence of unequal exchange is to adopt *another* abstract measuring rod by which to represent exchange in different terms from the illusory reciprocity of market prices. Without recourse to such an alternative "grand narrative," the Marxian concept of fetishism loses its meaning and its efficacy as an emancipatory theory.

For Marx, this measuring rod was labor time. In chapters 3 and 6, I argued that a more inclusive measure is the content of available energy. Drawing on the Second Law of Thermodynamics, it can be analytically demonstrated that the quantities of available energy flowing to and from industrial centers must be inversely related to the flows of exchange values. Whereas the imports of natural resources must have a higher content of available energy, or productive potential, than the exports of industrial products, the latter must be priced higher than the former. This is the fundamental condition of profit-oriented capitalism in a world obeying the Second Law of Thermodynamics. In effect, the more energy that has been dissipated by an industrial infrastructure today, the more new energy it will be able to command tomorrow. This expanding net appropriation of available energy within a restricted social space is the very foundation of industrial growth and "technological development." Because available energy is a measure precisely of the ability to conduct mechanical work, it is reasonable to propose that the work ostensibly conducted by machines in reality is the work of asymmetric, socially orchestrated energy flows, and in the last analysis by the price relationships (terms of trade) effecting this orchestration.

Such an analysis might ultimately transform our perception of the ontology of mechanical work, indeed the very *phenomenology of the machine*. Let us return to Taussig's (1980:36) formulation, but now with the image of a bulldozer on our retinas:

> If we "thingify" parts of a living system, ignore the context of which they are a part, and then observe that *the things move*, so to speak, it logically follows that the things may well be regarded or spoken of as though they were alive with their own autonomous powers. (emphasis added)

Let us also, with the bulldozer still in mind, again consider Sahlins's (1976:170) conclusion that "no object, no thing, has *being or movement* in human society except by the significance men can give it" (emphasis added). The bulldozer would literally not move, were it not for the semiotic mediation of the world market. When it *does* move, moreover, it seems essential for the viability of industrial capitalism that this mediation should not contaminate our image of the machine as powerful in itself. For would it not have the potential to change our perception of the very essence of mechanical movement to realize that as tangible an ingredient of our reality as the bulldozer exists and is propelled not by its "own autonomous powers" but by the power of social forces as intangible as global terms of trade?

An alternative and potentially quantifiable abstraction with which to gauge the occurrence of unequal exchange, mentioned in chapter 4, is the economy of time and space. From the point of view of the user, a machine can be defined as a device for saving time and/or space (by increasing velocity and/or intensifying the use of space). Time and space can be approached as commoditized human resources that the market and the machine render interchangeable, so that time can be converted into space and vice versa. It is no coincidence that the machine and the market have conquered the world hand in hand, because it is precisely the commercial interchangeability of human time (wage labor) and natural space (commoditized land) that has made the machine possible. Unequal exchange can be identified in discrepancies between the market prices of commodities vis-à-vis labor and natural resources, on one hand, and the investments of human time and natural space that they represent, on the other. In line with my previous argument on available energy, the very rationale of world trade seems to boil down to net transfers of time and space between different categories of people in global society. In this perspective, industrial technology emerges as an institution for *redistributing* time and space. One party's gain in disposable time or space is generally another party's loss.

Let us exemplify this zero-sum approach to technology by suggesting that the time saved by nineteenth-century railway users, compared to using the stagecoach, should be weighed against the labor time spent to build the railroads, engines, and railway cars; produce the iron and steel; mine the coal; fell the timber; and so on. I am not convinced that, for any specific stretch of railway, the balance would show a net liberation of human time. The fact that the railways were still good *business* derives from differences in the prices assigned to different people's time. The same applies to space. The total balance should include the spatial resources consumed by the railroads far beyond the spaces occupied by the rails themselves: the distant forests, mines, and coalfields that were thus transformed into gains of time for those who could afford the tickets (cf. Cronon 1991). Beneath the illusory reciprocity of market prices we may discern an unequal exchange of time and space between different sectors of world society. This becomes even clearer when we consider more recent and more exclusive transport technologies such as air traffic.

MACHINE AS EMPEROR, EMPEROR AS MACHINE

Can modern machinery really be compared with premodern fetishes? Let us again consider the Inca emperor, who appears to have been perceived by his subjects as a divine source of wealth and fertility (cf. Murra 1956 [1980]; Godelier 1986). The economic structure of the Inca state was a prototypical example of what Polanyi called "redistribution." The divine son of the Sun based much of his power on the strategic deployment of distantly imported *Spondylus* shell and other valuables such as cloth. He also engaged local populations to work in his maize fields by mimicking traditional, communal working bees and offering his guests generous servings of maize beer. We know that the maize beer with which he appeased his laborers could have represented only a fraction of the harvest of maize which he gained from their labor. Yet, in all these transactions, involving massive flows of goods and services to fill the royal warehouses, the Inca emperor was represented as a cornucopia. Following Godelier's (1986) and Friedman's (1979 [1998]) studies of the fetishization of political offices, I would not hesitate to classify the emperor as a fetish in the Marxian sense: his person was a *concrete reification of a wider system of material exchanges, attributed with autonomous productivity*. (This illustrates, incidentally, my earlier argument that the criterion of "personification" [Ellen 1988:213] is irrelevant or inadequate to the Marxian definition of fetishism. The emperor is not increasingly "personified" but rather the opposite: it is his *office* that is perceived as inherently productive.) Moreover, the appearance of autonomous productivity was *contingent on specific and asymmetric terms of exchange*. In this precise sense, his modern equivalent is indeed the industrial machine. It, too, is contingent on a net input of resources yet presents itself to us as a cornucopia.

As a heuristic device, the simplest image that I can offer that might convey the core of such a concept of fetishism is the old European folk tale of the tramp who made soup out of an object such as a stone or nail:

> The tramp is reluctantly admitted into a kitchen, but the housewife has no intention of serving him any food. He pulls a stone out of his pocket, asking merely for a pot of water to boil some soup on it. The housewife is too intrigued to deny his request. After a while, stirring and carefully tasting the water, the tramp observes that it could do with some flour, as if this was the only missing ingredient. The housewife consents to offer him some. Then, one by one, he similarly manages to lure her to add the various other ingredients, until, finally, she is amazed to find a delicious soup *cooked on a stone*.

The stone in the soup is the prototypical fetish. It *transfers our attention from the wider context to its imaginary center*. No more than the stone contributed to the soup was the Inca king himself the source of his people's affluence. Similarly, like the emperor in Cuzco, the industrial machine is but a fetishized "node" in a global system of resource flows. Yet, in all cases, the fetishized objects are in some sense *constitutive*—not just misrepresentations—of accumulation. In all three cases, we are dealing with a concrete object that is visualized as intrinsically generative or productive. In all three cases, the fetishized objects are indeed responsible for processes of accumulation, by orchestrating them, but this orchestration hinges precisely on obscuring their social basis in unequal exchange. The machine has obviously become a *symbol* of productivity (cf. Adas 1989), but the ideological illusion that I have challenged here is that it is an *index* of productivity.

"Symbolism" and "technology" generally have been treated by anthropologists as phenomena belonging to completely separate spheres of reality, yet few if any technologies would be able to operate without the mediation, in their very constitution, of what we might call *semiotic moments*. By "semiotic moments" I mean symbolic (communicative) events that may be crucial components of a technological system, although not likely to be recognized as such, owing to our tendency to think of technology as constituted exclusively in terms of principles of physical engineering. Such semiotic moments can be of several kinds. It is trivial to point out that the operation of machines generally presupposes communication (labeled buttons, warning lights, meters, etc.). It is somewhat less trivial to observe that many items of technology, from pre-industrial hunting equipment to modern automobiles, tend to be symbolically embellished so as to enhance the mental calibration of their users. When the human being is an important element in the technology, it is not altogether easy to distinguish between pragmatic function and "superfluous" symbolism. This is particularly clear in the case of architecture (cf. Hornborg 1990). The most opaque, semiotic elements in technological systems, however, are the various symbolic strategies that are employed to generate and maintain the social structures of exchange (of labor, materials, fuels, etc.) that are *requisite* for the very existence of those technologies. The modern phenomenon that I refer to as machine fetishism tends to represent such structures of exchange as external to the technologies "themselves." I argue that this is an illusion. "Prices," "wages," "interest": all these categories are symbolic constructs that are essential elements in the material operation of modern, industrial technology. No less than the ritual shell sacrifices or beer parties of the Inca emperor, they represent culture-specific, symbolic strategies for making claims on other people's resources. As such, they are inextricably interfused with the material aspects of the accumulative processes that they orchestrate. No less than Inca ritual, the vocabulary of our economic institutions and the concomitant structures of exchange are *an integral part of the technology*. If technologies are in part symbolically constituted, symbolic events can be "technological" in the sense that they are components in a total, social machination including kinematic as well as communicative moments, interfused to an extent where *the two cannot be clearly demarcated*. The point that Sahlins (1976) makes about consumption can be extended to production. He observes that "everything in capitalism conspires to conceal the symbolic ordering of the system," and that only the particular nature of this concealment—the abstract categories of economics—is what is "finally distinctive" of Western civilization (*Ibid*.:220).

The concealment of the symbolic (and thus arbitrary) foundation of human economies is ubiquitous, because their operation hinges on their being perceived as non-arbitrary. To propose that we are no less bedazzled by the machine than the Inca peasant was by his emperor certainly defies common sense. After all, the machines *do* work, don't they? Yes, but in the eyes of the participants, so did Inca ritual. In neither case is there a doubt that these social arrangements were or are efficacious; the question is *how* they work, namely whether their productivity is inherent in particular persons or artifacts or instead relies on socially negotiable rates of exchange. In both cases, it seems essential for their viability that technical agency and material bounty are represented as a result of autonomous productivity rather than unequal social distribution. To expose the agency of a "productive force" as a transmutation and deflection of the agency of other humans is to render morally suspect that which had been couched in the deceptive neutrality of the merely technical.

When an engineer expounding on the benefits of a particular technology is confronted with the objection that this technology is available to only a fraction of humankind, he will generally respond that this is something that can be amended politically, through technology transfer and other "development" policies. It would not occur to him that the unevenness of distribution could be inherent in the very nature of the technology itself. But if technology is in fact the form in which surplus is "stored" in modern society, his response can be seen to be no less naïve than would be an aspiration, expressed in fifteenth-century Peru, that one day all the Inca's subjects will have access to warehouses equal in size to those of the emperor. The technological benefits of industrial society cannot be generalized for the total population because the very constitution of these technologies, no less than the productive capacitation of the Inca elite, relies on unequal exchange between different sectors of that population. Modern technology is precisely a strategy of *elite capacitation*, no less inherently skewed in distribution than the ability to command armies of corvée laborers. It is a subset of a wider category of social strategies for capacitation of certain sectors of the population through systematic appropriation of resources from other sectors. In the absence of recourse to a divine genealogy, perhaps the crucial difference vis-à-vis earlier such strategies is exactly the modernist pretense that one day in the future, the disempowered will catch up to the levels of capacitation now enjoyed by the elite. As this myth of "development" continues to fade, it would thus not be unreasonable to expect that the inequalities of the contemporary world system will require other ideologies of legitimation, supported by yet stronger technologies of coercion and exclusion.

Are we really completely aware of the social mechanisms that keep our machines running? Or has a crucial dimension of our technology systematically escaped us, just as the ancient Andean peasant was unable to grasp the totality of the system that fueled the royal cornucopia? Have we even begun to spell out the implications of the fact, traumatically illuminated by the so-called oil crises of the 1970s, that what ultimately animates our machines are global terms of trade? If we really exert ourselves to bracket our own, cultural variety of common sense, we might glimpse the *possibility* that the machine presents itself to our consciousness as—to paraphrase Taussig—"*something other than what it basically is.*"

II

MONEY, MODERNITY, AND PERSONHOOD

9

Money, Reflexivity, and the Semiotics of Modernity

Throughout Part 1, I hope to have shown that one reason why "machine fetishism" continues to delude us is our pervasive inability to recognize how cultural constructs such as concepts and social relations in very tangible ways remold our material environment. A major example of this potency of culture, of course, is the phenomenon of money. Chapters 1 and 3 observed that the idea and institution of money is a fundamental prerequisite to industrial technology. In this chapter, I will argue for a semiotic approach to the problematic interface of economics and ecology. I begin by reflecting on the origins of materialist science and discussing strategies for transcending Cartesian dualism in the study of human ecology. Premodernity, modernity, and postmodernity are conceptualized as transformations of semiotic relations with implications for identity and culture as well as human-environmental relations. The phenomenon of money is identified as a vehicle and epitome of the processes of semiotic abstraction we know as modernity. Various analogies between money and language are scrutinized and rejected. The tendencies of money to dissolve cultural and natural systems are understood as two aspects of a single, *ecosemiotic* process. Finally, a very general suggestion is offered as to how the idea and institution of money could be transformed so as to check the continued devastation of the biosphere.

MATERIALIZED MEANINGS AND THE
MEANING OF "MATERIAL"

The distinction between "material" and nonmaterial aspects of human life is a reflection of the Cartesian compulsion to find a bedrock of unquestionable truth with which to fill the void left by crumbling, premodern certainties. As we noted in chapter 7, it seems revealing that synonyms for "material" include "essential" and "relevant," whereas the word "immaterial" is generally used to mean "unessential" or "irrelevant." I suggested that we may in fact have been using the category of "material" *prescriptively*, to cover that which is beyond question and once and for all given. It appears to denote a reality posited as fundamentally "objective" and immune to the intervention of human consciousness. As such, it may have served to alleviate some of the *horror vacui* generated by modern reflexivity (Bauman 1992) and the gradual disjunction of language and reality in European history (Szerszynski 1996). With God no longer at the helm, the specter of a plastic universe had to be kept at bay. The existential significance of the notion of an immutable, objective substratum of reality grew out of the modern acknowledgment of a subject-object dichotomy. The sovereignty of God was succeeded by the sovereignty of the material. Even as reluctant a dualist as Marshall Sahlins (1976:207) concedes that "thought can only kneel before the absolute sovereignty of the physical world."

The notion of a distinct, material reality continues to provide the foundation for objectivist "grand narratives" in natural science, even though the most cogent evidence against objectivism has come from Nobel Prize-winning physicists such as Heisenberg. The human sciences, on the other hand, have increasingly confined their attention to the images and projections of human subjects. Objectivism and constructivism thus represent two opposite responses to the Cartesian dilemma. Human cognition is viewed either as an increasingly exact representation of reality or as a contingent construction of meaning-creating humans (Bernstein 1983). One position takes the object as its point of departure, the other the subject. Although from the outset coeval and defined by the same Cartesian matrix, the two alternative approaches have come to be associated with social conditions of "modernity" and "postmodernity," respectively, suggesting a temporal sequence in which objectivism yields to constructivism and grand narratives to a plurality of language games (Lyotard 1979 [1984]).

References to the "material" world are grand narratives *par excellence*. To the extent that postmodernists recommend an abandonment of universalizing knowledge, they will thus inevitably have to deal with the conception of a "material" dimension as such. Although it would be inadvisable to try to jettison the notion of constraints and circumstances external to human consciousness, major advances can be made in conceptualizing ways in which consciousness and the world are interfused. This move will require a reconsideration of both the potency of consciousness and the permeability of the material. Beyond a general, post-structuralist acknowledgment of what Ardener (1989:169) called "language-category-object simultaneities," the challenge seems to be to trace some of the specific kinds of recursivity that link culture and language, on one hand, with material circumstances, on the other.

Much contemporary theorizing suggests a "relationist" theory of knowledge somewhere between the representationism of the natural sciences and the solipsism of much of the human sciences (cf. Maturana and Varela 1987 [1992]). In this view, pioneered by Bateson (1972, 1979) and now evident in a number of convergent approaches from both the natural and human sciences, knowledge is neither a representation nor a construction but a *relation* between the knower and the known. Halfway between von Uexküll's *Umwelt* and Gibson's "affordances" (cf. Ingold 1992), knowledge is the relation through which subject and object are mutually specified. This insight is particularly relevant to the various discourses on human ecology (i.e., human-environmental relations), including the field known as environmental history (Bird 1987). Although not implying a regression to premodern monism, in which the world was pure Subject and Word and as such susceptible to incantation, the acknowledgment of recursivity between subject and object suggests a *neomonism* that promises to transcend the Cartesian dilemma (cf. next chapter).

It seems that the only way to admit this recursivity into our models of society and environment would be to include the *person* as a crucial counterpart to both. Anthropology, with its accumulated insights about all three corners of what Steiner (1993) calls the "human ecological triangle" (i.e., ecology, society, and personhood), ought to be uniquely equipped to develop such an approach. Regrettably, the discipline suffers internally from the same dichotomies and fragmentations that riddle the academic community as a whole. Anthropologists tend to be either objectivists or constructivists, specialized for example in ecological anthropology, economic anthropology, or the anthropology of personhood. Only by putting the pieces together will we come closer to the holistic ambition that general anthropology shares with general semiotics (M. Anderson et al. 1984). The ecological crisis of modern society will then be recognized as having two aspects that are ultimately connected: one objective and generated by the general-purpose market and its axiom of universal interchangeability, the other subjective and founded in the alienation of the disembedded, modern individual. In whichever direction we choose to

trace the recursive logic of commoditization, abstraction, and disenchantment, the environmental crisis forces upon us the insight that Descartes
expelled from view, that the human *subject*, with its bundle of concepts,
anxieties, and aspirations, is recursively interfused with the planetary
landscape.

TRANSCENDING DUALISM AND
ADDRESSING REAL PROBLEMS

A generalized semiotics provides a counter-narrative to the materialist or-
thodoxy. Charles Sanders Peirce probably exaggerated when suggesting
that the universe may be "composed exclusively of signs" (Sebeok
1994:14), but it certainly can be argued that the production and interpretation of signs is a criterion of all *life* (*Ibid.*:6). Living things can be defined
by their capacity to respond as *subjects* (J. von Uexküll 1940 [1982]; Bateson 1979). From cells to ecosystems, their material reproduction is contingent on communication. Language, the mode of communication with
which we as humans are most familiar, is but one of the most recent additions (along with, e.g., money) to the semiotics of ecosystems. Because
language belongs to a wider family of communicative phenomena, the
formal analyses of linguistics can be extended not only to various aspects
of culture (Lévi-Strauss 1963) but also to semiotic dimensions of fields as
diverse as economics (Baudrillard 1972 [1981]; Sahlins 1976; Ahonen 1989;
Lash and Urry 1994), ecology (T. von Uexküll 1982), and even biochemistry (Hoffmeyer 1993 [1996]). Wherever there are living subjects, their fundamental condition is defined by the problem of interpreting signs. The
penetrating analyses of Peirce (1931–1958) and Saussure (1916 [1966])
have indicated that there are certain formal possibilities that generate the
different varieties of signs. Important parameters include the nature of
the relations between sign, object, and interpretant (Peirce) or between
signifier and signified (Saussure). Peirce's framework, in particular, suggests that such formal properties of sign relations are variously identifiable for example in the biochemistry of organisms, in plant and animal
communication in ecosystems, and in the various sign systems of human
societies. Formal parallels can be established between, for example, a
virus, zoological mimicry, and confidence tricks.

The major challenge for a generalized semiotics, as I see it, is to apply
such tools for formal analysis to the pressing problems of communication
that are increasingly evident at the interface of ecology and economics.
Such a line of inquiry was pioneered by Bateson (1972) and Rappaport
(1979), but the thrust of their argument has been shunned by mainstream
anthropology as functionalist and simplistically cybernetic (e.g., Fried-

man 1974a, 1979; cf. next chapter). A formal, semiotic approach would be better equipped to avoid the functionalist pitfalls of cybernetics. To speak of communicative or adaptive "disorder" (Rappaport 1979) is to invite criticism for implying a normative state of harmony or "order." At some point, however, even the most skeptical of relativists would have to concede that an economic signaling system that systematically destroys the material conditions of the species that devised it represents a *problem* of communication. In identifying the formal sources of this problem, a semiotic approach could in fact help us visualize a remedy. Such a problem-oriented semiotics would not be susceptible to challenges of "idealism" (cf. Sebeok 1994:14–15), as its very focus would be on the *interfusion* of the symbolic and the material. Rather than restrict itself to the analysis of culture, it would investigate how the logic of culture impinges on nature. The ambiguities and ambivalences that riddle postmodern culture, identity, and epistemology are closely connected to the runaway economic processes that generate accelerating environmental degradation worldwide.

Although often excruciatingly vague, Baudrillard's (1972 [1981], 1973 [1975], 1976 [1993]) intuitions about the transformations of capitalism may be a good starting point. I would use the "premodern," the "modern," and the "postmodern" as analytical (rather than historical) categories corresponding to distinct kinds of subject-object relations. As such, they also represent distinct ways of relating to signs. These modes of signification, furthermore, are relevant to various levels of experience: the perception of commodities, the perception of human identities, and the perception of the world in general), including, of course, the perception of nature. Baudrillard is primarily concerned with the transition from "modern" to "postmodern," but the complete set of transformations would have to include the "premodern."

Let us begin by suggesting that a premodern condition is one of naïveté, where signs appear as straightforward indices of essential identities, the crown indicates a king, and there is an identity of word and world (cf. Szerszynski 1996). It will immediately be obvious that no society we know of has ever been completely "premodern" in this sense: sources such as the Old Testament and the pervasive myth of the Trickster clearly indicate a profound and archaic familiarity with fraudulence. Premodernity in the sense of *constitutional* naïveté could perhaps only be established for infants (and irrespective of cultural context). In this sense, premodernity is a part of everyone's biography and thus also of everyone's frame of reference. It represents the unmediated and unreflexive being-in-the-world glorified by the phenomenologists. A *society* classified as "premodern," however, would be one where key relations of power— *seen from a distance in time or space*—appear to be "immunized" or opaque to skeptical scrutiny. It is important to recognize the relativity of this category. If the power structures of ancient monarchies and empires now strike us as premodern in their immunity to rational critique, we may very well at this very moment be submitting ourselves to other power structures that will strike our descendants as no less fetishized by "tradition," yet no less susceptible to deconstruction.

The modern condition is one of *reflexive uncertainty*: the crown is understood as a symbol (conventionally) representing the king, and human language as a (provisional) representation of the world. This is the historical space of the subject-object dichotomy and of the possibility of fraudulence or falsehood, where the wearer of the crown may be an impostor and Scripture may be mistaken. It has historical coordinates but is essentially more of a structural condition than a period in history. It is the moment of doubt that follows every major deconstruction of power. It is a source of tremendous existential anxiety and creativity that can either be harnessed in the production of new hegemonies to substitute for the old (e.g., science instead of religion) or assume the form of solipsism, disengagement, and indifference.

The latter alternative is what we have come to know as the "postmodern." It is a condition where the exhausting attitude of radical skepticism tends to give way to a structurally enforced *feigned gullibility*. All hope of certainty has vanished, but precisely because no pretense to power or truth can be admitted, any pretense is as good as any other. Signs are once again perceived as indices of identity, but now simply by virtue of positing themselves as such, rather than through assumed correspondences with essences. Again there is an identity of word and world, not, however, because the world is thought to be immediately known, but because the hope of really knowing it has been abandoned. If the modern condition recognizes the *symbol* as founded on convention, the postmodern represents a return to indexicality, but now stripped of phenomenological depth. A continuous exposure to signs (e.g., commercials, politicians, and manipulative messages in general) claiming to stand for qualities that they may not stand for tends to numb the ability to distinguish between different kinds of sign relations. There is an atrophication of the critical pursuit of truth and authenticity, resulting not so much in a reconflation of attribute (sign) and essence as in an abandonment of essence, or, in Baudrillard's (1973 [1975]:127–128) words, an autonomization of the signifier. This is the structural space of Baudrillard's (1972 [1981]) "political economy of the sign," Goffman's (1959 [1969]) "impression management," and Lasch's (1980) "culture of narcissism." It is also characterized by an intense reflexivity concerning the "constructed" nature of every feature of existence from personal identity to (perceptions of) the natural world.

In conditioning people to superficiality, late modern or postmodern capitalism also conditions them to disenchantment with nature. The abandonment of essence in the way we approach words and identities is paralleled in the way we approach the nonhuman environment. I will argue that it is also paralleled—perhaps paradigmatically so—in the way we approach money. Consciousness of the constructed nature of social reality generates fear of imminent collapse, whether of identities, meanings, or stock markets. The movement from naïve realism through the hazards of reflexivity and the threat of deconstruction has resulted in structurally similar responses at all these levels. There is thus a fundamental connection between the "anything goes" of New Age spirituality and the final abandonment of the Bretton Woods gold standard.

To understand these processes, we need to focus on the *disembedding*, decontextualizing forces that are inherent in modernity and are the common denominator of markets, universalizing science, and the ecologically alienated individual. There is a fundamental, "modern" tendency toward abstraction in the economy, discourse, and personhood, which encourages superficiality in relation to place and paves the way for environmental destruction. As Bateson (1972) and Rappaport (1979) argued, the subjective and the objective dimensions of environmental crisis are inseparable. If ecological relations are communicative, and ecosystems thus contingent on a plurality of subjective, species-specific perspectives (J. von Uexküll 1940 [1982]), the dissolution of cultural meaning and the dismantling of ecosystems are two aspects of a single process.

The concept of "disembedding," in signifying the alienation of persons, objects, or concepts from the *contexts* from which they have previously derived their meaning, is a thoroughly semiotic concept. It was applied by Karl Polanyi (1944) to the process whereby capitalist economic institutions achieved their own, autonomous logic vis-à-vis other dimensions of modern society. More recently, the term has been much used by Anthony Giddens (1990) and his followers in sociology. The phenomena that it tries to capture, of course, have been central concerns of sociology for more than a century (e.g., Weber, Marx, Simmel, Durkheim, Tönnies). We know much about what "disembedding" means in terms of identities and social relations, but the concept still has a lot of analytical potential to be explored in relation to problems of ecology and sustainability. The challenge for a monistic, post-Cartesian human ecology is to develop perspectives that humanize nature and naturalize society in the same move, and the concept of ecological (dis)embeddedness suggests an avenue in that direction.

There is another way of expressing the process of "disembedding," one that might make more sense to those who prefer stories closer to natural science. It would have to begin with a critique of what has been referred to as universal selection theory—that is, the argument of Richard Dawkins (1976) and others suggesting that cultural ideas and artifacts are subject to selective processes formally similar to those operating in nature. In anthropology, the closest may be Dan Sperber's (1985:30–31) notion of an "epidemiology of ideas." The problem with universal selection theory is that it seems to assume that the meanings of words or artifacts are embodied in those words or artifacts. We all know, however, that meanings emerge in *contexts*. We need only go back to Peirce's triadic definition of the sign, which always includes the interpretant. Selection theory has no way of handling these interpretive contexts, yet they must be crucial for the process of selection itself. Semiotics is a necessary corrective to selection theory (cf. Sahlins 1976:208; Bruun 1997).

With this much established, however, an interesting new perspective suggests itself: jointly, selection theory and semiotics provide us with another way of understanding modernity and postmodernity. Bateson (1979) suggests that an *explanation* is a description mapped onto a *tautology*. It is possible to identify such fundamental tautologies underlying theoretical frameworks such as the Entropy Law ("what is most likely to happen is most likely to happen") and the Darwinian theory of natural selection ("those most likely to survive are most likely to survive"). A similar, paradigmatic tautology may apply to the cultural sociology of modernity. From the point of view of universal selection theory, the specifics of local contexts of interpretation can be seen as *constraints* on reproductive success. Logically, the ideas, artifacts, and human persons that should thus be selected for are those that are least dependent on context. ("That which is most likely to spread is most likely to spread.") Abstract language, universalizing knowledge, general-purpose money, globalized commodities, and cosmopolitan personalities all share one fundamental feature: they are free to transcend specific, local contexts. They are not committed to *place*. There is thus an inverse relation between experiential depth and spatial expansion, between meaning investment and market shares. McDonald's is testimony to the ecology of cultural diffusion.

MONEY, MEANING, AND THE
OPERATIONAL LOGIC OF EMPTY SIGNS

Selection thus tends to increase the arbitrariness of the sign-object relation, suggesting a continuous movement along Peirce's well-known scale from index to icon to symbol. Inevitably, we have to scrutinize that paramount artifact of modernity, money itself. The sequence from the premodern through the modern to the postmodern can be traced in the evolution of the money sign, and it corresponds to the spectrum of interpretations ranging from *realist* to *nominalist* theories of money. The former posits intrinsic meaning or value in money, whereas the latter denies it (cf. Ahonen 1989:15). The movement toward semiotic abstraction, discussed at length by Simmel (1900 [1990]), can be described in different terms, depending on whether we are using the concepts of Saussure or of Peirce. If our point of departure is Saussure's dyadic model of signifier and signified, we can observe that money has had a historical tendency to repeatedly convert signifiers into signifieds. To begin with, gold signified exchange value. The signification was indexical to the extent that value was perceived as an essential quality of gold. With time, paper money came to signify gold. The ambiguities surrounding the value of paper money have generated, in the past century, various crises and negotiations concerning the relation between money and gold, until the gold standard was finally abandoned in 1971 (for historical details of these transformations, cf. Corbridge and Thrift 1994). Presently, electronic money can be said to signify paper money. We are thus faced with a chain of signifier-signified relations in which increasingly abstract signifiers tend to eclipse their more tangible predecessors, and in which the connection to the original and most concrete signified (gold) has dissolved.

The same process can be approached from the perspective of Peirce's notions of "firstness," "secondness," and "thirdness":

> The first is that whose being is simply in itself, not referring to anything nor lying behind anything. The second is that which is what it is by force of something to which it is second. The third is that which is what it is owing to things between which it mediates and which it brings into relation to each other. (Peirce 1931–1958, quoted in Ahonen 1989:17)

These conditions are not to be seen as properties of particular phenomena, but as various ways of perceiving signs. Whether gold, paper, or digits on a computer screen, of course, money risks being fetishized into intrinsic value ("firstness"), but the increasing ethereality (and volatility) of the money sign undoubtedly has been associated with greater reflexivity concerning its "secondness" in relation to what it is understood to represent. It could be argued, finally, that consciousness of the "thirdness" of money emerged in Marx's deconstruction of *money fetishism*, revealing how social relations between people assume the form of a relation between things. In the first interpretation, the sign *is* the object or essence to which it refers (the value of gold). In the second, the sign *represents* the object (paper money referring to a gold standard). In the third, the sign *mediates a relation between* objects (money representing not an essential value but a relation of exchange between humans). In this final understanding of the sign nature of money, it becomes obvious that money is nothing in itself, nor does it even refer to an object; it only mediates social relations. In the movement from firstness through secondness to third-ness, money metamorphosed from index to symbol and then into an "empty" sign that stands only for itself.

Ahonen's (1989) application of Peirce's categories to money is at times confusing. He thus classifies gold coins as "iconic" while money backed by the state or by a stock of bullion is classified as "indexical" (*Ibid.*:26). I would argue that the former are indexical and the latter (if backed by bul-lion, as in the Bretton Woods system) either iconic or symbolic, depending on the form or iconography of the money items themselves (for examples of iconic money, cf. Simmel 1900 [1990]:144–145). The specific reference to a gold (or other) standard is the only (and very restricted) sense in which money can serve as a *symbol* of something that it can be converted into.

A peculiar, semiotic conundrum posed by money is that it represents *a code with only one sign*. It is like imagining a language with one phoneme, an alphabet with one letter, or a DNA molecule with only one kind of nucleotide. As such, it is a sign with a completely arbitrary referent, lack-ing even a conventional relation (as in Peirce's definition of symbol) to any specific thing that it signifies. Nothing meaningful can be expressed with it because meaning emerges in contrasts, or in differences between what something stands for and what it *doesn't* stand for. In fact, if there were two kinds of money instead of one, it would make all the difference in the world. Recall the multicentric economy of the Nigerian Tiv that Paul Bohannan (1955) described fifty years ago and that—in theory, at least—recognized three distinct kinds of values. I believe that it could be argued that an economic transaction among the Tiv in the 1940s embod-ied more meaning—in a formal, semiotic sense—than ordinary market exchanges. In widening the reach of general-purpose money, we have, in a sense, divested ourselves of the possibility of investing the economy with meaning. Although more or less exotic exceptions certainly can be found (Parry and Bloch 1989), they do little to invalidate the long-stand-ing sociological conclusion that, by and large, modern money has had a tendency to render social relations increasingly abstract (cf. Simmel 1900 [1990]; Giddens 1990; Corbridge and Thrift 1994:20).

Let us more systematically address the uniqueness of money as a semi-otic phenomenon. From the perspective of general systems theory (e.g., J. G. Miller 1965), we might compare the circulation of money with informa-tion flows at other levels of integration in living systems. In market econo-mies, money functions as "markers" or "signals" that at first sight seem analogous to linguistic messages in groups, neural impulses in organ-isms, or RNA molecules in cells. These latter information flows, however, transmit patterned "ensembles" of signals (e.g., sounds or letters of the alphabet, nucleotides) in accordance with some kind of *code*. Miller (*Ibid.*:350) defines code as

> a language or convention used by a system, whereby one ensemble of signals is represented by, coupled with, or "mapped" upon another ensemble according to some regular rules. Transmitter and receiver must speak the same language or have established a prior convention, be coded alike, in advance, or the transmission will convey no information to the receiver.

As a signal, money obviously has no such ensemble from which to compose messages. Money passing from one person or group to another does not refer to a common language or convention that regulates its "meaning," that is, the impact that it will have on the receiver. It can be given any meaning that the owner chooses to convert it into. It might be argued that the market itself is the "convention" to which money refers, but reference to such a convention—in failing to specify how the money is to be used—is mere tautology. Money reinforces the activities paid for and transfers "power" or "freedom" between actors, but it does not itself convey meaning. The economic signals at our disposal do not enable us to transmit messages according to some code comparable to the systems of organized differences we know as languages or genes. To be sure, money is employed to reproduce elaborate, cultural codes (Baudrillard 1972 [1981]; Sahlins 1976), but these meaningful differences in consumption are external to the money system itself. According to Saussure's linguistic theory, meaning is based on difference and opposition. In view of the binary basis of information and meaning, it is evident that a unicentric economy (i.e., one based on the use of a single, general-purpose currency) renders money itself incapable of conveying meaning.

Semiotic approaches to money have repeatedly compared it with language, but generally without clarifying the proper levels and units for comparison. Saussure (1916 [1966]) compared coins and words, showing how both kinds of units relate to *unlike* units for which they may be *exchanged* (commodities and concepts, respectively) as well as to *like* units with which they may be *compared* (other coins and other words). The first relation is that between signifier and signified (which jointly constitute Saussure's concept of *sign*), the second (called "value" by Saussure) that between different signs in a semiological system. Saussure's comparison of money and words, however, is problematic with respect to both significance and value. A unit of money does not relate to a specified commodity in the way that a word relates to a specific concept, nor does it relate to other denominations in any other sense than a purely quantitative one. In both respects, money obviously lacks the kind of meaning invested in words. Karl Bühler's comparison of words, commodities, and coins (cf. Nöth 1996:4) fares no better. His suggestion that coins signify monetary value is no more enlightening than to say that words signify meaning. The crucial difference is that *specific* words signify *specific* concepts, but no similar statement can be made for a specific unit of money. Nor are we helped in this respect by Bühler's argument that the materiality of coins or bills qualifies them as commodities (*Ibid.*:5), first because such materiality has nothing to do with specificity of signification, and second because a very small percentage of circulated money today assumes such material forms. Commodities are certainly signs in the Saussurean sense, and the study of consumption is founded on this important observation, but money is not a commodity. In fact, according to Saussure's definition—*contra* Saussure himself as well as, for example, Ahonen (1989:23)—money should not even qualify as a sign, for a (Saussurean) sign is founded on the intimate and reciprocal relation between signifier and signified, and no such relation is possible with as nonspecific a signifier as money.

Yet Polanyi (1968:178) also suggests that modern money offers "a striking resemblance" to language and writing. He sees it as a "system of symbols" and a "semantic system" linking "symbols to quantifiable objects" (*Ibid.*:175, 194). To Polanyi, general-purpose money "appears as an almost complete parallel to language and writing with its all-purpose sounds and signs" (*Ibid.*:179). But the comparison is as unsatisfying as Saussure's. Polanyi finds the relation between money and its uses analogous to the relation between sounds and words; however, the former is a relation of interchangeability, as Saussure observed, whereas the latter is not. Sounds and words are merely two successive levels of integration *within* the domain of signifiers; an analogy with the uses of money would have to include, as did Saussure, the *concepts* signified by words. Polanyi elsewhere recognizes the limitations of his comparison. For one thing, "only quantifiable objects" can serve as money (*Ibid.*:180), a restriction obviously inapplicable to language. Second, the "purpose served by the system as a whole must be inferred from the actual uses, and can hardly be said to be as clear as that of writing or language" (*Ibid.*:194). Clearly, the sense in which money signifies something is different from that implied by the linguistic sign.

But several authors have continued to fall for the temptation to posit a complete correspondence between money and linguistic symbols. Codere (1968:559), for instance, writes:

> Money is a symbol. It functions as a sign, it is semiotic. It is a symbol of both past and future exchangeable goods, the idea of goods being understood to include services. As a symbol its particular physical character is arbitrary within certain practical limitations, as are all symbols.

Crump (1981:16) similarly suggests that "money is a symbol signifying what it can be converted into." He recognizes, however, "the chameleon-like property of money" (*Ibid.*:122) and the fact that it "gives no information about itself" that is not "cultural tautology" (*Ibid.*:1). Saussure's distinction between *value* and *significance* resurfaces in several corresponding, conceptual pairs applied to the two alleged dimensions of money. When referring only to the tautological, arithmetic system of which they are a part, Crump argues, the denominations of money should be seen as *metonyms*; when used in transactions beyond the boundaries of the money system, however, he suggests that their relation to whatever they are converted into could be seen as *metaphorical* (*Ibid.*:272–273). Similarly, Schacht (1973:127) has used Saussure's concepts of *syntagmatic* and *associative* relations for transactions within and beyond the money complex, respectively.

There are flaws in these claims that money can be viewed as a symbol or as a metaphor. Saussure would not have agreed with Codere that money is a symbol, for to the former, a symbol is never entirely arbitrary, and there are always remnants of a natural connection between signifier and signified. Clearly, there are no such connections between money and what it can be converted into. Even if, like Codere, we adopt Peirce's definition of a symbol as an arbitrary association of sign and object (which distinguishes it from an icon or index), this does not warrant classifying money as a symbol. In the case of money, arbitrariness characterizes the relation between sign and object not only in Peirce's sense, where that relation—however arbitrary—is at least codified as a cultural convention, but also in the sense that the relation is totally contextual and unpredictable *over time*. There is, in other words, no convention connecting the money sign with any specific object. In fact, it would be more reasonable to say that a commodity, because it is assigned a specific price, signifies a certain sum of money, than to say that a sum of money signifies an unspecified commodity (cf. Nöth 1996:3–4).

Finally, it seems unwarranted to think of the conversion of money into goods (or vice versa) as metaphorical, because metaphors juxtapose substantial, cultural domains, and money simply does not constitute a domain in this sense. To qualify as a cultural domain, the category of abstract exchange value would have to be internally differentiated so as to exhibit some kind of structure. This was indeed the case in traditional, multicentric economies documented by anthropologists. Thus, the three spheres of exchange among the Tiv (Bohannan 1955) would have entailed transactions and relations that could be viewed as metaphorical. It could, for instance, be argued that, for the Tiv, chickens were to cattle what utensils were to cloth; chickens and utensils belonged to the sphere of subsistence items, cattle and cloth to that of prestige items. Within the prestige sphere of the Tiv, brass rods functioned as a special-purpose currency. If some other medium of exchange (say, cereals, as in ancient Babylonia) would have operated as a similarly restricted currency within the sphere of subsistence items, we would have been able to say that it related to brass rods as subsistence to prestige, or perhaps as individual to society. The relation between the two kinds of money could then be seen as a metaphor for the relation between short-term and long-term values (cf. Parry and Bloch 1989) and would not be reducible to a simple matter of quantity. Each kind of money would derive its meaning from that opposition. The undifferentiated nature of modern money, by reducing itself to tautology, appears to preclude any such metaphorical messages.

THE VACUITY OF ABSTRACTION

Viewed from outer space, money is an *ecosemiotic* phenomenon that has very tangible effects on ecosystems and the biosphere as a whole. If it were not for general-purpose money, nobody would be able to trade tracts of rain forest for Coca-Cola. Much as Bateson and Rappaport did, we could regard money as a communicative disorder. The ecologist Crawford Holling (e.g., Holling and Sanderson 1996) notes that natural systems tend to show a kind of correspondence between temporal and spatial scales, so that the more inclusive a system is, the longer its time span. A forest is thus more permanent than a tree, a tree more permanent than a leaf, and so on. The reproduction of the more inclusive systems naturally has a higher priority than that of its component subsystems. To trade rain forests for carbonated beverages obviously does *not* agree with this pattern.

The recognition of more than one kind of money or exchange value, as among the Tiv, can serve to codify the recognition of different levels of social integration. The subsistence sphere among the Tiv, for instance, pertained to the physical reproduction of households, whereas the exchange of prestige goods and people represented the reproduction of larger social units. From the point of view of communication theory, the relative autonomy of such social levels may be as important as that of the levels of integration studied by the biological sciences. Parry and Bloch (1989:25–27) suggest that the fundamental problem confronting all societies is the mode in which individual (short-term) and social (long-term) goals and projects are to be articulated. The two spheres, they argue, must be kept *separate* but *related*. They concede that it is arguable that the uniqueness of capitalist ideology is that "the values of the short-term order have become elaborated into a theory of long-term reproduction" (*Ibid.*:29).

A similar understanding of capitalism—as a confusion of levels or logical types—is evident in Sahlins's (1976) conclusion, inspired by Baudrillard, that the success of capitalist institutions can be attributed to the fact that they are disembedded from any of the specific, cultural codes that define the contents of consumption at particular times and in particular places. It is precisely in its *unspecificity*—its lack of an object (Peirce) or signified (Saussure)—that the notion of a growing GNP manages to disguise as "rational" the arbitrary production of symbolic value. In this system, "the economy is the main site of symbolic production" (*Ibid.*:211). "Compare," says Sahlins (*Ibid.*:213 n. 1), "the economist's 'utility' with C. S. Peirce's general notion of the sign as 'something which stands to somebody for something in some respect or capacity.'" The conceptual cornerstone of economic science is thus as vague as the most abstract definition possible of the most elementary unit of communication. It specifies absolutely nothing about the substance of economic processes. The all-engulfing character of modernity is generated by this tendency toward abstraction—that is, by the use of signs (including concepts such as "utility") that can stand for anything to anybody. The core of our "culture" is a black hole; at the heart of our cosmology are empty signs.

But is not this a general human condition? Are not religious ideas universally based on signs designed to accommodate everything (Rappaport 1979)? There is a peculiar relation between money and the Sacred, two ideas—or "memes" in Dawkins's (1976) terminology—that both signify encompassment, abstraction, and the transcendence of context. In a complex sense, money is a transmutation—and an inversion—of the Sacred. We can think of the biblical Mammon or of Marx's concept of money fetishism. The same capacity for abstraction that gave us the Sacred, the ultimate, the irreducible, also gave us money, for which nothing is sacred and everything reducible. The Sacred is abstraction rooted or embedded in local resonance; money and science are *disembedded* abstractions. And the universal selection theorists could no doubt observe that human history has selected for money and science, at the expense of the Sacred.

Crump (1981:274) is certainly right when he observes that "language and money are both means of communication." This is what justifies a semiotic analysis. His "one general conclusion," however, is simply that money is a "means for transmitting signals" (*Ibid.*:291). But then, so is air. What do we make of this vacuity? It seems that the only way to deal with such a tautological medium is through a tautological theory. Thus, Gudeman (1986) shows that neoclassical economics, like the money it purports to understand, is uniquely self-referential and nonmetaphorical, and suggests that this very vacuity has made it the ideal accomplice of imperialism.

A RECOVERY OF SPECIFICITY?

Crump (1981:125) concedes that "there is no theoretical objection to a system in which all commodities are divided into *n* classes, . . . each with its own money." The only rationale he seems to be able to see for such monetary boundaries, however, is political. He suggests that "the primary function of any boundary is control" and that "every boundary represents a conflict of interests" (*Ibid.*:131–132). This is a simplistic perspective deriving from neo-liberal economic ideology and thus in itself political. A much more profound view is offered by Kopytoff (1986), who shows that *all* societies recognize spheres of human life that are not to be mediated by money—that is, the values of which are incommensurable. All societies struggle to find a balance between *commoditization* and *singularization*, between the totally homogeneous and the totally heterogeneous economy. The counterdrive to total commoditization is the cognitive discrimination we know as *culture* (*Ibid.*:73). In undermining cognitive discrimination, commoditization is fundamentally "anticultural," but culture tends to resist total commoditization by processes of singularization and sacralization. The fact that *power* often asserts itself in this way (*Ibid.*; cf. Crump's view, above) is only one aspect of this phenomenon of culture. Kopytoff discusses various ways in which commoditization now tends to threaten the only major discrimination still adhered to in the modern West, namely that between objects and persons. He suggests that exchange and commoditization is a "fundamentally seductive idea" (1986:72) and asks,

> how secure are the Western cultural ramparts that defend the human sphere against commoditization, especially in a secularized society that finds it increasingly difficult to appeal to any transcendental sanctions for cultural discrimination and classification? (*Ibid.*:85)

Responding to Kopytoff, Parry and Bloch (1989:16) instead emphasize the political and coercive background to commoditization:

> If money is really such a "fundamentally seductive idea" it is perhaps strange that the colonial powers in Africa should have repeatedly found that they needed to tax people in order to draw them into the wider economy.

It is true that traditional cultures generally did not dismantle their systems of meaning voluntarily, without struggle, but the general tendency in history suggests that commoditization, once introduced, is not very likely to be reversed. The political dimension of these processes of abstraction is obvious but does not refute the "seductive," cultural inertia through which they are continuously being reproduced. How does one *reverse* a process of categorical abstraction? By means of which selective pressures can abstract categories be *undone*?

From different perspectives, I regard both Kopytoff's (1986) and Parry and Bloch's (1989) contributions as arguments that could lend support to a normative vision of a multi- or at least bicentric economy. The tendency to distinguish between the short-term and the long-term is related to what Kopytoff calls singularization. Space will not permit me to here pursue the various institutional practicalities of a bicentric economy, but I hope to have suggested some of its theoretical foundations. It is as much within the capacity of our species to devise such a system as it is to create a global currency. Perhaps the two projects could be articulated: local currencies for subsistence and short-term reproduction, a global currency for telecommunications and long-term social projects. The primary objective of such a distinction between incommensurable, local and global currencies should be to inhibit exploitative exchanges of labor time and natural space between local ecosystems. In the present, general-purpose market, such exchanges permit seemingly limitless capital accumulation to the detriment of global peripheries (cf. Emmanuel 1972; Bunker 1985). A bicentric economy would be a way of "immunizing" the specific and local from the dissolvent logic of the abstract and global. It would represent an acknowledgment of those other forms of humanity, to quote Sahlins (1976:221), "whose difference from us consists in having discovered not merely other codes of existence but ways of achieving an end that still eludes us: the mastery by society of society's mastery over nature."

I hope to have shown that a recovery of specificity and locally embedded economies is, more than anything else, a communicative or *semiotic* challenge. To achieve sustainability, the money sign will have to be reequipped with a certain capacity for discrimination. We could begin by reminding ourselves that general-purpose money is a relatively new phenomenon and that multicentric economies were once ubiquitous rather than exotic. One of the more philosophical accounts of such a system is de Coppet's (1968) description of the role of money among the traditional 'Are'are of the Solomon Islands:

> The circulation of these moneys is subject to precise rules, so that, together with men, women, children and other goods recognized in the local culture, they form a system of exchanges which maintains and perpetuates the established patterns of social organization. The implicit immortality of the society, as such, is thus maintained by the mortality of the people and goods which, momentarily, cross its path. Both the living and the dead combine in the eventual destruction of all things, so that in the end nothing remains save these strings of money, and the unceasing ballet which they perform. (Translated passage quoted from Crump 1981:19)

If in the end nothing remains save the code itself, this is a recognition of the predicament of living systems. Like all structures, the biosphere is composed of differences. If it is humankind's mission to devise a coded system of signals to integrate this most inclusive of living systems, our monetary system must recognize those differences or continue to annihilate them.

In his rich discussion of environmental justice and the social construction of space and time, Harvey (1996) draws on Munn's (1986) classic study of the exchange of *kula* valuables in Melanesia. It is as if the socio-material logic of money protrudes with greater clarity in its earliest (i.e., least abstract, most discriminatory) form, where the money objects retain distinct identities and prescribed channels of circulation. The *kula* valuables suggest material signs poised on the very threshold between the realms of personalized gifts and abstract exchange values, that is, between economies of genuine symbols and economies of empty signifiers. The circulation of these material objects generates specific structures of claims and reciprocities in space and time. The push and pull of such relations constitute gravitational fields that variously extend the social reach of individual persons. It becomes clear that money signs are generative of social space and time and, by implication, that differently designed money institutions will generate different kinds of spatio-temporal worlds. This should be a crucial implication of Harvey's struggles to reconcile particularism and universalism, constructivism and objectivism, phenomenology and historical materialism. The scope of material agency in human worlds hinges on the organization of sign relations. Any attempt to reorganize the material dimension of global society will have to proceed by means of a reorganization of the semiotics of money. If there is to be any hope of achieving "the mastery by society of society's mastery over nature," we must be prepared to rethink the very foundations of economics. I believe that this is an insight with which any struggle for environmental justice and ecological sustainability will have to begin.

10

Ecology As Semiotics: A Contextualist Manifesto

In this chapter, I would like to use some of the ideas in the previous chapter to discuss and connect two recurrent themes in ecological anthropology. One is the epistemological polarization between "dualist" and "monist" approaches to human ecology. The other is the issue of whether or not traditional, pre-industrial human societies have something to tell us about how to live sustainably. As a shorthand for this latter polarity, I will use the categories "contextualist" (for the position that they do have something to tell us) versus "modernist" (for the position that they do not). I believe that the interconnectedness of these two polarities deserves to be clarified. As the limitations of dualist and modernist perspectives are inexorably revealing themselves all over the world, I will try to take stock of some of the theoretical foundations on which a normative, monistic, and contextualist stance can be articulated.

I choose to speak of "contextualism" (rather than, say, "traditionalism") because it suggests, in positive terms, the logical antithesis to *modernity* as defined, for instance, by Giddens (1990). Giddens's observations on the "disembedding" (i.e., decontextualizing) tendencies in modernity subsume a long line of concepts offered by social philosophers such as Weber, Marx, Tönnies, and Simmel. Processes of decontextualization pervade all aspects of modern society. They are as representative for the construction of scientific knowledge as for the organization of economic life. Against this background, a "contextualist" stance is one that denies the capacity of abstract, totalizing systems such as science or the market to

solve the basic problems of human survival, recognizing local and implicit meanings as the essential components of a sustainable livelihood.
All this is of much more than academic significance, considering its implications for the role of what is often referred to as "traditional ecological
knowledge" or "traditional resource management" in the public discussion on "sustainable development."

VULGAR MATERIALISM OR
HEGELIAN ECOLOGY?

My point of departure in this chapter is the contextualist position of Roy
Rappaport's *Pigs for the Ancestors* (1968). This is not so much to defend his
early, cybernetic formulations as to briefly trace the career of a pioneer
contextualist message through three decades of shifting anthropological
paradigms. Moran (1990:15) suggests that "no work has had a greater impact on the development of an ecosystem approach in anthropology"
than Rappaport's study, "nor has any other study attracted as many critics of the ecological approach." I will discuss only one of his critics (Friedman 1974a, 1979) and instead concentrate on the convergences between
Rappaport's contributions and more recent components of what could be
articulated as an increasingly elaborate, contextualist framework.

In economic anthropology, much of the modernist-contextualist polarity was evident in the debate between formalists and substantivists in the
1950s and 1960s, and many of us will associate the concept of "embeddedness" with Karl Polanyi. In the 1970s, I would suggest, the same underlying polarity that had organized the anthropological discourse on
economics was projected into its discourse on ecology. Representing the
contextualist pole, Rappaport (1968, 1979) suggested that traditional, de-
centralized social systems tended to develop means of regulating local
ecosystems that were better geared to sustainability than modern economies.

Rappaport's urge to bring nature and society into a common framework should be understood against the backdrop of two diametrically opposed approaches to ecological anthropology, the materialist "cultural
ecology" pioneered by Julian Steward and Leslie White, and the mentalist
"Ecology of Mind" of Gregory Bateson (1972). His argument may be
viewed as an attempt at reconciliation but has been criticized in the very
dualist language it had hoped to transcend. Jonathan Friedman, for instance, in 1974 asserted that Rappaport's work belonged to a "functional
ecology entrenched in the ideological matrix of vulgar materialism"
(Friedman 1974a:445). Five years later, Friedman (1979) described the
same work as "Hegelian Ecology," suspended "between Rousseau and

the World Spirit." To have been charged, for the same work and by the same critic, with both "vulgar materialism" and Hegelianism suggests that Rappaport's attempt at monism may not have been altogether unsuccessful and that Friedman's two critiques, though contradictory, remain entrenched in the matrix of dualism.

To be sure, a number of formulations in ecological anthropology deserve criticism for their materialist or functionalist bias. Rappaport's (1968) own formulations are far from flawless in this respect, as he himself concedes (Rappaport 1979, 1990). In retrospect, however, we may observe that these shortcomings largely derive from a failure to more decisively extricate the contextualist argument from a dualist vocabulary, a task that would have been more demanding in the 1960s than at present. I hope to show that the underlying intuition then couched in the functionalist terms of cybernetics can now be elaborated in the light of more recent paradigms such as post-structuralism and practice theory, and of theoretical developments in areas such as cognitive science, metaphor theory, and semiotics.

HOMEOSTATS AND CONSCIOUS PURPOSE

The positions of Rappaport and Friedman are diametrically opposed with respect to the role of conscious purpose in maintaining social and ecological systems within the "goal ranges" defining their viability. Rappaport (1979:169–170) follows Bateson (1972:402–422) in suggesting that the linear structure of purposive, problem-solving consciousness is incapable of grasping the circular connectedness of living systems, and that explicit knowledge and rationality are insufficient tools for the sustainable management of ecological relations. Both advocate a more holistic human involvement in the natural environment that would include the engagement of unconscious aspects of the human mind, as in religion, ritual, and aesthetics. Friedman (1979), on the other hand, seems to distrust the regulatory significance of any cultural institution that is not organized by conscious intention.

Whereas Bateson and Rappaport are explicitly concerned with discovering principles for providing human societies with greater capacities for self-regulation and for avoiding catastrophes, Friedman seems to share no such hopes. In his view, offered against the backdrop of I. Prigogine's far-from-equilibrium thermodynamics and of R. Thom's "catastrophe theory," social systems are inherently and once and for all incapable of self-regulation. This fatalistic view is difficult to reconcile with his warnings that Bateson's and Rappaport's "religious solution" is "dangerous, to say the least" (1979:266). One wonders in what sense anything can

be more "dangerous" than regarding catastrophe as inevitable. The paradox here is that in advocating social policies serving to revitalize local,
cultural autonomy, Bateson and Rappaport (1979:262) emerge as the
champions of conscious purpose (though at another level), whereas it
could be argued that Friedman's fatalism at times assumes a religious dimension. Again, the problem seems to be Cartesian dualism. Whereas
Bateson and Rappaport consistently deal with human cognition and information processing as active aspects of evolutionary processes (which
agrees very well with Prigogine's fundamentally optimistic position; cf.
Prigogine and Stengers 1984), Friedman's objectivist approach to cycles
of social transformations suggests very little scope for human agency.

Another aspect of Friedman's argument that deserves scrutiny is his
view on homeostasis. He suggests that the cycle of ritual pig slaughter
among the Tsembaga Maring does not qualify as a homeostat because the
reference values that trigger the slaughter (women's complaints) are not
identical with the goal ranges set by the carrying capacity of the local ecosystem. Thus, there is "no homeostatic regulation of the environment but
rather the maintenance of certain environmental variables as a *non-inten-
tional* result of the ritual cycle" (1979:256; emphasis added). As an instance of a real homeostat, where goal ranges and reference values do coincide, Friedman offers the mechanical thermostat. A thermostat, it
seems, qualifies as a homeostat because it is "a mechanism that must be
set by a human regulator" in purposive or teleological fashion (*Ibid.*:256),
and purposiveness or teleology means that "there exists a sentence in the
programme specifying the goal to be attained" (*Ibid.*:267).

If homeostatic processes are to be defined in terms of conscious intention, as Friedman suggests, at least two major problems arise. The first is
whether the myriad homeostatic processes within living organisms from
amoebas to mammals (including their body thermostats) are no longer to
be considered homeostatic, and the concept is henceforth to be restricted
to human-made machines. Second, the concepts of intentionality and purposiveness, defined as the existence of "a sentence in the programme
specifying the goal to be attained," evoke an increasingly outmoded epistemology according to which it would be feasible for us to judge whether
or not the "sentence" stands in some exact relationship to the "goal."
Conscious purpose would have to be buttressed with an objectivist epistemology to justify such a clear-cut distinction between teleology and teleo-
nomy. Intentionality does not imply transparency. If the goal is as complex as ecological viability, a vast number of different sentences could
conceivably work toward that same goal. Traditional cosmologies may
codify very relevant observations of (and participation in) ecological processes without corresponding to the vocabulary or even the logic of modern science. If it were not so, the premodern human colonization of every

ecological biome on the planet would have been inconceivable. In concentrating on the *adequacy* of cultural models rather than on their literal "truth" as defined by the categories of modern science, Rappaport's work in 1968 in a sense foreshadowed the postmodern deposition of the master narrative.

Consciousness, like teleology, is not an "either/or" but a gradient, partial and amenable to various formulations. What else but the stochastics of long-term survival are to judge which "sentence" most adequately represents the "goal"? In Rappaport's (1979:98) words, "the criterion of adequacy for a cognized model is not its accuracy, but its adaptive effectiveness." If we consider the feeding behavior of various kinds of living organisms, Friedman's supposedly clear-cut distinction (*Ibid.*:254, 267) between teleological and teleonomic processes begins to fade. An adult and not too absent-minded human reaching for food would surely qualify as an example of purposive behavior ("where the goal is itself an integral and explicit part of the activity"), but foraging invertebrates decidedly less so, and as we approach unicellular organisms and plants the absorption of nutrients from their surroundings seems increasingly teleonomic (where the goal of the activity is not an explicit part of the program but merely "a predictable result of that programme.") Teleological processes, in other words, are an arbitrarily defined subset of teleonomic processes.

Recent studies in cognitive science (Maturana and Varela 1987 [1992]) serve to downplay the distinction between human intention and other forms of systemic directionality in living systems. Recognizing the continuity means not only to acknowledge the elaborateness of goal orientation in living systems generally but also to deconstruct the illusion of transparency projected by the concept of "conscious purpose." As psychoanalytic theory might underscore, there is no point at which purpose or goal-oriented behavior becomes "conscious" in any absolute sense. As human beings we remain constrained by the specific forms of perception and cognition that our genetic and cultural endowments will permit.

If the crucial issue in defining a homeostat is whether "there exists a sentence in the programme specifying the goal to be attained," we must ask ourselves on which criteria—other than survival—we could possibly base an assessment of the degree to which the "sentence" accurately specifies the "goal." If we follow the meta-perspective on cognition offered by Maturana and Varela (1987 [1992]:136–137), the only way to assess such a correspondence is to approach the relationship between program and environment from a detached position, like that of people on the shore congratulating a submarine navigator for avoiding reefs that he himself could only detect as indicator readings. Maturana and Varela's (*Ibid.*:172–174) pragmatist definition of "knowledge" does not assume an internalization of the environment but "an effective (or adequate) behavior in a given context." In a nutshell, these authors conclude, "to live is to know."

From this perspective, in discussing the prospects for sustainability, the issue is not the exactitude, in terms defined by modern science, of the relationship between program and goal (reference values and goal ranges), but the feasibility of maintaining some kind of feedback of information that might continuously calibrate one with the other. The crucial issue then becomes the nature (and origin) of the program that defines the reference values and thus governs local resource use. This is a recurrent theme in Rappaport's (1979) discussion of adaptation versus "maladaptation." With the loss of local self-sufficiency, he argues (*Ibid.*:162), there is also loss of homeostatic capacity. Not surprisingly, he identifies "all-purpose money" as one of the major causes of such maladaptive trends (*Ibid.*:130–131, 167). The economic terms in which reference values are expressed "may be alien to and inappropriate for the systems being regulated" (*Ibid.*:100). Another but structurally related source of maladaptation is the objectivism of modern science, a mode of knowledge construction that apotheosizes "facts" and systematically destroys meanings (*Ibid.*:128–130). Rappaport concludes that the decontextualized rationality of science and the world market is ill-suited to the task of deriving a sustainable livelihood from local ecosystems:

> Given the complexity of natural ecosystems it is unlikely that we will ever be able to predict the outcome of all of the actions we undertake in any of them, even if we do understand the principles of ecosystemic operation generally. Because knowledge can never replace respect as a guiding principle in our ecosystemic relations, it is adaptive for cognized models to engender respect for that which is unknown, unpredictable, and uncontrollable, as well as for them to codify empirical knowledge. It may be that the most appropriate cognized models, that is, those from which adaptive behaviour follows, are not those that simply represent ecosystemic relations in objectively "correct" material terms, but those that invest them with significance and value beyond themselves. (*Ibid.*:100–101)

THE MONIST FOUNDATION OF CONTEXTUALISM

It is interesting to consider the extent to which more recent developments in anthropology, sociology, and related fields might serve to solidify a critical, contextualist framework. A brief selection of references will suffice to indicate the thrust of this convergence. Rappaport's concern over the loss of local autonomy, for instance, is shared by a growing number of anthropologists and development theorists addressing the dominance of "disembedded" over "embedded" knowledge systems (Gudeman 1986; Apffel Marglin and Marglin 1990; Shiva 1991; Croll and Parkin 1992; Banuri and Apffel Marglin 1993). We might even include Habermas (1987:151), for whom the relationship between "system" and "life-world" is nothing less than "the fundamental problem of social theory."

The connection between monism and contextualism is particularly evident in the collection of papers edited by Croll and Parkin (1992). The argument that people, their indigenous knowledge, and their environment exist inseparably "within each other" (*Ibid.*:i) is fundamental to their critique of external "scripts" for development. When the environment is "separated out from human agents and perceived as an exterior non-human habitat," subjugated by specialists imposing outside distinctions and categories in the interests of order, rationality, and standardization, it is opened to "appropriation, domination, attack, conquest and domestication" (*Ibid.*:32). Even as benevolent a discourse as that of "global" environmentalism, we might add, is largely founded on the same, "Western" inclination toward objectification and decontextualization (Evernden 1985; Ingold 1993).

If contextualism is served by a monist epistemology, we may conversely conclude that the disembedding tendencies of modernity are part and parcel of Cartesian dualism. The interrelations between the different dimensions of modernity (e.g., market institutions, "Western" personhood, and dualist epistemology) deserve to be more fully illuminated. Croll and Parkin's argument might have proceeded further in what Bourdieu (1990) has called "objectifying objectification," that is, in conceptualizing and defamiliarizing the "Western" outlook that is undermining the "inside wisdom" of traditional ecocosmologies. If their book represents the discovery that people, discourse, and environment may be inseparable, it does not reflect back on the discoverers—that is, on why this should be news to us "Westerners." It does not connect its concerns in any way with the sociological concepts of modernity and disembeddedness, nor even with Polanyi's early observations on the modern economy as being less embedded than premodern modes of livelihood. It is a sign of the times that ecological anthropology is beginning to investigate the "difficult, negotiable and contested relationship between person and environment" (Croll and Parkin 1992:9) but unfortunate that it seems so altogether disengaged from sociology and economic anthropology. A more profound understanding of modernity would have provided these crucial links between economy, discourse, personhood, and ecology. Decontextualization and objectification can be understood as two sides of the same coin. The decontextualization of social relations, knowledge production, and identities can also be expressed as the objectification (and fetishization) of exchange, language, and the self. Moreover, objectification (of the body, the landscape, labor, women, the colonies) can be identified as the ultimate prerequisite of power, repression, and exploitation. Paradoxically, this becomes visible to us only as we turn the logic of modernity against itself, by objectifying objectification, achieving a distanced view of the distanced view, and encompassing the ambition to encompass.

Post-structuralism, in recognizing the unity of discourse and practice, could well serve to buttress the contextualist argument that Rappaport presented in *Pigs for the Ancestors* more than thirty years ago. Indeed, in his later texts we find the same underlying message couched in an updated and more persuasive vocabulary. Rappaport writes, for instance, that human

> meanings and understandings [do] not only reflect or approximate an independently existing world but participate in its construction. . . . Language has ever more powerfully reached out from the species in which it emerged to reorder and subordinate the natural systems in which populations of that species participate. (Rappaport 1994:156)

Lines such as these suggest Foucault applied to ecosystems. They also harmonize well with the perspective of cognitive scientists such as Maturana and Varela (1987 [1992]:234), who conclude that "it is by languaging that the act of knowing brings forth a world." A similar view is emerging in the field of environmental history, where "knowledge" is being recognized neither as a representation of something that exists outside it, nor merely a social construction, but as a negotiated *relationship* with nature that actually reconstructs nature in the process of representing it (cf. Bird 1987). This emergent, monist view of knowledge is explicit in the work of Maturana and Varela, whose position is

> not the mere negation of representationism—namely, that the organism invents or constructs its own world at whim—but, more interestingly, that animal and environment are two sides of the same coin, knower and known are mutually specified. (Maturana and Varela 1987 [1992]:253)

Such a "relationist" conception of knowledge offers a middle road between the Scylla of representationism and the Charybdis of solipsism (*Ibid.*:133–134), each in its own way a product of the dualist matrix. Beyond the paralyzing, late modern stalemate between objectivism and relativism (cf. Bernstein 1983), it suggests a *rapprochement* of subject and object that might restore a sense of involvement and responsibility to the production of knowledge.

THE CASE FOR A RECONTEXTUALIZATION
OF KNOWLEDGE

Monistic approaches are increasingly explicit in recent, ecological anthropology (e.g., Bennett 1990; Croll and Parkin 1992). Rappaport's own formulations, however, at times seem unnecessarily dualistic. Consider the following distinction between ecosystems and cultures:

> An ecosystem is a system of matter and energy transactions among populations of organisms of various kinds, and between each of them and all of them on the one hand, and non-living substances, things, and processes on the other. Culture is the category of phenomena distinguished from others by its contingency upon symbols. (Rappaport 1979:59–60)

My conviction that this dichotomy may be unnecessary and misleading largely stems from the work of Jakob von Uexküll (1940 [1982]) and from Ingold's (1992) discussion of the significance of von Uexküll's concept of *Umwelt* for ecological anthropology. In the words of Thure von Uexküll (1982:7), *Umwelt*-theory amounts to "the fact that living organisms (including cells) respond as subjects, i.e., they respond only to signs. . . ." Each organism in an ecosystem lives in its own subjective world (*Umwelt*) largely defined by its species-specific mode of perceiving its environment. "The question of meaning," says Jakob von Uexküll (1940 [1982]:37), is therefore "the crucial one to all living beings." The implication is that ecological interaction *presupposes* such a plurality of subjective worlds. Indeed, ecological relations are based on meaning; they are semiotic. Even if *symbols* in Peirce's sense are indeed restricted to humans, ecosystems, no less than cultures, are contingent upon communication. Rappaport's aspiration to bring the objective and the subjective into a common framework is paralleled by the interdisciplinary field of semiotics, the aim of which is to "reintegrate the natural and human sciences in the higher synthesis proper to a doctrine of signs" (Anderson et al. 1984:8).

At one point, Rappaport (1979:158) does concede that "all organisms behave in terms of meanings" (the crucial difference being that humans "must themselves construct those meanings"; cf. also Ingold 1992:43), but apparently this does not prompt him to revise his definition of an ecosystem as fundamentally "a system of matter and energy transactions" (1979:59). Here he clearly remains constrained by the categories of dualism. There is really no reason to emphasize the material over the communicative aspect of ecosystems, or, for that matter, to do the reverse with respect to human societies. Once we recognize that human subjectivity, along with the subjectivity of all the other species, is an aspect of the very *constitution* of ecosystems, we have a solid foundation for the conclusion that the destruction of meaning and the destruction of ecosystems are two aspects of the same process.

In trying to visualize the process by which meanings and ecosystems are simultaneously dismantled, we come back to the concept of decontextualization. As Rappaport (1979:142) suggests, the confusion of hierarchical relations among different levels of understanding (e.g., specific versus general, concrete versus abstract, etc.) may "lead not only to the destruction of meaning but of the material world as well." Decontextualizing models, such as the universal rationality of the Green Revolution or the formalism of neoclassical economic theory, alter the relation between person and world by subordinating or eclipsing the non-objectifiable, local specificities that render meanings everywhere so implicit and inextricable. The neoclassical concept of "utility," for instance, imposes on local worlds everywhere the axiom of universal interchangeability, dissolving complex codifications of resource flows and paving the way for a system the blind logic of which is simply to reward an accelerating rate of destruction. As we saw in chapter 6, such a cosmological shift was a prerequisite to industrialism: the notion of a decontextualized "utility" has very tangible material repercussions. The dissipative and fetishistic nature of the accumulation of industrial technomass is clearly also a part of Rappaport's paradigm:

> The product tends to become a by- or even waste-product of what might be called the "industrial metabolism" which is, ultimately, simply the operation of machines. . . . The ultimate consequence is not merely that the short-run interests of a few powerful men or institutions come to prevail, but that the "interests" of machines—which even powerful men serve—become dominant. (*Ibid.*:163–164)

Rappaport's observation (*Ibid.*:164) that short-run interests have "usurped" the places of long-run needs and values is echoed in Bloch and Parry's (1989:29) suggestion that, in capitalist ideology, "the values of the short-term order have become elaborated into a theory of long-term reproduction." The list of convergences continues. For instance, much as Bateson and Rappaport contemplate a return to religion and restoration of local autonomy, Giddens writes that, whether a postmodern world "would imply a resurgence of religion in some form or another is difficult to say, but there would presumably be a renewed fixity to certain aspects of life that would recall some features of tradition" (Giddens 1990:178). Bateson's and Rappaport's emphasis on the implicit and nonlinguistic aspects of culture and experience, moreover, harmonizes well with Bourdieu's (1990) influential theory of "practice" and with recent developments in cognitive science (cf. Bloch 1994).

Romanticist critiques of Western rationality have a long history, but studies in human ecology seem now to be in a position to articulate a *rational* critique of that rationality. The contextualist position is not romanticism or mysticism but a sober recognition of the limitations of totalizing institutions and knowledge systems. Because of the sheer complexity and specificity of ecosystemic interrelationships and fluctuations, it is not unreasonable to expect that optimal strategies for sustainable resource management are generally best defined by local practitioners with close and long-term experience of these specificities, and with special stakes in the outcome. Yet it is clear that actual management strategies are today generally informed by entirely different sets of conditions. This structural contradiction in the organization of human society is an adequate point of departure for any anthropological contribution to ongoing deliberations on "sustainable development."

METAPHOR, MORALITY, AND POLICY

The argument for a recontextualization of the production of ecological knowledge necessarily leads to a consideration of the significance of metaphor. This issue is central to the contextualist argument inasmuch as it suggests an answer to the general question of what it is in the nature of traditional understandings that might make them more meaningful and at the same time more conducive to sustainable resource use than modern representations. I am referring here not to the capacity of traditional knowledge systems to register complex ecological relations, which has been amply documented (cf., e.g., Johannes 1989; Posey and Balée 1989; Moran 1993) but to their capacity to constitute prescriptive "models *for*" sustainable resource use. Rappaport, having traced the complex metaphorical structure of Maring ritual cosmology (1979:103–116), observes that metaphors convey not "information in the digital sense" but meanings that may be "affectively more powerful" (*Ibid.*:156–157). In their inclination to codify normative, practical attitudes, metaphorical understandings of nature assume the responsibilities that must always adhere to the very act of "knowing." If "knowledge" is a *relationship* with nature that is constitutive both of the knower and the known, then metaphor is a mode of knowing that incorporates the very conditions of knowledge.

The connection I want to make here is with Gudeman's (1986) important observation that neoclassical economic theory distinguished itself from all local models of livelihood by its ambition to abandon metaphor. Rather than positioning the knowing subject by investing economic practices with meanings deriving from other spheres of life (e.g., respect for the ancestors), Ricardo's "derivational" representations turn inward on themselves in a closed, self-referential, and thus ultimately tautological web of concepts. This act of decontextualization dispelled morality from human livelihood and provided a vocabulary (e.g., "utility") for engulfing all local systems of meaning.

Metaphor is a mode of knowing that positions the human subject by *evoking* non-objectifiable inner states associated with specific forms of practice. The significance of metaphor for the contextualist argument thus lies in its capacity to activate tacit, practical knowledge based on experience of highly specific, local conditions. This position accommodates Ingold's (1992:52–53) proposition that cultural constructions of the environment are secondary to practical action ("the practitioner's way of knowing"), while recognizing the capacity of such constructions to codify and reinforce a specific, ecological *habitus*, not least in the transmission of such dispositions between generations. A metaphorical "cognized model" does not so much encode ecological information as provide "cues" for the activation of specific, practical repertoires appropriated in the context of action. Metaphor, in implying participation, would thus have to be granted a central, epistemological status in the "postmodern science" envisaged by Rappaport:

> Whereas modern science has attempted to develop "theory," that is, detached intellectual understandings derived from "objective" or "outside" knowledge of particular constituents of the world, leaving "praxis" to farmers, carpenters, engineers, priests, or politicians, a postmodern science, recognizing that participation in the world it observes is inescapable, will incorporate into itself considerations of practice. (Rappaport 1994:163)

Metaphorical understandings of subsistence practices and ecological relationships have been richly documented in the anthropological literature (for general discussions cf. Gudeman 1986; Ingold 1986; Bird-David 1993). Bird-David (1993:112, 121) notes that hunter-gatherer cultures all over the world tend to represent "human-nature relatedness in terms of personal relatedness," within a "subject-subject" rather than a "subject-object" frame, and suggests that "since these tribal peoples share an intimate and time-proven knowledge of their respective natural environments, their representations cannot be dismissed outright in favour of the Western one." The application of social metaphors to practices of livelihood is not limited to hunter-gatherers but seems to be a pervasive aspect of premodern subsistence production. Descola (1994:327) demonstrates, for instance, how the Achuar conceptualize different subsistence practices in terms of different kinds of social behavior: "the women's consanguine mothering of cultivated plants and the affinal charming of game practiced by the men."

Descola further suggests that if social relationships provide the conceptual model for human-environmental relations, a modification of the latter will generally begin with "prior mutation" of the former (*Ibid.*:330). It may not be necessary to establish such a generalized priority, among other things because metaphors are known to predicate meanings in a reciprocal manner (cf. Jackson 1983; Isbell 1985). However, Descola's observation on the congruity between social relations and human-environmental relations is clearly relevant to the argument advanced here, that several features of modern life generally treated as distinct (namely, market exchange, "Western" personhood, Cartesian dualism) are but the social and epistemological aspects of a single phenomenon of modernity. Rather than treat plants and animals as categories of kinsmen, a society of strangers will breed "natural aliens" (cf. Evernden 1985). In other words, a society founded on objectification of self and others will tend to project the same, hierarchical mind/body dichotomy onto the relationship between self and the natural world.

Among the implications of such a conclusion is yet another argument for the postmodern resurrection of some kind of "fixity" (Giddens 1990:178) within a local sphere of social life. If the predominant, modern mode of human-environmental relations can be improved only in conjunction with a transformation of the predominant, modern mode of sociability, the discussion on "sustainable development" will have to incorporate considerations of how to revitalize that aspect of human existence which Tönnies (1887 [1963]) called *Gemeinschaft*. 7

Another implication is that our choice of metaphors in the discourse on "sustainable development" deserves very careful consideration. It is exceedingly interesting to compare the new social metaphors for human-environmental interaction, which are being articulated by different parties in this discourse, with their premodern counterparts. Whereas traditional subsistence cultures commonly conceptualized human-environmental relations in terms of their own social practices of gift-giving and reciprocity (cf. Ingold 1986; Århem 1996), the recent discourse on ecological economics suggests that ecosystems are a form of "capital" that humans should "invest" in and that they provide humans with "services" that need to be evaluated properly in monetary terms (e.g. Folke and Kåberger 1991; Jansson et al. 1994). Hitherto unpaid ecosystem services are thus said to have generated, for human society, an ecological "debt" of immense proportions, and concepts such as "green taxes" and the "Polluter Pays Principle" have been advanced to rectify the situation. As we shall see in the next chapter, this is clearly a modern instance of the projection of a social metaphor on human-environmental relations, where the latter are accordingly conceptualized as market transactions. Inasmuch as it serves as a literal understanding of the environmental crisis, however, it is an extremely misleading metaphor, because monetary phenomena such as "investments," "services," and "debts" remain relations between human beings and could not possibly denote human-environmental relations. Ecosystems are not offering their "services" on the market, nor do they have any use for monetary compensation. Money is a claim on other people. Thus, contrary to the tenets of conventional discourse, it cannot restore damages to the biosphere, only redistribute them among sectors of global society. Nevertheless, the metaphorical understanding of nature in terms of "services" to be paid for serves the crucial ideological function of marshaling the adverse effects of economic "growth" merely to reinforce our faith in it (WCED 1987).

CONCLUDING REMARKS ON
CONTEXTUALISM AND IDEOLOGY

In an otherwise very persuasive critique of modernity, Marglin (1990) at one point draws an unnecessarily sharp line between the domains of what John Maynard Keynes called "organic" and "atomic" propositions, respectively. The former are propositions "the truth of which depends on the beliefs of agents," whereas the latter are propositions "the truth of which is independent of these beliefs." In Marglin's view, "propositions about the world of things and plants are atomic, while many if not all propositions about the world of human beings, the world of social relationships, are organic" (Marglin 1990:15).

In light of the various arguments sketched in this chapter, such a clearcut distinction between nature and society should be difficult to maintain. To a greater extent than we normally recognize, even the natural sciences generate propositions "the truth of which depends on the beliefs of agents." Rappaport provides a persuasive example:

> In a world in which the lawful and the meaningful, the discovered and the constructed, are inseparable the concept of the ecosystem *is not simply a theoretical framework* within which the world can be analyzed. It is itself an element of that world, one that is crucial in maintaining that world's integrity in the face of mounting insults to it. To put this a little differently, the concept of the ecosystem is not simply descriptive. . . . It is also "performative"; the ecosystem concept and actions informed by it are *part of the world's means for maintaining, if not indeed constructing, ecosystems.* (Rappaport 1990:68–69)

In this sense, debates over the self-stabilizing capacities of ecosystems (e.g., Friedman 1979; Vayda 1986) are as ideologically committing as the polarization between proponents of traditional "environmental wisdom" and those writers who "now dwell singlemindedly on examples of bad natural resource management among traditional peoples, advancing the opposing notion that traditional environmental practices were basically unsound" (Johannes 1989:7).

In this chapter, I have explored some of the possible theoretical foundations for the former of these two positions. I have argued that a number of advances in recent social and cognitive science converge in a critique of modernity's *decontextualization of knowledge*, and that this critique coincides with an increasingly successful ambition to transcend Cartesian dualism.

The contextualist argument, however, will need to look out for the pitfalls inherent in our conventional vocabulary. Proponents of ecological economics, for instance, have suggested that "cultural diversity and traditional ecological knowledge are part of the cultural capital into which society needs to invest to provide the raw material for the process of sustainable development" (Berkes and Folke 1994:18). Although it should be clear by now that I share the underlying evaluation of indigenous knowledge expressed in this quotation, I remain hesitant about the industrial metaphor in which it is couched. It is ironic that parts of the abstract and nonmetaphorical terminology that has been responsible for muting the local metaphors (cf. Gudeman 1986) are now being used metaphorically to understand these local constructions as yet another "raw material" in which to "invest." Considering how the contemporary economic system actually operates, it is easy to share Baines's (1989) apprehensions that traditional ecological knowledge will continue to be converted into just that: a raw material for profitable commercial enterprise such as the pharmaceutical industry. The objectification of indigenous knowledge as "capital" and "raw materials" to "invest" in represents a hierarchical, modernist perspective with no indications of respect for the social context and irreducibility of local experience.

The discussion on "traditional ecological knowledge" and "traditional resource management" (cf. Johannes 1989; Berkes, Folke, and Gadgil 1993; Berkes and Folke 1994; Gadgil 1991; Posey and Balée 1989; Moran 1990, 1993) is thus intrinsically paradoxical to the extent that it hopes for an appropriation and application of local knowledge by the very modernist framework by which such knowledge is continually being eclipsed. In advocating what he calls "epistemological decentralization," Banuri (1990:97–99) recognizes that an increasing contextuality of knowledge will render "the expert, trained in universal sciences, an anachronism." Clearly, an "expert" in an abstractly conceived field of "local knowledge" is a contradiction in terms. But this paradox, of course, is a pervasive aspect of the anthropological condition. We can engage in a meta-discourse on knowledge, but in terms of concrete expertise we can at best become awkward apprentices to specific, local practitioners.

Rather than approach indigenous knowledge as another "resource" to be tapped, ecological anthropology might concentrate on the sociocultural contexts that allow ecologically sensitive knowledge systems to evolve and persist over time. There are reasons to believe that the best conditions for such local calibrations occur precisely when they are *not* being subjected to attempts at encompassment by totalizing frameworks of one kind or another. In recognizing implicit and inextricable local meanings as the very stuff of ecological resilience, a critical inquiry into human ecology might begin to confront the agents of destruction by modifying its own ambition to encompass.

11

Exchange, Personhood,
and Human Ecology

In this chapter, I will try to put together some theoretical jigsaw pieces that might help us get a fuller picture of the relation between human beings and their natural environment in different cultural contexts. I will discuss some general issues of method and analysis in human ecology and then try to apply some of these thoughts to the much discussed contrast between traditional Amerindian and modern ways of approaching nature. I will suggest a correlation between varieties of personhood, ways of engaging nature, and ways of engaging other human beings through exchange. Finally, I will argue that a theoretical conflation of these three aspects of human life and cosmology is facilitated by recognizing their various *spatial* dimensions. In comparing the spatial coordinates of personhood, nature, and exchange, we may surmise a structural logic that permits us to juxtapose as disparate contexts as premodern Algonquian hunter-gatherers, modern scholars in the field of ecological economics, and the "postmodern" deep ecology movement.

THE HUMAN ECOLOGICAL TRIANGLE

Recent years have witnessed a proliferation of discourses on human-environmental relations. It seems as if each traditional discipline in the human sciences has been developing a "green" territory of its own (e.g., environ-

mental history, environmental sociology, environmental law, environmental ethics, ecological economics, ecological anthropology, and so on).
Proponents of these discourses are faced with the perennial problem of
whether to adopt the language of "Humanists" or "Scientists" (cf. Ingerson 1994). The former tends to imply a focus on how particular humans
experience their environment, adopting the terminology of phenomenology, hermeneutics, or constructivism, and stylistically often verging on
literature. The latter generally means assuming an objectivist stance, typically involving more exact analytical procedures as well as quantification
of various aspects of human-environmental interaction (cf. Bates and Lees
1996:9). I need not dwell on the mutual antagonism that proponents of
the "two cultures" often feel vis-à-vis each other; suffice to say that they
seem to live in different intellectual universes (cf. Bernstein 1983). I suspect that, in this book, I have taken something of a middle road. I am
definitely a humanist insofar as I am concerned with the subjective and
semiotic dimension of human-environmental relations (and in my lack of
interest in quantification), yet I share the natural scientists' predilection
for conciseness and analytical precision. The result may seem awkward
and sterile to the humanist but vague and fanciful to the natural scientist.
This probably is an inevitable cost of trying to deal objectively with subjectivity.

It has often been recognized that the study of human-environmental
relations is a "triadic" research field involving what we could provisionally refer to as *nature, society*, and *consciousness*. Environmental historians
such as Merchant (1989:3), McEvoy (1988:229), and Worster (1993:5) tend
to use "production" for what I have called "society," and "ecology" for
"nature," but the general scheme is the same. The greatest variation is in
categories pertaining to "consciousness." Merchant speaks of "forms of
consciousness," McEvoy of "cognition," and Worster of "structures of
meaning" (cf. Worster 1988:293 for a more elaborate explication). Geogra-
pher Dieter Steiner (1993:56) suggests a "human ecological triangle" of
environment, society, and *person*. The recurrent, triadic scheme is not arbitrary but reflects the complementarity of perspectives on human-environmental relations deriving, respectively, from the natural sciences, the social sciences, and the humanities. It may seem curious to let the concept
of "person" stand for that aspect which the environmental historians call
"consciousness," "cognition," or "structures of meaning," but there are
good reasons for doing so. The person is the only conceivable entity that
is both a locus of consciousness, cognition, and meaning *and* a source of
tangible agency. Although it is possible to visualize abstract patterns of
"culture," "ideology," or "symbolism" that transcend the individual person, it is through concrete persons that such abstract phenomena intervene in the world.

It is important to recognize that these three dimensions of human-environmental relations are not to be arranged into some kind of causal hierarchy reminiscent of the Marxist model of a "mode of production," with nature and production as "base" and consciousness as "superstructure." Steiner instead speaks of a *recursivity* between the different corners of his triangle. They are three, mutually reinforcing *aspects* of a single, socio-ecological phenomenon. If, for instance, we want to use Steiner's model to understand a process of emergent modernization of human-environmental relations, I believe that an adequate way of going about it would be to identify specific structures and relationships representing the three *sides* of the triangle, because the sides are what connect the three dimensions in mutually reinforcing (recursive) ways.

Although Steiner does not detail such a procedure himself, I have tentatively "filled in" the corners and sides of the triangle to make it applicable to a generalized condition of modernity (figure 8). The three corners of the triangle in modern society could perhaps be crudely characterized, respectively, in terms of *environmental problems, market economy,* and *individualism.* The task is then to identify the structures and relations that connect them. The notion of a connection between the market economy and individualism has a long history in sociology, and we might use the concept of "disembedding" (cf. Giddens 1990) for that side of the triangle. The connection between market economy and environmental problems, on the other hand, is being explored for example in the field of ecological economics. It is not unreasonable to identify the market principle itself—the notion of generalized interchangeability—as ultimately responsible for accelerating environmental problems, because, as we saw in chapter

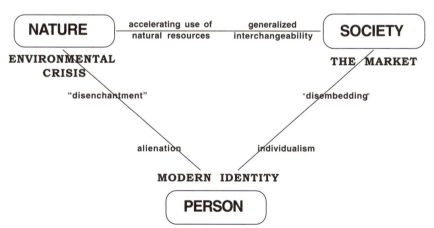

Fig. 8   Modernity as a recursive process of decontextualization

3, the market in effect rewards the dissipation of resources with ever more resources to dissipate. The connection between modern, individualistic identity and environmental crisis, finally, could perhaps be summed up in the concept of "alienation" or in Max Weber's concept of "disenchantment." This is the phenomenological or existential dimension of human-environmental relations: that intangible and hard-to-theorize aspect of reality that has to do with how human beings experience the world.

In closing the triangle, we are able to conclude that ecological, sociological, and existential phenomena together form a whole that no single, conventional discipline can encompass. Modern environmental problems have a subjective dimension that has to do with the constitution of the modern person, as well as an objective dimension that has to do with the organization of the market economy, but the triangle suggests that these two dimensions are ultimately aspects of a single phenomenon of modernity. Instead of arranging different aspects according to some linear, causal chain, we must visualize how a specific trajectory at one level is accompanied by structurally cognate trajectories at the other two levels. These three, specific trajectories of nature, society, and personhood (which are really a single trajectory) accompany each other historically because they are mutually reinforcing. In fact, without this recursivity between them, there would be no historical movement. (To depict such a movement, the triangle should perhaps be drawn in three dimensions, as a series of triangles laid on top of each other.) It is by recognizing their mutual interpenetration that we can see, for instance, how a society of strangers will tend to foster "natural aliens" (cf. Evernden 1985).

HUMAN ECOLOGY AND PERSONHOOD

Whether we call ourselves environmental historians, environmental sociologists, or ecological anthropologists, we probably have had to struggle with some habitual dualisms of Western thought such as the dichotomies of culture/nature, society/nature, subject/object, mind/body, mental/material, and so forth. To replace a rigid dualism with a triadic scheme, as in Steiner's triangle, may be one way of transcending some of the problems. The dichotomy of mental and material, for instance, requires a third category—the *social*—to accommodate the kinds of mutual interpenetration that arguably exist between the two traditional poles. As was argued in the previous chapter, it is also essential to understand human "cognition" or "knowledge" neither as pure representation nor as pure construction, but as a recursive *relationship* that constitutes both the knower (subject) and the known (object). Such a perspective is fundamental to the work of Bateson (1972), to cognitive scientists like Maturana and Varela (1987 [1992]), and to environmental historians such as Bird (1987). An implication that this "relationist" approach to knowledge shares with constructivism (which it subsumes) is that essentialist notions of nature will have to be more or less abandoned. If natural landscapes virtually everywhere carry traces of human activity (cf. Simmons 1993), the conclusion must be that "nature" is imbued with human culture and that human language intervenes in ecological processes (cf. Rappaport 1994; Ingerson 1994:62). It can also be argued, conversely, that ecological relations have always been communicative phenomena, and that human symbolism and language are only the latest additions to the semiotics of ecosystems (cf. the two previous chapters).

Let us say that the challenge for a post-Cartesian theory of human-environmental relations is to recognize the significance of the human *subject* without that theory itself becoming a direct expression of some specific variety of *subjectivity* (as, for instance, in poetry). The only conceivable way to achieve this—that is, an analytical acknowledgment of the recursivity between subject and object—may be to include the *person* as a ubiquitous counterpart to both "society" and "nature." Considerations of the "person" as an analytical category is essential to any study of human-environmental relations that seeks to understand the cultural incentives that generate particular modes of resource management rather than restrict itself merely to their material repercussions.

It is, in fact, symptomatic of Western thought that we should at all have to argue for the significance of personhood in human dealings with the rest of the natural world. Ingold (1996) questions the Western consignment of the notion of "person" to an exclusively human, sociocultural domain that is conceived as distinct from a natural, material world of "organisms." Such a distinction between persons and things (subjects and objects) is alien to hunter-gatherer groups like the Algonquian-speakers of northeastern North America, who tend to view *all* living beings as undivided centers of awareness, agency, and intentionality. For the Waswanipi Cree of Quebec, as mentioned in chapter 8, nonhuman animals are " 'like persons' in that they act intelligently and have wills and idiosyncrasies, and understand and are understood by men" (Feit 1973:116, quoted in Ingold 1996:131). Much as was understood by ethologist and semiotician Jakob von Uexküll (1940 [1982]), a crucial corollary is that even for animals, "the world exists as a meaningful place" (Ingold 1996:135).

If we are willing to concede that humans relate to their environments as persons, not merely as organisms—or more precisely that their aspect of "personhood" is of significance for ecology—it is only natural to consider the ecological significance of cultural *variation* in personhood. This has long been a subject of Western self-reflection, based on observations of culture- or class-based contrasts between different varieties of personhood in space and time (Indians versus Europeans, traditional peasants versus modern city-dwellers, etc.). Environmental historians such as Martin (1978), Cronon (1983), and Merchant (1989) have interpreted the ecological transformations of northeastern North America during the past few centuries in terms that could be translated into changes in personhood. In explaining the transitions from native Amerindian to colonial and capitalist land use, they focus on cultural differences between Indians and Europeans, whether in the cosmology of hunting (Martin), in conceptions of property (Cronon), or in different "forms of consciousness" (Merchant). All these "cultural" differences pertain to the phenomenological side of the human-ecological triangle.

But references to "culture" seem unsatisfactory to the extent that the identified contrasts can be generalized for a great number of comparisons between middle-class, urban Europeans and their primitive Other. Although some anthropologists caution against such dichotomous "constructions," others try to provide analytical frameworks for validating them. Sahlins (1976:216), for instance, sums up a complex argument by concluding that "money is to the West what kinship is to the Rest," while Shweder and Bourne (1984) identify a contrast between Western and non-Western concepts of personhood, noting that the latter typically are based on more context-dependent and concrete modes of thinking. Rather than essentializing typically non-Western features as characteristic of specific, exotic "cultures," such approaches ultimately imply a structural definition of "the West" as a (geographically indeterminate) condition of modernity.

The two dichotomous characterizations of "the West and the Rest" just referred to have bearings on two sides of the human ecological triangle. Sahlins's observation pertains to mechanisms for social exchange and thus to the link between society and person, whereas Shweder and Bourne's, in focusing on modes of thinking about (and thus of *relating* to) the world, is of great relevance for the interface of person and nature. Particularly interesting, of course, are perspectives that explicitly connect these two dimensions by suggesting that the modern inclination toward abstract thought, decontextualization, and objectification is structurally related to money, market institutions, and the fetishization of abstract exchange value. Such insights, formulated for example by Horkheimer and Adorno (1944 [1972]), Whorf (1956 [1978]), and Baudrillard (1976 [1993]), can be traced back to nineteenth-century social philosophers such as Marx, Weber, and Simmel.

I suggested that references merely to "cultural" differences, taken as given, are insufficient to account for the different ecological perceptions and practices of the Indians and colonists in North America. In consequence with the tenets of our human ecological triangle, it should be incumbent on us to demonstrate structural connections between its phenomenological, social, and material dimensions. In particular, we should be able to show, in specific instances as well as in general terms, how the person/nature interface is connected to the interface of person/society. A possible point of departure, discussed by Gudeman (1986), Descola (1992), Bird-David (1992), and Ingold (1996), is that the different ways in which humans engage other creatures in nature somehow correspond to different ways of engaging each other in society. Gudeman, Descola, and Bird-David suggest that this occurs through the medium of *social metaphors* applied to human-environmental relations—for example, when the land is conceptualized as ancestors, the forest as parents, crops as children, game animals as affines, and so on. In transferring meanings and feelings from the world of social relations onto relations with nonhuman nature, such metaphors codify specific ways of relating to the latter (cf. the previous chapter). These authors seem to assume that social relations here conceptually precede ecological relations and serve as templates for them in a unidirectional way.

Ingold (1996), drawing on Jackson (1983), challenges this approach by suggesting that such metaphors can point to real commonalities between the two kinds of relations. Instead of merely observing that some ecological relations could be *likened* to specific kinds of social relations, the metaphors can draw attention to their essential *unity*. Such unities or equivalences presumably would pertain to the attitudes, moods, and emotions—in short, what Bourdieu (1990) calls the *habitus*—generated in these relationships. It is of course possible to experience similar feelings and adopt similar postures with respect to phenomena that are categorically quite distinct, such as "land" and "ancestors." The unity evoked in such metaphors, then, is that aspect of the *person* that constitutes the nexus of the conflated relations. Metaphors refer to experiential commonalities that transcend categorical disjunctions. In this sense, Ingold's objection is certainly valid. But the conflation of categorical domains is in itself the source of specific kinds of cultural logic because the metaphors may have categorical implications that go beyond the experiential level. There are undoubtedly social metaphors that do transfer meanings from relations in the human world to relations with the nonhuman one, committing societies to specific trains of thought that transcend the experiential commonalities. In the next section, I will discuss two very different examples of this that I briefly mentioned in the previous chapter.

FROM ANIMAL MASTERS TO
ECOSYSTEM SERVICES

Throughout northeastern North America, as in many other parts of the
world, ethnographers have identified a pervasive inclination among premodern hunting peoples to project onto nature their own conceptions of
society. Such cosmologies are particularly well documented among the
hunting peoples of northern Asia and North America (cf. Hultkrantz
1961; Ingold 1986), but similar beliefs have been reported, for example,
from Amazonia (cf. Århem 1996). The various species of game animals
are conceptualized as being organized into social groups similar to those
of the hunters themselves, complete with leaders responsible for negotiations with human leaders. These supernatural leaders have been referred
to as, for example, "animal guardians" (Hultkrantz 1961), "owners of the
animals" (*Ibid.*), "lords of the animals" (Zerries 1987), "animal masters"
(Ingold 1986, chap. 10), or "keepers of the game" (Martin 1978). They are
often visualized as striking specimens of their species, by virtue of their
size or (white) color. Hunting is understood as a form of reciprocal exchange between human and animal societies, in which game animals
agree to surrender to human hunters in exchange for sacrificial offerings
and observances of specific rules relating to the treatment of their remains. The mutual prestations of animals and men are clearly modeled
on the predominant principle of intergroup exchange in these societies.
The relationship between human and animal communities could thus be
said to be construed as one of "balanced reciprocity" (cf. Sahlins 1972).
The delicate pact between humans and animals is contingent on the ful-
fillment of mutual obligations, mediated by esoteric communication between human shamans and the animal masters.

In many premodern societies, we might add, the phenomenon of "sac-
rifice" evokes similar ideas about balanced reciprocity between humans
and nonhuman nature even in relation to (what Westerners perceive as)
inanimate sources of livelihood, such as mountains. Thus, for instance,
Taussig (1980:224) reports how Andean peasant miners exchange gifts
with the "spirit owners" of their mines.

Before moving on to our second example, let us reiterate what the notion of animal masters is an example *of*. It represents a projection of a predominant principle of social exchange (here, reciprocal gift exchange)
onto the realm of human-environmental relations. It is as if humans seek-
ing guidance for behavior in their uncertain negotiations with nonhuman
nature have no recourse but to look to their experience of human social
life. In these ecocosmologies, both the morphology (group structure) and
physiology (exchange relations) of human society are extended into nature. In the process, familiar varieties of social personhood are also recog-

nized in the behavior of game animals. The latter are assumed to exhibit attitudes (resentfulness, indebtedness, etc.) similar to those regularly generated in the normal course of human affairs.

I will now turn to a very dissimilar social context, namely the Institute for Ecological Economics in Solomons, Maryland, in the 1990s. Geographically we have not moved very far from the New England forests where the Passamaquoddy and other Algonquian hunters once negotiated with the masters of their game animals, but rather than the shamans of a tribe of hunter-gatherers, we are listening to the wisdom of scholars in the midst of industrial society, published in a recent issue of *Nature*:

> The services of ecological systems and the natural capital stocks that produce them are critical to the functioning of the Earth's life-support system. They contribute to human welfare, both directly and indirectly, and therefore represent part of the total economic value of the planet. . . . For the entire biosphere, the value (most of which is outside the market) is estimated to be in the range of US$ 16–54 trillion (10^{12}) per year, with an average of US$ 33 trillion per year. (Costanza et al. 1997:253)

Let us attend closely to this "cultural text." Clearly, like the Algonquian hunters, the authors are concerned about the sustainability of human-environmental relations. But there are several significant differences. Although nonhuman nature is still granted a kind of benevolent agency ("services," "contribute"), it is no longer conceived as a *personal* agency. Nature has changed from a community of persons to a machine-like assemblage of things ("systems," "produce," "functioning"). Moreover, the perspective has shifted from the local to the global ("Earth," "planet"). Finally, and most intriguingly, the relations between humans and nonhuman nature are couched not in terms of reciprocal gift exchange but in the language of the market economy ("services," "capital stocks," "welfare," "economic value," "US$").

Perhaps none of these differences comes as a surprise to the reader, but I believe that they are worthy of reflection, for in their very differences the two groups reveal a fundamental commonality. We may observe that the Algonquian hunters and the modern scholars, in their different conceptualizations of nature, are pursuing a similar strategy. Both resort to their specific understandings of social exchange to construct the relation between humans and nonhuman nature. In their constructions of nature, furthermore, they reveal the different, basic modes of *relating* to the world that characterize the social contexts that they are respectively accustomed to. Where the premodern hunters concern themselves with concrete, contextualized subjects (cf. Shweder and Bourne 1984), the modern scholars visualize abstract, decontextualized objects. In this way, it could be argued, the two groups also project onto the natural world their different conceptions of the human person. Paradoxically, the ecological economists bring nature into the modern world of social interaction *precisely by objectifying it*. The experiential commonality that underlies their metaphorical conflation of nature and society is not interpersonal engagement, but detachment.

Yet—and this would no doubt surprise the ecological economists—according to the definition proposed by Descola (1992, 1996), their conceptual strategy (no less than that of the Algonquians) should be classified as an example of *animism*. Descola (1996:88) defines animism as the use of "the elementary categories structuring social life to organise, in conceptual terms, the relations between human beings and natural species." This is precisely what the ecological economists are doing when couching the discussion of human-environmental relations in terms of "natural *capital*," "ecosystem *services*," "environmental *costs*," and "environmental *debts*." Through a peculiar structural inversion, it seems that we should classify as "animistic" the pricing of the world at US$ 33 trillion, or, to take another example, the 1992 Swedish estimate of its national, environmental debt at 260 billion crowns. It should be obvious that Descola's definition of animism is slightly beside the mark. Because the term connotes a "subjectification" rather than objectification, it covers only a particular *kind* of meaning transfer from society to nature.

Social metaphors applied to human-environmental relations can become problematic when used as guidance for ecological practice in times of environmental crisis. Martin (1978) has suggested that the complex of ideas about animal masters was largely responsible for the self-destructive response of the Algonquians to the encroachment of European fur traders. He posits that epidemics introduced by the Europeans, but thought to be inflicted on the Indians by the animal masters, unleashed a war of retaliation on the game animals, which merely aggravated the emaciation of these peoples by destroying their resource base. This is a highly unlikely explanation for the Indian role in depleting North American game stocks and has been extensively criticized (cf. Krech 1981). The brunt of the responsibility must rather be borne by the European market cosmology that converted communities of animal kinsmen into abstract exchange values. The recursive (positive feedback) structure of Martin's argument is more applicable to the market cosmology than to the (ecologically restraining) animal master complex it displaced. Only by converting all things into abstract exchange value can the illusion be created that ecological deterioration may be alleviated by more of the same. This continues to be the alarming logic of human-environmental relations in the periphery of the world system, now as then. Money is simultaneously a measure of, and a (short-term) remedy for, the dissipation of resources.

SPACE, EXCHANGE, AND THE SELF

In juxtaposing principles of exchange and modes of relating to nonhuman nature, I am advocating a renewed dialogue between economic and ecological anthropology. The relevance of fundamental economic principles such as "reciprocity" and "market," delineated by Karl Polanyi, obviously extends beyond the domain of human society into relations with other species. Descola (1992, 1996) and Pálsson (1996) have thus analyzed different varieties of human-environmental relations in terms of different permutations of reciprocity. In this section, I would like to consider the *spatial* dimensions of the notion of "nature," different principles of exchange, and personhood as they relate to cultural constructions of human-environmental relations.

Ellen (1996:104–105) has observed that concepts of "nature" (or notions approximating it) are commonly defined in spatial terms, as "some realm outside humans or their immediate living (cultural) space." He suggests that the notion of nature as an external space is one of three "cognitive axes or dimensions" that in various combinations generate specific models of nature. In this view, society and nature are concentrically arranged, with nature the more distant, a "spatial other" (*Ibid.*:120) defined in opposition to society. But Ellen also observes that "very few languages have words which easily translate as 'nature' " (*Ibid.*), and Ingold (1996:127–129, fig. 5.2) shows that the dichotomy of nature and society is quite alien to the worldview of hunter-gatherers.

It seems to me that the presence or absence of a concentric dualism of society versus nature would have implications for the principles of exchange that organize constructions of human-environmental relations in a particular society. My reason for speculating along these lines is that a similar, concentric arrangement organizes Sahlins's (1972) analysis of generalized, balanced, and negative reciprocity. The innermost space is the realm of Malinowski's "pure gift," for which "an open stipulation of return would be unthinkable and unsociable" (*Ibid.*:191). With increasing social distance, generalized reciprocity yields to balanced reciprocity, which involves a conscious reckoning with return, and finally negative reciprocity ("the unsociable extreme"), which means trying to "get something for nothing" (*Ibid.*:195). This continuum necessarily also has bearings on personhood. Contemplating the Maori *hau*, Mauss (1923–24 [1967]) observed that to extend a gift means extending something of one's own person (cf. also Munn 1986). Negative reciprocity, on the other hand, is "the most *impersonal* sort of exchange" (Sahlins 1972:195, emphasis added). The emergence of money, accordingly, most likely occurred in "peripheral social sectors" (*Ibid.*:229). As mentioned in chapter 6, this idea has a long tradition in anthropology (cf. White 1959).

Toward the innermost end of the continuum, then, we have true sociability defined in terms of intimacy, gift-giving, and personal trust; toward
its outer end we have money, impersonality, avarice, and—in societies
such as the Western—an asocial "nature." Where nonhuman nature is
conceptualized as external and opposed to society, as in the West, it
seems unlikely that human-environmental relations should assume the
sensitive and balanced form that so intrigues us in the ethnography of
the Algonquians. In the Western conception, productive engagement with
wild species tends to be relegated to a marginal space where human sociability has been attenuated to the point where it is reduced to predation.
Among the Algonquians, on the other hand, humans and nonhumans apparently may share the entire extent of the social continuum, without any
concern for a dichotomy of society versus nature (Ingold 1996). It is thus
quite feasible for these groups to experience closer kinship with local
populations of beavers or moose than with neighboring populations of
humans, engaging with the former in compliance with the principle of
balanced reciprocity while subjecting the latter to predation. Thus, for instance, the Recollect missionary Le Clercq (1691 [1910]:276–277) reported
that

> the [Micmac] Indians say that the Beavers have sense, and form a separate
> nation; and they say they would cease to make war upon these animals if
> these would speak, howsoever little, in order that they might learn whether
> the Beavers are among their friends or their enemies.

Other reports from the same period tell of seemingly unprovoked assaults
on neighboring (human) tribes (cf. Hoffman 1946:643).

Sahlins's continuum of reciprocities suggests that, in modern society,
the social space of gift-giving has contracted while the "peripheral" domain of money transactions and negative reciprocity has imploded
toward the shrinking, domestic bastions of the "pure gift." The readiness
to give away their possessions is one of the features of the Algonquian
hunting peoples most often commented upon by European visitors. Consider the early seventeenth-century reflections of the French lawyer Lescarbot (1609 [1928]:262–263):

> Our savages are praiseworthy in the exercise of this virtue [liberality], ac-
> cording to their poverty. For, as we have said before, when they visit one
> another they give mutual presents one to the other. And when some French
> Sagamos [leaders] cometh to them, they do the like with him, casting at his
> feet some bundle of beavers' or other furs, which be all their riches. . . . This
> custom of the said savages proceedeth but from a liberal mind, and which
> hath some generosity. And, although they be very glad when the like is done
> unto them, yet so it falleth out that they begin the venture and put them-

selves in hazard to lose their merchandise. And who is he amongst us that doth more than they, that is to say which giveth but with intention to receive? . . . And for to show the gallantness of our said savages: they do not willingly cheapen, and do content themselves with that which is given them honestly with a willing mind, disdaining and blaming the fashions of our petty merchants, which be an hour a-cheapening for to buy a beaver-skin, as I saw being [done] at the River Saint John . . . that they called a young merchant of Saint Malo *mercatoria*, which is a word of reproach among them borrowed of the Basques, signifying, as it were, a haggling fellow. Finally, they have nothing in them but frankness and liberality in their exchanging. And, seeing the base manners of some of our men, they demanded sometimes what they came to seek for in their country, saying that they came not into ours; and, seeing that we are richer than they, we should give them liberally that which we have.

If the gift is indeed an extension of the person, this means that personhood has in a sense contracted along with it, yielding the "atomistic" individual whom we tend to associate with modernity. In other words, and perhaps paradoxically, the more we have been implicated in global networks of market exchange, the less "outreaching" have we become as persons. The notion of the person as something that can be more or less extended in space (and time) has an elaborate theoretical foundation in phenomenology and semiotics (cf. Relph 1976; Evernden 1985:44–45; Singer 1984). Singer (1984:3, 57) quotes C. S. Peirce's conclusion that "each self has a distinctive and 'outreaching identity,' an 'essence and a meaning subtile as may be' that is 'the true and exact expression of the fact of sympathy, fellow-feeling—together with all unselfish interests,—and all that makes us feel that he has an absolute worth.' " According to Peirce, a "man's circle of society (however widely or narrowly this phrase may be understood), is a sort of loosely compacted person, in some respects of higher rank than the person of an individual organism" (quoted in Singer 1984:64). Singer (*Ibid.*:65) concludes that

> Peirce's theory of personality and of personal identity has the important consequence that the self . . . is not identical with the individual organism. The self may be less or more than the individual organism, less when in the flow of time the inner dialogue brings a new phase of the self into life, and more when in dialogue with other organisms there emerges one loosely compacted person.
>
> Under these circumstances, personal identity is not confined to the consciousness of one's body, the "box of flesh and blood," but extends as well to "social consciousness," the consciousness of living others with whom one is in sympathetic communication. . . . The boundaries of personal identity, in Peirce's theory, are somewhat indefinite and variable and depend on the social and cultural "outreach" of a particular individual's consciousness.

Against the background of our argument so far, it is significant that the remedy for environmental problems advocated by the so-called deep ecology movement should be an expansion of the human self:

> Spiritual growth . . . begins when we cease to understand or see ourselves as isolated and narrow competing egos and begin to identify with other humans and friends to, eventually, our species. But the deep ecology sense of self requires . . . an identification which goes beyond humanity to include the nonhuman world. (Devall and Sessions 1985:67, quoted in Cheney 1989:317 n. 69)

Cheney (1989) and Szerszynski (1996) express hesitation about this strategy, arguing that, like the similar ambition of the ancient Greek Stoics to identify with an abstract cosmos, it would imply an even deeper retreat into alienation. Hans Jonas writes: "Grand and inspiring as [the Stoic] conception is, it must not be overlooked that it represented a position of retreat inasmuch as its appeal was addressed to a human subject that was no longer a part of anything *except the universe . . .*" (quoted in Cheney 1989:301). Cheney (1989:300–302) posits a structural similarity between the metaphysics of Stoicism and deep ecology as reactions to the alienation resulting from, respectively, the fall of the Athenian city-state and the demise of Western modernity. In both cases, there is an attempt to retain a sense of abstract hegemony and "containment of the other" when previous securities shatter into (Alexandrian and postmodern) "worlds of difference."

What needs to be recognized here is the difference between an abstract, verbal *representation* of embeddedness in the world, on one hand, and the concrete phenomenology of the *practice* of such embeddedness, on the other. The epistemology of Spinoza, which has served as a major inspiration for deep ecology, appears to accommodate both possibilities. The former (abstraction) is evoked in Spinoza's ideal of "seeing the universal in all the particulars of one's existence" (Cheney 1989:321), the latter (phenomenology) in his ideal of "direct intuitive knowledge of individual things" (Devall and Sessions 1985:239–240, quoted in Cheney 1989:306–307). The former is a product of intellectual reflection, whereas the latter evokes practical, bodily experience. Devall and Sessions appropriately continue by quoting Wittgenstein: "What we cannot speak about we must pass over in silence." The intellectual constructions of deep ecologists risk sharing with those of phenomenologists like Heidegger and Merleau-Ponty the paradox posed by an *excessive reflection over the bliss of nonreflective existence*. It is one thing to posit an abstract, spiritual embeddedness in the world, another to practice embeddedness as concrete, bodily experience. The philosophy of deep ecology risks remaining a very Cartesian form of communion, an embeddedness of the mind but not of the body.

The duality of language and experience or mind and body reproduces the modern rift between abstract systems and local life-worlds. To see the specifics of our direct experience as instances of more general categories may at times be poetically inspiring but always risks *detracting* from the phenomenological depth of that particular experience. The pursuit of a renewed embeddedness would thus seem to have to involve something else than a cosmically expanded sense of identity. As Ingold (1993:40) has observed, for instance, many of the global environmental problems may "have their source in that very alienation of humanity from the world of which the notion of the global environment is a conspicuous expression." The reestablishment of an ecologically more outreaching kind of person-hood would need to be grounded not so much in abstract, Stoicist self-effacement as in the specifics of concrete, place-based *practice*, that is, a reimmersion into what Ingold (*Ibid.*) refers to as a local "mode of apprehension" based on "an active, perceptual engagement with components of the dwelt-in world, in the practical business of life."

Characteristic of modernity is the movement from concrete and place-based to more abstract reference points for identity construction. The premodern person is moored to *specific* faces, landscapes, and artifacts, whereas the ideal-typically modern person is constituted in terms of abstract *categories* of people, spaces, and commodities. The modern identification with abstract communities has tended to eclipse the identification with specific places (cf. Relph 1976), but the process may in some respects be reversible. The two structural options seem to open the person to completely different versions of the expanded Self: the *anthropocentric cosmopolitan* versus the *ecocentric local*. The deep ecology movement suggests a third possibility: the *ecocentric cosmopolitan*. But to identify oneself with an abstract, planetary whole, whether the human species or the biosphere, is not the same kind of self-expansion as the immersion into a local life-world. The difference between "local" and "global" is a difference not in scale but in kind (see next section).

Another matrix for classifying varieties of human-environmental relations could be constructed from the intersection of two different dimensions of being "local" or "global." One is the phenomenological dimension that we have just outlined—the extent to which a person identifies with a specific place. The other is the tangible, material dimension of consumption—whether a person's lifestyle draws on resources from a local ecosystem or the far corners of the biosphere (cf. Dasmann 1976). Juxtaposed, these two dimensions suggest four ideal types:

1. People who are "local" in both respects (premodern locals),
2. People who are "global" in both respects (cosmopolitans),

3. People who are "local" in identity but "global" in consumption (modern locals), and
4. People who are "global" in identity but "local" in consumption (postmodern locals; e.g., back-to-the-land deep ecologists attempting self-sufficiency).

For a person in category 3, a modern local, access to the world market has extended a person's material agency beyond her field of identification, whereas for a person in category 4, a postmodern local, an extended field of identification has prompted her to restrict her ecological footprint by withdrawing from the market. A crucial issue in these transformations is the degree of fit or congruity between different kinds of "reach"—economic, ethical, existential, and so on. An implication of this analysis is that the phenomenology of being "local" is *ecologically relevant* only when such congruity is strong. A local sense of identity need not have anything to do with sustainability, if consumption is globalized.

"LOCAL" VERSUS "GLOBAL" IDENTITY
AND THE VARIETIES OF
ENVIRONMENTALIST CONCERN

The distinction between society visualized as a concrete community or as an unlocalized abstraction has inspired a number of conceptual dichotomies throughout the history of social science. What I refer to as the local/global polarity has previously been expressed in terms, for example, of *Gemeinschaft/Gesellschaft*, mechanical solidarity/organic solidarity, *societas/civitas*, consensus/contract, and personal/impersonal. The resiliency of this dichotomy throughout social science history indicates its significance as well as some of the difficulties in pinning it down conceptually. I have chosen the terms "local" versus "global" to underscore its spatial dimensions. Viewed concentrically from the vantage point of any individual, the social universe can remain organized on a generalized, face-to-face basis only within a proximate spatial field. Social systems generating relations beyond that field will develop unlocalized, abstract sodalities such as professional associations, ethnic groups, or nations. In terms of social reference points for identity, this means that neighbors and kin are eclipsed by, for example, occupational colleagues. In terms of space, an ego-centered centrality anchored in a specific segment of rural landscape is eclipsed by the generalized, socio-centered centrality of urban-dominated society. The movement from local to global identity thus involves a movement from the concrete to the abstract and, in terms of relations to space, from the specific to the generalized. Whereas local delineations of

selfhood incorporate tangible reference points (specific places, people, artifacts) from which they cannot be extricated, the global self is founded
on conceptual abstractions (e.g., occupation) and thus are more detachable, both practically (by being more mobile) and philosophically (as the
European *individual*; cf. Dumont 1986; Geertz 1983:59). Needless to say,
the degree to which the physical environment is internalized in personal
identity should be important for understanding different versions of environmentalism.

A "local" construction of identity is anchored in *specific* places, objects,
and relationships. The major difference vis-à-vis "global" constructions
is that these elements are experience-based and irreplaceable, that is, not
susceptible to verbal abstraction. In this sense, "global" identity is more
generalized. On the other hand, "global" identity necessarily involves an
existential specialization—an occupation. Thus, a movement from "local"
to "global" identity implies a shift from a concrete, spatial specificity to
an abstract, existential specificity, or from an existential generality to a
spatio-contextual generality. The professional, like the market commodity, is, as it were, socially *generalized*. There is a transformation in the nature of sociability itself.

The generalization of sociability so fundamental to civilization is far
from unproblematic. The contemporary pursuit of historical, genealogical, and ethnic "roots," "primitivism" (Friedman 1983), and the nostalgia
for "nameable places" (Stewart 1988) are only the most explicit of the
myriad indications that the exchange of a "local" for a "global" identity
leaves many people unsatisfied. Modern civilization seems to rely on
what we might call a strategy of minimal meaning investment. It general-
izes the purpose of human life into abstractions (such as "utility," "development," and so on) but remains mute as to the meaning of individual
existence. To fill this vacuum, modern people construct themselves by
pursuing the narrow, occupational meanings and self-defining consumption patterns that the market has to offer them. To the outside observer, a
person thus "occupied" by the obscure specificities of professional or lei-
sure-time meanings evokes the cognate concept of being "possessed."

Urbanization and standardization tend to minimize the specifics of
physical environment onto which meaning and identity can be anchored,
thus facilitating mobility and individual autonomy. Existential matters
are relegated to the vicissitudes of individual circumstances. The effect is
to stimulate an active groping for specific meanings. Instead of anchoring
identity in the specifics of place, the "global" individual expresses his autonomous self through the use of abstract symbols. The rapid turnover of
consumption goods indicates some of the difficulties in defining a self
thus constituted. In highlighting the *replaceability* of objects used as refer-

ence points for identity, it also presents a parallel to the spatial and social aspects of "global" identity (figure 9).

Needless to say, the polarity I wish to illuminate is not meant as an either-or dichotomy, but as a difference in inclination. "Local" identity construction, for instance, occurs in urban environments, as do "global" identities in rural contexts. A more important difference is that local identity is more directly based on sensory experience, rather than verbal construction.

Meaning has to do with a perception of order, intelligibility, and familiarity based on a relationship of compatibility between past and present experience. Fundamental to meaning are experiences of recognition and reassurance. Its opposite is an experience of chaos or arbitrariness variously referred to as anomie, alienation, or anxiety. If culture process is essentially synonymous to meaning construction, it is propelled by a fear of chaos. The human species is uniquely "unprogrammed" (or rather, it is programmed to construct its own programs), and the multiplicity of alternative ways in which to attribute meaning to human existence indicates how extremely *specific* any one system of meaning must be. The polarization of "local" versus "global" identity, however, suggests two fundamentally different kinds of specificity, geared to different kinds of reference points.

Against this background, different versions of environmentalist discourse can be understood as "local" versus "global" formulations of anxiety. At which points do chaos and arbitrariness threaten? If the specifics of meaning serve to expel chaos, we should expect experiences of arbitrariness to appear whenever this specificity threatens to reveal itself. This happens whenever the individual distances herself from her own frame

	LOCAL/ IRREPLACEABLE	GLOBAL/ ABSTRACT
SPACE	Specific community Natural landscape	Mobility Urbanism
SOCIAL RELATIONSHIPS	Kin Neighbors	Colleagues Peers
OBJECTS	Handicraft Heirlooms	Consumption goods Money

Fig. 9   Local versus global reference points for identity

of reference. "Local" specificities of meaning are thus jeopardized by literal dislocation itself or by traumatically expanded horizons such as have evoked so-called revitalization movements in many parts of the Third World (cf. Worsley 1957). It may also be threatened by a threat to the concrete landscape in which it is anchored. Occupational specificity, on the other hand, is continually challenged by exposure to other occupational meanings and may be jeopardized by mere personal sensitivity. In both instances, relativization and arbitrariness must be actively suppressed, primarily by various ways of drawing symbolic boundaries around the different sectors of meaning, local or occupational (cf. Douglas 1966; Cohen 1985). Such defensive strategies will, however, produce very different kinds of human beings depending on whether local or occupational specificities of meaning are being underpinned. Whereas the boundaries of local identity naturally align with fields of face-to-face familiarity, civilization requires a specific competence at maintaining boundaries around abstract sodalities cross-cutting the spheres of regular social interaction. "Global" contexts thus encourage the cultivation of a specific kind of social insensitivity that goes hand in hand with individualism.

If meaning and order are the antithesis of anxiety and chaos, we might expect anxiety to appear where meaning ends (cf. Douglas 1966, 1975). The cultural construction of threat and anxiety will vary with the construction of identity, as "local" or "global." In a local context, the realm of meaning and order could be visualized concentrically as an ego-centered, inner circle, beyond which lurks the unknown. In a "global" context, on the other hand, meaning and anxiety run parallel and diffuse through the entire extent of the social fabric. This may be important to an understanding of the "global" construction of an abstract environment. From a local viewpoint, the threat of chaos is located in the external *social* environment, whereas identification with such an abstract, "global" society may imply a projection of threat or chaos onto the nonsocial (i.e., natural) environment.

The "global" delineation of the detached individual is a social phenomenon but has significant implications for human-environmental relations, not least through the accelerating turnover of consumption goods. If people are conceived of as discrete, bounded entities, then all living things may similarly be perceived as distinct and atomistic, rather than as interconnected and overlapping fields (cf. Evernden 1985). Finally, the abstract, global notion of the environment, detached from concrete landscapes and the activities of specific humans, may in various ways be counterproductive to the intentions of the environmentalists (cf. Ingold 1993). There is a risk in identifying "issues" and "problems" so as to reproduce an abstract, "environmentalist" sector of meaning. In the words of a radical, New England environmentalist,

Environmentalism always was a human-centered movement that viewed "the environment" as something out there that we had to save from ourselves, for ourselves because it was "our" environment. It became an ego trip to be identified with such noble, selfless labour. Yuppies loved to view themselves as saviors of the environment. (Sayen 1990).

These are matters to be further explored in the next chapter.

I have indicated how a series of transformations in human personhood may provide a theoretical link between principles of social exchange and varieties of human-environmental relations. One conclusion might be that a reestablishment of relations of reciprocity with nonhuman nature is conceivable only in the practical engagement of complete persons in concrete places. The abstract concerns with global ecology, though undoubtedly justifiable in rational terms, might at another level be read as projections of human persons alienated from such embedment. The greatest challenge for environmental policy may be to find ways of transposing these concerns back into the specifics of human life-worlds *without* jeopardizing the struggle for abstract human solidarities that is the hallmark of modernity. To bring these aspirations together into a single, socio-ecological equation would undoubtedly entail radical changes in the institutions that govern economic life. It would probably require some kind of institutional insulation of (more localized) subsistence practices vis-à-vis (global) communication flows, much as I have previously suggested as a remedy for unequal, global exchange.

The ecological economists have done us the service of estimating the price of our planet at US$ 33 trillion per year. These are the lengths to which we are prepared to go in order not to have to surrender the fetishized abstractions that rule our lives and jeopardize "the Earth's life-support system." But let us not despair. Beneath the jargon on underpaid "ecosystem services" and mounting "environmental debts," however convoluted and misleading it is as a literal understanding of environmental crisis, we may recognize an ancient concern with reciprocity and an aspiration to bring nonhuman nature back into the community of humans.

12

The Abstraction of Discourse and Identity: A Case Study

In recent years and throughout the world, environmental movements and indigenous movements have been developing a kind of conceptual symbiosis. In the media and in several popular books (e.g., Suzuki and Knudtson 1992), environmentalists have used the image of the ecological native to bring their critique of industrialism into sharper focus. Conversely, indigenous activists increasingly have employed environmental arguments in their struggle for the rights of native minorities. In this chapter, I would like to reflect on the convergence of environmental and indigenous activists as it relates to larger issues of modern identity construction, discourse, and power. Although it could be argued that both these movements ultimately represent a critique of modernity, the articulation of that critique itself risks remaining but one of its expressions. The adoption of decontextualizing modes of discourse and self-definition generates ambivalences and contradictions in any movement launched against a social structure founded on such modes. For such contradictions to be resolved, they must first be made transparent by identifying modernity as the ultimate target of critique. My empirical point of departure is the movement to stop a proposed granite quarry on Cape Breton Island, Nova Scotia, but in trying to situate this movement in a larger field of discourse on "development" and the "environment," my aims are primarily theoretical.

As elsewhere in North America in recent decades, the indigenous people of Nova Scotia are re-evaluating their cultural identity. Fourth World

211

consciousness is gaining momentum as the self-confidence of Western civilization is challenged by the environmental movement and other forms of internal critique. The growth of a "red consciousness" has also been inadvertently encouraged by Canadian Indian policy (Lithman 1978). The increasingly articulate Fourth World stance serves as an "external" vantage point for social critique in native communities strongly ambivalent about participating in what national society defines as "development." This was dramatically highlighted in the summer of 1990 by the militancy of the Mohawk Warriors in the Kahnesatake reserve of Quebec, an incident that prompted demonstrations of sympathy among indigenous nations throughout Canada, including the Nova Scotia Mi'kmaq.

THE MI'KMAQ: A BRIEF
ENVIRONMENTAL HISTORY

Five hundred years ago, Cape Breton (called *Unama'kik* by the Mi'kmaq) was one of the seven districts of the Mi'kmaq nation (*Mi'kma'kik*), which embraced the modern Canadian provinces of Nova Scotia and Prince Edward Island and adjoining parts of New Brunswick, Quebec, and Newfoundland. The Mi'kmaq are an Algonquian-speaking people who have inhabited the area for at least three thousand years. Prior to the arrival of Europeans, they were primarily fishermen, hunters, and gatherers, spending the warmer half of the year fishing along coasts and rivers and moving inland to hunt moose, beaver, and other game in the winter. One of the best sources on Mi'kmaq subsistence practices is a text published in 1672 by the French fur trader Nicholas Denys (1908), who gives us a glimpse of how their daily life was being transformed by the fur trade in the mid-seventeenth century. To be sure, there is nothing in Denys's account to suggest that the aboriginal Mi'kmaq were overexploiting their natural environment. On the contrary, he mentions several taboos and other beliefs that indicate that they perceived their interaction with non-human life-forms as constrained by a delicate pact. This sense of respect for the game animals and their supernatural masters, however, seems to have been undermined by the very fur trade that Denys himself promoted. Spurred by the trade, the natives were important agents in the depletion of game stocks in much of eastern Canada.

The ambiguity surrounding native hunting ethics has created much controversy all over Canada about the ecological validity of restoring to First Nations their aboriginal hunting rights. *The Mi'kmaq Treaty Handbook*, compiled by the Grand Council of the Mi'kmaq (1987), uses recent court victories to argue for the Mi'kmaq right to rely on their own traditional judgment (*netukulimk*) as the exclusive constraint on native hunting. But when in September 1988 the Grand Council sanctioned a two-week "Treaty Moose Harvest" in the Cape Breton Highlands, some of the hunters were charged with violations of the provincial Wildlife Act (Marshall, Denny, and Marshall 1989). From a European perspective, it is ironic that in November of 1995, a delegation of Canadian Indians and Inuits was compelled to go to Europe to convince the European Union to continue to import furs from animals caught in traps found inhumane by the Europeans.

As was mentioned in the previous chapter, environmental historian Calvin Martin (1978) has tried to explain how the hunting ethics of the Mi'kmaq and other Algonquian peoples could be so rapidly transformed upon European contact. He argues that much of the intensity with which they came to deplete stocks of beaver and other furbearers derived from the aboriginal notion that human disease was inflicted by the animal masters, the "keepers of the game." According to this interpretation, the disastrous epidemics introduced by the Europeans thus unleashed a war of retaliation on the animals, which in turn well served the European fur traders. But Martin comes close to contradicting himself by showing how various other components of the European invasion undermined the very belief system that he holds responsible for the slaughter. The commodity market, new technology, Christianity, and the marginalization of shamanism all contributed to a *secularization* of hunting. This is undoubtedly the more fundamental cause of the demise of aboriginal environmental ethics. The notion of retaliation sounds more like a transitional rationalization than a real incentive. Critics of Martin's work have emphasized how incentives to participate in the fur trade would have been linked to political and economic structures that were already part of native Amerindian societies, although destined to be transformed by it (cf. Krech 1981; Kay 1985). But on one point Martin and his academic critics tend to agree: they are all very careful to reject the popular notion of the American Indian as what Martin (1978:157) calls "the great high priest of the Ecology Cult." If indigenous resource management was conservationist in practice, its cosmological foundation would have had very little in common with modern environmentalism.

The European colonization of coasts and rivers in the seventeenth and eighteenth centuries had pushed much of the Mi'kmaq population permanently inland to hunt. Many retreated to the district of *Unama'kik*, now known as Cape Breton Island, which long remained a wilderness with few European settlers. As game was depleted and the fur trade moved West, the Mi'kmaq resorted to craft production for the European settlements. The raw materials for baskets, barrels, handles, oars, snowshoes, and so forth were almost exclusively derived from the forest. Nicholas Denys in the 1640s had documented the Mi'kmaq's skill in exploiting forest products, whether marveling at their birchbark canoes or deploring their cumbersome wooden kettles. Now that neither hunting nor fishing was a viable mode of subsistence, history would turn the Mi'kmaq into a nation of basketmakers. Baskets, produced mainly for tourists, are still emblems of their ethnic identity.

During the Second World War, the Department of Indian Affairs attempted to concentrate the native population of Nova Scotia into two large reserves, Eskasoni on Cape Breton and Shubenacadie on the mainland. In 1958, it divided the Nova Scotia Mi'kmaq into twelve "bands," five of them on Cape Breton. The Mi'kmaq population of Cape Breton now numbers about 5,000 people. Except for formal contact—for example, with storekeepers, teachers, doctors, and police—their five reserves are socially isolated from the rest of the population of the island. They are ethnically marginalized pockets of *Gemeinschaft* in an economically marginalized part of Canada.

ACTORS AND ARGUMENTS IN
THE PUBLIC PROCESS

In the days of the fur trade, North America as a whole was reduced to a periphery in an economic "world system" centered on Europe (Wallerstein 1974–1989). Today, economic centers and peripheries are somewhat harder to delineate in geographical or political terms. The relationship between industrial "core" areas and their dependent, raw material-producing peripheries is a structural one, and though generally speaking a part of the twentieth-century "core," both Europe and North America also have their peripheral sectors. Cape Breton Island is definitely such an area. The unemployment rate is among the highest in Canada, and provincial politicians have long invited external, usually American, capital to exploit its natural resources.

In 1989, a local corporation called Kelly Rock announced its plans to open a so-called superquarry—one of the three largest in the world—on Kelly's Mountain, which is located on a peninsula between St. Ann's Bay and the Great Bras d'Or inlet to the Bras d'Or Lakes, on Cape Breton Island. Kelly Rock planned to annually ship 5.4 million tons of crushed granite gravel (for use, for example, as concrete aggregate and asphalt topping) to the eastern United States. The quarry would start as a strip mine 2,300 feet across and 200 feet deep, and the granite would be transported to a shipping wharf by means of a 600-foot shaft. This so-called "Glory Hole" method would be used to minimize the visibility of the operations. Almost invisibly, the company maintained, the mountain could keep yielding 2,500 tonnes of rock every working hour for the next 20 to

40 years. It would provide an estimated total of 103 jobs. Once a month, about half a million tons would be blasted loose. The seven shoreline crushers would be at work 24 hours a day. The crushed gravel would then be washed in sizable settling ponds. The shipping wharf would be equipped to receive 60,000-ton ships about twice weekly, and to stockpile perhaps a half million tons of gravel (equivalent to almost five football fields piled 30 feet high.) Space would also be required for the 30-ton trucks, conveyor belts, and administrative buildings. Kelly Rock estimated that the project would require about 40 acres but negotiated "an agreement in principle" to obtain almost 4,000 acres of Crown land on the mountain from the provincial government.

Opposition to the quarry was immediately evident, primarily from some local residents organized as the Save Kelly's Mountain Society (SKMS) and from Mi'kmaq traditionalists affiliated with the Grand Council of the Mi'kmaq. The SKMS was organized within weeks of Kelly Rock's announcement, which was made at a public meeting for the residents of the St. Ann's Bay area, on September 5, 1989. Also in September 1989, Mi'kmaq traditionalists organized a demonstration in Englishtown, the community closest to the proposed quarry site. The protesters told the press that they represented the Grand Chief of the Mi'kmaq Grand Council (*Cape Breton Post* 26/9/89). They arranged a ceremony with drumming and chanting, and they requested a major historical and archaeological study of the mountain, emphasizing that it is the sacred abode of the Mi'kmaq god Kluskap and the point of his prophesied return.

In response to the debate on the status of the mountain, staff from the Nova Scotia Museum laid out the facts in October 1989:

> Traditionally, Cape Breton is the site of three "doors" into the World Beneath The Earth, the place where the Micmac spirit-helper and culture-hero Kluskap went when he left the Earth World behind. . . . The third door, which is considered quite an important site due to the presence of the rock called "Kluskap's Table," and the rock called "The Mother-in-law" or "The Grandmother," is a cave in a cliff washed by the sea, on Kelly's Mountain at Cape Dauphin. Traditionally, it is called Kluskap's Cave, Kluskap's Door, or Kluskap's Wigwam. Although known to the Micmac for generations, this cave was first recorded in anthropological literature only in 1923. (Whitehead 1989)

The museum staff continued by quoting one of Elsie Clews Parsons's (1925:87) informants almost seven decades earlier:

> At Cape Dolphin (Dauphin), Big Bras d'Or, there is a door through the cliff, Gluskap's door. Outside, there is a stone like a table. Indians going hunting will leave on it tobacco and eels, to give them good luck. They do this today.

Finally, the museum report concludes:

> Offerings are said to have been made at this cave for generations, up into the twentieth century, and it is a tradition still being carried out today. Traces of gifts made to Kluskap have been noted in the presence of deposits of fish bones on the rock in front of the cave entrance ("Kluskap's Table"). On a recent visit to the site, Museum staff noted offerings of tobacco and sweet fern inside the cave itself, and in holes in the rock of the "Table." (Whitehead 1989)

A year later, in October 1990—only weeks after dramatic confrontations between soldiers and natives at Oka, Quebec—a more militant demonstration made the headlines. At an information meeting called by the Victoria County Committee for Development and attended by the Kelly Rock president, members of three separate Mi'kmaq bands turned up, all wearing army camouflage dress. "At all costs," they said, "we will blockade the road to the quarry. We are preparing for war" (*Harrowsmith* January/February 1991). This group of militant Mi'kmaq activists, some of whom had assisted the Mohawk Warriors at Oka, became known as the Mi'kmaq Warrior Society. The Warrior Society later also operated under the name Sacred Mountain Society (SMS). The SMS presents itself as "the only First Nations environmental organization in Atlantic Canada," declaring that "funds will be utilized to support environmental struggles affecting all peoples within the Mi'kmaq territory" (*Nova Scotia Environmental Network News* April/May 1993).

Opponents to the quarry have pointed to at least seventeen different ways in which it might harm the environment, including the nearby Bird Islands seabird sanctuary, the Bras D'Or Lakes spawning grounds, local lobster stocks, and the bald eagles on the mountain itself. Critics add that the project was proposed in Nova Scotia only because U.S. environmental laws would never allow it to be built in New England. A national magazine (*Earthkeeper* 3.91) says that "the province is reported to have the most relaxed environmental legislation and lowest prosecution rates for environmental crimes in the country, and word is spreading." The issue thus immediately emerged as a problem of environmental justice as well.

Whereas SKMS immediately began listing a number of separate concerns about the impact of the proposed quarry, the Mi'kmaq organizations initially focused on the threats to Kluskap's Cave. As the discussions continued, however, the SKMS and the SMS increasingly pooled their arguments. The chairman of the SKMS realized that "the challenge by the Cape Breton Micmacs may pose an even tougher hurdle for the company to cross" than purely environmental arguments (*The Inverness Oran* February 1991). He emphasized that "more study is needed to look at Mi'kmaq concerns" (*Micmac News* 19/4/91). In an article in *Earthkeeper* (January/February 1991, p. 56), he makes the Mi'kmaq argument his own:

> This mountain is Sacred. It contains a Sacred Cave. Even the absurdities of the proposal pale in comparison with this reality: what is threatened for the People of the Dawn is not Kelly's Mountain, but Glooscap's Mountain.

Conversely, the SMS's "information package" lists many of the arguments advanced by SKMS. It even concludes with the observation that "the super quarry is contrary to the concept of sustainable development." According to a survey conducted by members of the Victoria County Committee for Development early in 1990, however, only 34 out of 404 residents in the Englishtown area were opposed to the quarry. Many local people saw the 103 jobs Kelly Rock hoped to create as a dying community's chance to survive.

When Kelly Rock submitted its own environmental impact assessment to the provincial Department of the Environment in November 1989, SKMS successfully challenged its validity and requested a federal environmental review. The decision to conduct such a review took some time, but in early March 1991 the federal and provincial governments agreed to establish a joint federal-provincial Environmental Assessment Review (EAR) panel to review the quarry project. Later that month, the names of the five members of the panel were announced, and the final guidelines for the preparation of Terms of Reference for their report were completed on May 8, 1991.

The Union of Nova Scotia Indians (UNSI), based in Sydney, Cape Breton, actively participated in the review process from the start. In an April 1991 submission, it suggested a number of changes to the EAR guidelines, many of which were incorporated in the final version. In early May, UNSI also requested that an aboriginal person be added to the panel. The UNSI president wrote,

> The mountain is of cultural and spiritual significance to the Mi'kmaq of Nova Scotia as the site to which Glooscap will return and the location of his cave. We are concerned about the impact that the quarry would have on this interest, as well as its impact on fish and wildlife.

The provincial and federal Environment Ministers immediately agreed, and in December 1991 they appointed a Captain of the Mi'kmaq Grand Council as the sixth member of the panel. A few weeks earlier, moreover, the EAR panel had announced the hiring of a Mi'kmaq linguist as "technical specialist" to "provide the Panel with expertise in Micmac communication and interpretation" and to "advise on issues related to Micmac culture."

In late January 1992, Kelly Rock submitted its draft Terms of Reference for the EAR, but these were immediately returned, as they did not satisfy the final guidelines. In October 1992, the revised Terms of Reference were finally approved by the provincial Minister of the Environment. The proponent had "turned itself inside out" to demonstrate that it would consider all possible impacts of the quarry (*The Inverness Oran*).

A few months later, however, Kelly Rock announced that, for economic reasons, it would not be proceeding with the EAR. It is difficult to assess the importance of environmentalist protests in determining Kelly Rock's decision, but it is probably safe to assume that if SKMS and the Mi'kmaq traditionalists had not raised their voices in September 1989, construction would have begun as planned, in May 1990. The opponents of the quarry may have achieved their immediate aim as portrayed in the media, but there is definitely more to it than this. Reading the debate on Kelly's Mountain between the lines, I believe that we can unravel much of the cultural fabric and the structural tensions of modern civilization itself.

DISCOURSE AS NEGOTIATION OF
IDENTITY AND CREDIBILITY

To the Mi'kmaq traditionalists, the struggle against the quarry was not only a matter of keeping the mountain undisturbed but also an opportunity to redefine their identity as native people in ways to which most Cape Bretoners were unaccustomed. Journalists readily cooperated with the traditionalists in projecting the new image of Mi'kmaq culture, but the message was received with skepticism in many quarters. The president of Kelly Rock responded that radical natives were simply using the occasion to further their land-claims issue (*The Inverness Oran* February 1991). He was not alone in brushing aside the Mi'kmaq protests as part of a larger strategy. In a sense, of course, any behavior is strategic inasmuch as it aims to communicate something. But the little group of drummers who so effectively helped to turn public processes against the quarry had much more profound objectives in mind than land claims. Several questions come to mind if we focus on this meta-communicative dimension of Mi'kmaq environmentalism. What are the different levels of their message? Why is it so potent today? How are we to assess its authenticity?

A discourse continuously remolds its own framework of rules. In testing various messages on one another, the participants negotiate a shifting field of credibility. But the limits of credible discourse have a tenuous relationship to real motives and objectives. These two levels must thus be investigated separately. For instance, we can safely assume that the primary motive of Kelly's Rock was not to generate local opportunities for employment, yet this is the message continually presented in the media (*The Toronto Star* 20/6/91). The president of Kelly's Rock is thus an unlikely person to question the motives professed by the Mi'kmaq traditionalists. The issue is not whether all the motives of the participants have been exposed or truthfully presented, but whether those offered are accepted by the public (media, authorities, etc.) as legitimate. Suffice it to say that the struggle to stop the quarry on Kelly's Mountain suggests a shift in the range of credible public discourse, compared to environmental debate on Cape Breton a mere decade previously. The framework is no longer restricted to the "jobs-versus-the-environment" or "jobs-versus-health" debate. Nor is it even constrained by the rational-scientific "environmental assessment" approach. The pivotal contribution of indigenous activists to environmental discourse is to have redefined its framework so that it is becoming increasingly legitimate to evoke concepts of "sanctity."

Initially, there were attempts to define the spiritual approach as incomprehensible. An article in the *Micmac News*, covering a March 1991 meeting between Kelly Rock and Mi'kmaq representatives (UNSI and the Micmac Association of Cultural Studies), states that the "Micmac leaders view the proposed rock development as a cruel and disrespectful way to treat Mother Nature and the Great Spirit." The president of Kelly Rock is quoted as responding, "We don't fully understand each other's concerns at this time and we wish to see what steps can be taken to alleviate your concerns" (*Micmac News* 15/3/91). At another occasion, a representative of the Federal EAR office in Hull, Quebec, said that "the Panel is going to need help in understanding what is said here" (*Micmac News* 19/4/91). An UNSI executive told me in an interview that it had been very difficult to convey the significance of concepts such as the "spiritual impact" of the quarry. The concept is obviously a hybrid between two separate worlds of discourse. Problems of communication seem unavoidable when elements of traditionalist discourse enter into the rational, analytical discourse of the bureaucracy. A predictable problem, for instance, is how an assessment instructed to conceptually break down Kelly's Mountain into "Valued Ecosystem Components" will be able to deal with holistic perspectives such as are embodied in the Mi'kmaq view that the mountain is sacred. Referring to Beanlands and Duinker (1983), the EAR Final Guidelines for the Preparation of Terms of Reference propose that the study should "identify an initial set of valued ecosystem components (VECs) to provide a focus for subsequent activities." This approach immediately defines the proper relationship to the mountain as one of analysis, fragmentation, and objectification, rather than holism and participation. Turn-

ing a mountain into gravel is facilitated by first breaking it down conceptually. Recognizing this, a commentator wrote to a local newspaper (*Cape
Breton Post*), "It's a pity that a project like this can't simply be termed a
blight on the landscape and totally unacceptable in relation to the benefits, and that every slug and shrew on the mountain has to be counted in
an effort to stop it."

The approach of the Mi'kmaq traditionalists also exposed inadequacies
in the categories of the public framework for dealing with multifaceted
issues such as those concerning Kelly's Mountain. SMS turned to the
Nova Scotia Human Rights Commission (NSHRC), arguing that, "like
any other spiritual beliefs we have certain sites that are more important
than life itself." In its information package, SMS explains that "the degree
of offense would be equal to that felt by Christians if a super quarry were
placed at the Holy Sepulcher, or by Hebrews if the wailing wall were removed for a motel, or by Muslims if a casino were placed in Mecca." The
NSHRC replied that it did "not see the complaint as coming within the
confines of the Nova Scotia Human Rights Act" and referred it to the Department of Culture. The Nova Scotia Museum, in turn, responded that,
"since the cave is not an archaeological site, it does not fit within the usual
interpretation of the Special Places Protection Act" (correspondence from
the files of SMS).

Although many Cape Bretoners may have found the image of the ecological and spiritual native difficult to reconcile with ingrained local ste-
reotypes, at a more abstract level most were probably well prepared to
receive the new message. There was, so to speak, a conceptual space in
their worldview reserved for, and thus in fact conducive to, this kind of
media event. The Mi'kmaq traditionalists reenacted a message that rings
familiar to the nonnative majority of North America. In many people it
evoked a strain of collective guilt handed down through the generations
and reinforced by a whole genre of books and films from *The Last of the
Mohicans* to *Dances with Wolves*. I am not questioning the historical validity
of that sense of guilt, only suggesting that this archetype is one of the
reasons why indigenous environmentalists today are provided with so
much space in the media. It is as if native people are allowed, and indeed
encouraged, to say things that nonnative people cannot. The style of presentation and the meta-message it conveys are the prerogative of the native traditionalist.

The credibility of a claim that a mountain is sacred hinges on the identity of the speaker. Considering the extent to which our image of the ecological native is a projection of nonnative writers from James Fennimore
Cooper and on (cf. Francis 1992), it is as if native people are invited, by
the dominant culture, to protest against it. In an almost Jungian way, they
are offered a niche in the dominant cosmology as speakers of spiritual

truths of which everybody is at heart aware. Mainstream North Americans want them to say the things they cannot say themselves. If presenting themselves as protectors of Mother Earth is yet another emblem of their "opposition ideology" (Larsen 1983), the choice of this emblem is not entirely their own. This social constructivist perspective does not detract from the authenticity or significance of their critique. On the contrary, it recognizes that the First Nations, in articulating a new framework for environmental debate, are being assigned an important, historical mission. Their leading actors, I would add, are acutely aware of these processes, but rather than feel "deconstructed," they recognize a real opportunity to fill their sense of ethnic identity with new and profound meaning. A constructivist account of Mi'kmaq spiritual resurgence need not be de-authenticating. Giddens (1990:150) visualizes a "radicalised modernity" that, rather than succumb to the postmodern dissolution of the self, encourages "active processes of reflexive self-identity." Thus, in a sense, the "traditionalist" who in an interview reflects on the Mi'kmaq revival is radically modern:

> [T]he nativeness is growing. And it's fortunate. If I were to fight for this mountain fifteen years ago, I'd be locked up in one of the mental hospitals. My people would have signed me in. . . . Some of our elders . . . I would have never believed fifteen years ago would be walking around with eagle feathers, going to powwows, dancing.

THE AUTHENTIC AND THE CORRUPT

In positioning themselves as uncompromisingly opposed to the quarry, the Mi'kmaq traditionalists evoke a dualistic archetype of Indian-White relations. Native people are presented as the oppressed guardians of authentic, spiritual values, whereas the dominant, nonnative culture is identified with corrupt power and a materialistic greed for money. But when I discussed this polarity with several Mi'kmaq, I soon realized that it was applicable not only to the ethnic, Indian-White dichotomy. Precisely the same opposition recurs in the way many natives present the difference between the two forms of Mi'kmaq government, the traditional Grand Council, on one hand, and the system of band chiefs and councils organized and funded by the Department of Indian Affairs, on the other. The derogatory remarks about the "chief and council" invariably focused on corruption such as favoritism and mismanagement of funds. In the context of reserve life, where funding is a scarce resource to compete for, being entrusted with the allocation of funds seems sufficient to warrant suspicion (cf. Larsen 1983:79–81). It is obvious that the same "moral" polarity that at one level serves to define Indian-White relations can be applied at another level to divide native communities. The concept of native people who have adopted a White mentality is a commonly evoked archetype. The two parallel systems of Mi'kmaq government employ distinctly separate modes of self-presentation, in terms of both speech and dress. The Grand Council affiliates often appear in "traditional" dress and adopt a befitting, serene idiom, whereas "chief and council" tend to dress and speak like mainstream bureaucrats. It is evident that competence in bureaucratic discourse is an asset in careers funded by the Department of Indian Affairs. In effect, bureaucratic jargon is rewarded with funding.

Just as I believed that I had come to understand the major divisions of Mi'kmaq society in terms of an opposition between people affiliated with the Grand Council and with the band chiefs, respectively, I was, however, disillusioned. In various ways it was brought to my attention that a very similar opposition divided the affiliates of the Grand Council itself. From the perspective of some of these affiliates, there is a rift between the "traditionalists" and the "Catholics." The leading "Catholics," sometimes also referred to as the "academics," were those who had the best access to funding agencies such as churches, universities, the Department of Indian Affairs, and the United Nations. The division at times seemed to connote a kind of class difference, but I realized that it would be useless to try to delineate "sociocentric" factions on the basis of the criterion of funding, as the same dual opposition between funded and fundless seemed to be generated in every conceivable organization and context. It proved to be an "egocentric" and contextual mode of classification rather than a statement about definable groups. I even started to discern similar tensions among the "traditionalists" themselves, between the Mi'kmaq Warrior Society and the "pacifists," who were more easily drawn into various activities eligible for funding (e.g., cultural and spiritual events, musical recordings).

At four successive levels of integration, then, a single structural polarity was evoked to express resentment over one's own marginality and the uneven distribution of economic power. At each level, moreover, the people identified with power would emphasize the more inclusive contradiction on which their own position was built and downplay the opposition conceptualized by those challenging them at their own level. Thus, the band chiefs would concentrate almost exclusively on Indian-White relations, the Catholics on the difference between Grand Council and band chiefs, the pacifist traditionalists on the conflict between traditionalists and Catholics, and so on. The further "down," of course, the more perspectives there would be to choose from, according to context. But the characteristics projected onto the opposite camp were strikingly similar at all levels. The adversaries were people who betrayed fundamental values and sold themselves to money and power. Conspicuously often, they were also charged with mismanagement of the funds they had secured. From the perspective of some traditionalists, the adversaries were also impostors. Their most essential critique focused on lack of authenticity. At one level, this was simply a matter of observing that a successful fundraiser was not really Mi'kmaq, and that he should not be diverting funds that ought to be enjoyed by those who were. At another level, adversaries were characterized as "wannabes" whose self-construction as "traditionalists" was not accepted as credible or legitimate. One traditionalist said in an interview,

> We have a lot of what we call "plastic medicine people" also. They take treatment, or they sober up, or they go off in a fast four days, and they're coming down with all kinds of stories on what they've seen on their quest. . . . They're going much too fast. . . . Now we got so many pipe carriers, anybody who has the desire to whittle out a pipe, by the time it's finished, they're a pipe carrier.

Charges of low authenticity were common and sometimes reciprocal. These types of dismissal suggest a competitive struggle to appropriate whichever forms of recognition mainstream Canadian society is ready to confer on native voices. It seems to be structurally related to the situation Larsen (1983:126–131) has identified on Mi'kmaq reserves, where the scarcity of ethnic resources such as housing and welfare generates a continuous struggle over who is or is not to be defined as an Indian. The assertion of a collective, ethnic identity is thus undermined by the recurrent disavowal, among neighbors, of one another's Indianness. To Larsen's observations, I would add that the struggle over ethnic resources is not confined to tangible, material gratification. At stake may also be a publicly recognized but nonformalized *persona* (e.g., as an "elder," "pipe carrier," "traditionalist," or "spiritual leader") built on self-reflexive, ethnic construction. The greater the number of candidates for such public roles, the more competitive is the process of identity construction.

In view of all the internal divisions reflecting the ambiguity and contextuality of the Indian-White dichotomy, I should add, much of the significance of an issue such as Kelly's Mountain is that it united, at a higher level, virtually all those who define themselves as Mi'kmaq. Even though there has been overt disagreement on the methods to be used in the struggle, being opposed to the quarry became an expression of ethnic identity. The issue presented an opportunity to publicly define Mi'kmaq culture in opposition to mainstream values, an act of definition that may have been as helpful to many Mi'kmaq as it was instructive to nonnatives. Whether a band chief, a Grand Council Catholic, or a Mi'kmaq Warrior, at this level the message was the same.

ENVIRONMENTALISM AND THE STATE

Ever since the "budworm battles" (May 1982) against aerial forest spraying in the 1970s (cf. Hornborg 1998a), Cape Breton's environmental issues
have engaged a mosaic of *ad hoc* action groups and other organizations. I
had the opportunity to listen to what many environmentalists had to say
about other environmentalists and about green politics, and it struck me
how often, here too, feelings of antagonism focused on the issue of funding. Funding by government could be perceived either as conspirational
co-optation or as success and recognition, and the ambivalent attitudes to
it ultimately reflect an ambivalence about the possibilities of the political
system itself. Once again it was possible to discern a hierarchy of opposi-
tions expressing a polarization of funded and fundless, collaborators and
fundamentalists, power and marginality. Greens would sometimes also
dismiss other greens by focusing on inappropriate elements of lifestyle,
such as smoking. "Greenness" is thus obviously as contestable an identity as "Indianness." Moreover, the divisions within the environmental
movement similarly suggested a connection between funding and the
adoption of specific modes of discourse. For example, one activist observed that the concept of "sustainable development" served as a kind of
password for funding. In evoking phrases from key documents such as
the UN's Brundtland Report (WCED 1987), applicants were able to secure
their legitimacy. It seems as if public credibility is thus continuously defined by formal discourse emanating from the highest and most central
echelons. In the mainstream of government funding, according to this
view, success and recognition hinge on skills of discursive emulation. The
issue of funding is a tangible manifestation of the political aspect of modernity. In negotiations concerning funding, the trade-off between movement and state is sometimes quite explicit, as in a dialogue I recorded
between an environmentalist and the provincial Minister of the Environment. The essence of the dialogue is as follows: The environmentalist says
that if provincial funding for his organization is granted, the confrontations between environmentalists and politicians will not be as bitter as
previously, but the Minister of the Environment expresses doubts that the
"deal" will be as beneficial as the environmentalist suggests.

In comparing the divisions within the environmental and indigenous
movements, I was struck by how what appeared to be the same basic polarity between the "authentic" and the "corrupt" was dressed in different
interpretations of evil. Moreover, I realized that there were other, critical
movements, such as feminism and socialism, that seemed to grapple with
the same polarity in yet other terms. It struck me that all these various
movements may ultimately be directed at the same evil, although with
their separate vantage points they tend to dress it in different words. Be-

yond their various constructions, a new question emerged with increasing clarity: what is the common denominator of the elusive polarity that both stimulates and organizes their critique? Whether construed as the White Man, industry, patriarchy, or capital, the target of all their protests is perhaps nothing less than modernity itself. Although epitomized by the affluent, bourgeois, Caucasoid male, the sociocultural and political phenomenon of modernity cannot be reduced to a function of race, gender, or even class. In focusing on modernity, we may distill the essence of that pervasive polarity which continues to generate rifts in the most commendable of movements. At the same time, we may come to understand why these various movements have had such difficulties conceptualizing the enemy in ways conducive to its subjugation. For modernity is essentially a strategy for encompassment of the local; thus, it cannot be challenged in local terms, but only by turning its own logic against itself, that is by "encompassing encompassment," or what Bourdieu (1990:30–41) has called "objectifying objectification."

OBJECTIFYING MODERNITY: CONCEPTUAL ENCOMPASSMENT AS POWER

In the previous chapter I argued that, in realizing his own projects of identity construction, the modern person was required to redefine his or her relations to places and people. These could no longer constitute a definitive platform for identity construction *as particulars*, only as categories. This disembedding of social relations and of perceived selfhood is intertwined with the decontextualization of discourse on society and on the self. The self-definition of the professional goes hand in hand with the decontextualization of discourse on "labor," "production," and "economics." Objectification of self and objectification of social relations (i.e., alienation and fetishism) are part and parcel of the same phenomenon of modernity.

Let us recall that we are not suggesting that there has been a wholesale transition from a premodern to a modern state of affairs, but rather the emergence of a social *polarity*. Although its genesis could be traced to European history, it would also be misleading to refer to modernity as an aspect of "European culture," contrasting, for instance, with native "Amerindian culture." The polarity of local versus global identity is as evident in modern Europe as anywhere else in the world. It is generated by the systems of national and international integration (state, market, and movement; cf. Hannerz 1989) that require centralization, mobility, and specialized, supra-local interest groups. Finally, although there are great differences between people in terms of how far they have submitted to modernity, the polarity is not primarily a mode of classifying individuals but a tension that most people would recognize as running down the middle of their existence. It could be approximated by a series of linked conceptual dualities, thus:

Embedded	Disembedded
Local	Global
Irreplaceable	Interchangeable
Experience-near	Experience-far
Sensory	Cerebral
Subjectivity	Objectification
Holism	Fragmentation

We shall now discuss how these two polar modes of relating to the world interact with each other in terms of social processes, and what significance such processes have for the negotiation of environmental issues such as Kelly's Mountain.

I have already indicated that modernity is a strategy of conceptual encompassment of local life-worlds. When the cognitive approach of science and technology was applied to society, as in economics and administration, it was, as always, as a means of manipulation and control. The language of the administrators, in objectifying local life-worlds into abstractions such as "labor," "consumers," or "voters," constitutes a relationship of power. Because it provides access to supra-local power structures, proficiency in such abstract modes of discourse is a kind of social capital accumulated through what we know as "education." In spite of its emancipatory goals, the modern educational system remains fundamentally an institution for equipping a select minority of the world's population with the conceptual means to dominate the remainder. Modernist perspectives tend to objectify, encompass, and transcend the concrete realities of place.

At a public seminar on indigenous perspectives on "sustainable development," I recorded an interchange between a Canadian marine biologist (B), a local Mi'kmaq youth (M), and a UN observer from an indigenous minority in Russia (R) that highlights the role of education in the asymmetrical articulation of local and global identities:

B: From my experiences in all the countries that I've worked in, including Canada, one of the biggest problems that the aboriginal groups have is a lack of education. . . .

M: The thing I want to say is, the education part. . . . It's kind of a disagreement, when he says that, you know . . . that he's smarter than I am, you see? That's not the case. Are you smarter than I am? How much education do you have? . . . I might not be a biologist . . . but . . . it's really bullshit. It's the people inside, if they want to save the Mother Earth. It's the people inside, if they care, really. . . . It's the spirituality part. We have to treat each other with respect, show respect to people and to Mother Earth. . . . It's the other side, they have to take the false part away, the bullshit part, and open up their minds and their hearts and say, we're equal, we're equal, let's work together. . . . I don't stand up here and say, I have a master's. . . . All these things I have to say to prove, this is me, you know what I mean? I don't have to do that. . . . I'm just a human being. I speak from my heart, and that's the way it should be. Education, the biologists, and everything else goes out the window, and that's all I have to say, and thank you for listening to me.

R: Education is not bullshit. Education is a way . . . to go and achieve the goal which you need. . . . The United Nations . . . is not a god. . . . It's a very big building with very small rooms, and in each of the rooms there are very small people, and if you learn about those people, and if you learn the way to get in there, then you can use it. Because we live in a very strange world. The great warrior nowadays is not a brave with bow or tomahawk; it's a very sneaky lawyer with a fax machine.

To become a "great warrior" today generally means to adopt a modernist, "global" frame of mind. Ambitious local actors will appropriate abstract modes of discourse to gain access to external funding and other forms of recognition. Conversely, "global" actors from the outside will attempt to evoke local frameworks and reference points for purposes of political or commercial infiltration. Through such dialectical instrumentalities (local actors adopting global modes and vice versa), local and global language continuously intermingle and shade into one another. The relationship between local and global actors is not symmetrical, however. It is one thing to promote a local cause by adopting a language that outside powers will recognize, another to promote an abstract cause (such as share of voters or of the market) by adopting a language that local people will listen to. A local cause can at times be served by an abstract language, but an abstract cause masqueraded in local language deserves to be more closely examined. The essential difference is whether the actors themselves are ultimately guided by local or abstract motives. Here, of course, is a central problem of modernity: the adoption of a decontextualized discourse is itself a distancing from place, and if this means entering into one of modernity's specialized sectors for identity construction, there will be a corresponding shift of motives. If the individual has to *choose* whether to define himself in terms of local or abstract reference points, the movement from local to global will tend to be irreversible, and there will be a continuous co-optation of local voices into placeless, guild-like frameworks. Without the constant, experience-near resonance of place, these voices risk forgetting the contexts in which they were raised, devoting themselves to the perfection of their own, objectified intonation, echoing in the empty labyrinths of disembedded abstraction.

THE "GLOBAL" MINDFRAME AND THE SUBSUMPTION OF CRITIQUE

This brings us to the subsumptive nature of modernity's global language. The confrontation between the local Mi'kmaq youth and the educated few who would be spokespeople for indigenous minorities evokes the perennial paradox of power. Can local voices ever ring unadulterated in global institutions? To confront modernity through public discourse is, paradoxically, to be absorbed by it. This is the predicament of movements. Self-reflection and self-objectification tend to mold activists according to public images such as those of the "environmentalist" or the "indigenous" representative. Opposition to the ills of modernity is thus subsumed in the creation of a niche for each variant of critique, complete with formal channels for complaint and with chances of funding. There is a subtle transformation in motives as critique is progressively institutionalized and the focus is shifted from the source of indignation to the skills of self-presentation.

One hallmark of the "global" actor is to see the public definition of environmental problems as an *opportunity*. At the above-mentioned seminar on "sustainable development," a United Nations observer for the Mi'kmaq enthusiastically observed that the UN had

> created a *Department* of Sustainable Development, whatever that means, but anyway, it's a reorganization, creating new opportunities. We have all sorts of United Nations agencies suddenly wondering what indigenous peoples are all about, and looking for indigenous people to talk to. So, it's really a tremendous opportunity for what we call here in Canada First Nations, to push their elbows into things and say, Here we are . . .

He later continued, "Another example of the way in which there are international opportunities being created which we can take advantage of has to do with the fishery."

It is intriguing to discover how social contexts are created where the catastrophic collapse of the North Atlantic fishery in the early 1990s, which left 20,000 fishermen stranded in Newfoundland alone, can be re-

ferred to as an "opportunity." An opportunity for whom? Several participants in the seminar seemed to doubt that such global negotiations of sustainability ever yield any tangible improvements. At one point, the UN
observer for the Mi'kmaq mentioned as a "success" the "contribution that
the Mi'kmaq nation was able to make to the struggle against Stora Kopparberg, against the forest spraying, by triggering groups in Sweden to
demonstrate against the president of Stora Kopparberg," whereupon a
nonnative environmentalist in the audience, who had been heavily involved in that struggle (cf. Hornborg 1998a), offered a caution:

> I've spent a number of years now consulting with government agencies be-
> cause they like to grab an environmentalist to bring in to the table to find out
> just what's on our mind. To no avail, really: I can't say that, for all that time
> that we've spent at the table with government and industry, that we've really
> succeeded on changing one iota of forest practices or strategies in this
> country. . . . I would really caution us in terms of us legitimating our oppres-
> sors. I mean, basically, what has happened in these negotiations is that we've
> given government and industry the jargon that they can use in their public
> relations crap, to confuse and finesse the public into making it appear as if
> something's happening. . . . Those guys aren't going to do it for us, believe
> me, they will talk us, and basically it's a stalling game. If they can keep
> NGO's and environmentalists and indigenous peoples at the table, talking,
> meanwhile a hundred thousand acres is falling on Cape Breton Island, Kel-
> ly's Mountain is used for a causeway to Prince Edward Island.

Such feelings of resignation tend to be a recurrent outcome in movements as they are subsumed by the frameworks against which they were
launched. I would add that "extremist" positions are continuously being
generated by precisely this subsumptive nature of modernity. Within the
indigenous movement, the Mi'kmaq Warrior Society is a good example.
Among environmentalists, the "biocentric" position is similarly uncom-
promising (cf. Sayen 1990). In Nova Scotia, it is represented by the Green
Web, which presents itself as a "small independent research group serving the needs of the environmental and green movements." Significantly,
it explicitly does "not solicit or accept government or corporate funding."
Significantly, also, its critique tends to focus on the language of public
discourse itself. In a bulletin titled " 'Sustainable Development' and Conceptual Enclosure" (Orton 1992), it notes:

> In Nova Scotia, "development" means local environmental degradation and
> destruction, plus the erosion of community power from the community to
> provincial, national or international centers. Conflicts become "resolved"
> using the criteria of the developers, *which means the local affected community,*
> *if it can participate, can only do so using an alien language, e.g. cost benefit analysis,*

which does not reflect its concerns. . . . To successfully oppose ongoing environmental destruction, must mean to move power from the market and the state
back to the communities.

In evoking the "deep ecology" of Naess (1989) and others, the Green
Web converges with the Mi'kmaq traditionalists in demanding a radical
and spiritually informed reconceptualization of the role of humankind in
the biosphere. I will turn now to discussing the challenge this poses to
modernity and the "disembeddedness" of modern discourse. How
should we conceptualize the relation between money, language, identity,
and power in a way that suggests strategies for reempowering locally sustainable communities? What do the spiritual elements of native and nonnative environmentalism signify?

SPIRITUALITY AS REVOLT
AGAINST MODERNITY

I have suggested that modernity, while subsuming the mainstream of critique it generates, simultaneously pushes countercultural movements
toward extremist positions, including the threat of violence. When the
dominant word-games fail them, the chronically disempowered may seek
more potent forms of expression. In a television interview, a young Mi'k-
maq Warrior described the effects of his camouflage uniform:

> I walk into Woolco, and I have everybody's eyes watching me as I walk all
> through the store. People won't turn their back on me now, when I walk into
> a store.

To start discussing the historical and contemporary "facts" of the spiritual significance of Kelly's Mountain to the Mi'kmaq would be to miss
the point of their message. Theirs is a message about contemporary social
relationships, not about history. Evoking Hirschman's (1970) terminology
of "exit" and "voice," the new native voices pose an alternative to the
self-destructive patterns that for so long have crippled the indigenous minorities of North America. Their growing impact on the mainstream environmental debate fulfils an old prophecy of native revival. In drawing on
potent archetypes, their invocation of spirituality becomes a revolt against
the language of modernity, yet their mode of self-definition is radically
modern.

Local people tend to maintain a skeptical stance vis-à-vis the kind of
abstract formulations that are regularly championed to empower them.
The 1992 deliberations on a new constitutional accord, the idea of which

was to radically improve the legal situation of native groups, generated very little enthusiasm on the Mi'kmaq reserves. Can abstract language ever serve local interests? And where does this put anthropology? There is a real risk, I believe, that the discourse on "culture" and "identity" will remain but another modernist strategy for conceptual encompassment, objectifying local life-worlds for purposes of management and control. A successful fund-attractor in one of the Mi'kmaq reserves called for contributions to a United Nations report on the protection of the "cultural property" of indigenous peoples:

> Cultural property includes sacred sites, ceremonial objects, and places or objects of special historical and/or cultural significance, including historical documents and works of art. It may also include burials, human remains, and archaeological sites. Bongs, symbols, and ceremonies can be cultural property, if they are very essential to the identity of a people. (Letter accompanying Guidelines for Cultural-Property Case Studies, Apamukek Institute, Eskasoni Indian Reserve)

When a person begins to talk about his or her own "culture," it is a sign that another life-world is being objectified and decontextualized. It would seem that the only way to resist the power of modernity would be to refuse to let one's life-world thus be encompassed. From a purely theoretical perspective, such a strategy would have to be based on some kind of boundary-drawing between the local and the global. To pursue this line of reasoning, we must once again consider the extent to which discourse is a function of exchange. Concepts such as "development" and "employment opportunities" are part and parcel of the way in which the market is organized. The decontextualizing cosmology of the economists, which aspires to engulf all local systems of meaning, is a means to open local communities and ecosystems to outside exploitation. In other words, the impact of the disembedded language of modernity upon the material world is such as to facilitate ecological destruction. Against this background, we can appreciate why both the Mi'kmaq traditionalists and the biocentrics have chosen to revolt against mainstream language. They are both trying to redesign the definition space (cf. Ardener 1989) of environmentalist discourse.

The concept of "sanctity" is radically opposed to modernity and commoditization because it posits irreplaceable and incommensurable values (cf. Kopytoff 1986). But is not "sanctity" itself an abstract and disembedded concept? At this point, I would like to make a distinction between "abstract" and "disembedded." I would argue that these concepts represent two separate parameters, and that human cognition and practices can be broadly classified according to their intersections:

	CONCRETE	ABSTRACT
EMBEDDED	Ritual	Spirituality
DISEMBEDDED	Technology	Science

A living relationship to place, in the sense suggested previously in this chapter, can provide abstract thought with the sensory resonance and experience-near reference points that distinguish a spiritual from a completely secular frame of mind. The destructive tendencies in modernity are generated not by abstract thought in itself, but by the disembedding and secularization of abstraction. Grove-White (1993:24–25) calls environmentalism "a new moral discourse for technological society," suggesting that "some of the deeper shades of recent 'green' religiosity" can be read as a dissatisfaction with objectivistic, atomizing, and trivializing representations, and express a "need to address authentic human concern about deeper mysteries of existence." These, he adds, are "far from insignificant matters."

Modern, objectivist rationality claims a monopoly on legitimate knowledge construction, suggesting a confusion of map and territory. But to the extent that there is such a thing as an absolute truth, it will not allow itself to be encapsulated in any specific set of words. There will always be more than one way of drawing a map. We saw in chapter 10 that cognitive scientists are concerned not with truth but with the adequacy of representations, observing that the only measure of adequacy we will ever have is survival (Maturana and Varela 1987 [1992]). Foucault (1971) locates in classical Greece the point at which what words *said* started to become more important than what they *did*. Spiritual and "deep ecology" approaches to environmental issues suggest a renewed concern with the performative dimension of our narratives. It could be argued that they represent the logical next step beyond the paralysis of postmodernism. If there is a sense in which humans are indeed the authors of their world, the postmodern discovery that this is the case should ultimately inspire responsibility rather than nihilism. If we have to recover a metaphorical idiom capable of sustainably *relating* us to the rest of the world, the reflexive experience of modernity now leaves us no other choice than to learn how to handle the awareness that this is what we should be doing.

In trying to put into other words what the Mi'kmaq environmentalists actually meant with the concept of spirituality, I have felt that it signifies a propensity to *see beyond the surface*. Whereas the detached, late modern mind objectifies even cultural symbols (i.e., strips them of meaning), the spiritually inclined mind is attuned to signs and meanings even outside the realm of culture: in mountains, eagles, and sunrises. In the way that it is used among many Mi'kmaq, "spirituality" has to do with *relating*. It refers to the emotive states that are evoked in human subjects in the process of relating to each other and to the natural world. The fact that the concept is frequently used to describe a proposed difference between Mi'kmaq and White indicates that the former perceive the latter as somehow less apt to relate, that is, less sensitive to the emotive dimension of being-in-the-world. This observation is a cultural datum worth examining in its own right. If there is such a thing as cultural variation in personhood (cf. Shweder and Bourne 1984), it is not invalid to propose that such sensitivity may be one of the parameters to investigate.

There have been attempts in anthropology to shift our focus from symbols and surfaces to their extralinguistic "resonance" (cf. LeVine 1984:85–86; Wikan 1990), but given how thoroughly textualized our communication about these matters is, the methodological problems remain formidable. Increasingly, it seems, anthropology is trying to tackle things that it is not fully equipped to express. We are probably caught in the situation recognized by Geertz (1983:58), where the ethnographer generally "cannot perceive what his informants perceive," only "what they perceive 'with'—or 'by means of,' or 'through' . . . or whatever the word should be." We will keep taking notes on eagle feathers, sacred pipes, and the rhetoric about Mother Earth, but it is important not to confuse such "signs of the self" (Singer 1984:60) with the human essence trying to express itself through them.

Following post-structural theorists such as Foucault and Derrida, sociologists and anthropologists have observed how social discourse suppresses and conceals perspectives and modes of existence that disagree with hegemonic orders and ideals. Giddens (1991) writes that modern day-to-day social life is being "sequestered" from incongruous factors such as madness, criminality, sickness, death, sexuality, and nature. This view is as pertinent to Indian reserves as to prisons and mental hospitals. What is there about Mi'kmaq life that mainstream Canadian society needs to stow away? It is not difficult to see some of the subversive challenges that it poses to a rational *Gesellschaft*, most generally perhaps the refusal to submit one's anxious or euphoric body to modernist versions of self-discipline, whether imposed by clocks, contracts, or the gaze of impersonal authority. The relative lack of concern with property or accumulation is another such irregularity. To this list could be added the subversive implications of genuine spirituality. The concept of sanctity is diametrically opposed to the notion of generalized interchangeability on which modernity is founded. To suggest that a mountain or a person's time is not for sale is incongruent with the basic premises of the modern project.

BEYOND NOSTALGIA AND CYNICISM:
INDIGENOUS ENVIRONMENTALISM AND
THE POLITICS OF ECOLOGICAL IRONY

Most Mi'kmaq environmentalists that I spoke with explicitly referred to
the spiritual underpinnings of their struggle to safeguard Kluskap's sacred mountain. I am convinced that the concept of spirituality indeed signified an experiential reality for most of them; it was not just an instrumental accessory in their self-construction. But contemporary
anthropology would undoubtedly have difficulties "buying," as it were,
the image of themselves that the Mi'kmaq traditionalists were projecting
through the media. This is not only, I would add, because modern natives
are not accepted as representative of their premodern ancestors but also
because the whole idea of a "premodern" condition is increasingly dismissed as a modern construction. It is ironic that the image of the spiritual, ecological native, though widely disseminated by earlier generations
of anthropologists, is now being systematically dismissed as romanticism
by anthropology precisely when (or is it because?) it is gaining a popular
foothold. Perhaps an adequate representative of such earlier generations,
Lee (1988:253) has observed that there is now "a considerable industry in
anthropology . . . to show the primitive as a Hobbesian being—with a life
that is 'nasty, brutish and short.' " In the current climate of opinion, he
notes, "no one is going to go broke" by appealing to cynicism.

Naess (1995:134), widely recognized as the founder of the deep ecology
movement, notes that "since World War II, the general disrespect in the
West of non-industrial cultures has changed into deep and serious respect
among an increasing minority." It is indeed ironic—and psychologically
puzzling—that so many anthropologists should now choose to direct
their energies toward deconstructing the basis for this respect. Perhaps
part of the problem is that indigenous movements and nonnative environmental movements have increasingly pooled their arguments. Harries-Jones (1993:49, 52) found some native leaders in Ontario rejecting
nonnative attempts to cultivate a green spirituality, but generally speaking I think the relationship between the two movements can be seen as
one of symbiosis. When I returned to Nova Scotia for a longer period of
fieldwork in 1992, one of the Mi'kmaq environmentalists recommended
me to read a new book compiled by environmentalists David Suzuki and
Peter Knudtson (1992)—and enthusiastically endorsed on the cover by Al
Gore—called *Wisdom of the Elders*, with the subtitle *Sacred Native Stories of
Nature*. It popularizes anthropological data on traditional ecocosmologies
from various parts of the world and juxtaposes these data with modern
science, to bridge, as the cover says, "the shimmering gulf between the

shaman and the scientist" and to show "how we can create our own sacred ecology."

These quotations could today be used as a kind of shibboleth for the
anthropological profession. If you do not find them ridiculous, you are
not likely to be an anthropologist. The current fashion in anthropology is
to dissolve any distinction between the modern and the premodern as a
modern fabrication. *Gemeinschaft* is now nothing but a fabrication of *Gesellschaft*, the ecologically sensitive native merely a projection of industrial
society. The rather remarkable implication is that, in the course of the
emergence of urban-industrial civilization, no significant changes have
been taking place in terms of social relations, knowledge construction, or
human-environmental relations. The closely knit kinship group, locally
contextualized ecological knowledge, attachment to place, reciprocity,
animism: all of them are suddenly dismissed as myth. With the displace-
ment of the old narrative, represented most forcefully by Karl Polanyi
(1944), emerges the new but implicit message that we have always been
capitalists.

Ellen (1993:126) captures the currently fashionable opinion in his assertion that the "myth of primitive environmental wisdom" does not make
sense "except in relation to the recognition that such an illusion serves an
important ideological purpose in modern or post-modern society." But
cynicism, too, has its ideological purposes. Dwelling on examples of un-
wise natural resource management among indigenous peoples today is
not a very good argument because it rests on essentialist premises. The
opposite argument is not that indigenous peoples are somehow inherently (genetically?) prone to deal wisely with their environment, but that
the social condition and mindframe of premodern existence contains elements that may be more conducive to wise management than the modern
mindframe (Bateson 1972; Rappaport 1979; E. N. Anderson 1996). The instances investigated today can rarely be called premodern, for example
in the sense that their resource management is informed by traditional
metaphors of human-nature reciprocity (cf. Bird-David 1993) or pre-
Cartesian notions about the intervention of human meanings in the material world. Such are the parameters that might help us clarify, in an analytically more precise way, the cultural dimension of environmental problems.

A premodern condition is very much a matter of experiential immersion or embeddedness in a local, socio-ecological context. Even if, for the
moment, anthropologists have lost sight of any way of curbing the ongoing commoditization of the planet, we have no reason to terminate the
long-standing anthropological project of investigating the role of the capitalist world market in dissolving such conditions. Even less should we
have reason to adopt a cynical posture vis-à-vis people—indigenous or

not—who refuse to lose sight of the real changes that have been taking place in human-environmental relations worldwide. The world system may have started emerging five thousand years ago (Gills and Frank 1993), but that does not mean that we have always been capitalists. Rather than end up with essentializing distinctions between cultures, however, we would propose a structural definition that explains the polarization of "the West and the Rest" in terms of the differential infiltration of modernity and conditions of disembeddedness.

Paradoxically, the role of a "wise" social science would be to double back and *relinquish* its modernist claims for conceptual encompassment of local life-worlds. This most certainly applies to economics and political science but has implications for anthropology and sociology as well. Fortunately, anthropology has other options than to go on dissecting local worlds in terms of a uniform, conceptual tool-set. To side with the locals would be paradoxical but not impossible; it would mean objectifying not the local worlds but the modern project of which anthropology itself has been a part. To focus on the processes through which local experience is fragmented and absorbed by modernity could be a step toward the protection and resurrection of place.

Although my focus in this chapter has been on the conditions for political activism, the quarry conflict simultaneously illustrates issues of environmental justice and risk distribution. If carried out, the project would have reduced traffic risks in the United States while generating environmental as well as existential risks in its Canadian periphery. The controversy highlights how technology and spirituality represent two alternative sources of ontological security. The modern, secular culture of risk reduction (cf. Beck 1986 [1992]) in the economic centers of the world system aims to generate ontological security through, for instance, improved traffic technology, while the disempowered in the periphery resort to spirituality. In this particular case, it is obvious how the former strategy put the latter at risk by threatening to colonize and literally undermine a central point of reference for Mi'kmaq spirituality and identity. It illustrates how the domain of "technology"—in interfusing the political economy and phenomenology of risk—implicates questions of both power and culture. Although perhaps not quite as evidently as in raw material extraction in so-called developing countries (cf. Johnston 1994; Watts 1994; Rival 1997), the quarry controversy illuminates how the modern project of "development" pursues its utopian vision of security through local, technological risk reduction, while simultaneously generating and exporting other kinds of risk such as the deterioration of the natural environment.

Afterword

Culture, Modernity, and Power—The Relevance of Anthropology

In its pursuit of *difference*, anthropology has thoroughly acquainted itself with human universals, the most prominent of which is *culture* itself: the drive to experience the world as meaningful. The local specificities of such processes of meaning-creation cannot obscure this
fundamental, human commonality that underlies them all. It is not, then,
that anthropology is not interested in so-called human nature, only that
it remains justly skeptical of facile, ideologically grounded definitions of
what is genetically "natural" for our species, whether it be economic
competition, territorial aggression, patriarchy, or whatever. Such abuse of
biology, which *naturalizes* the arbitrary, is very often the language of
power. For more than a century, anthropology has thus been providing
counternarratives to power. Whether we like it or not, our discipline carries some inherently subversive implications. It celebrated cultural diversity even as European high modernity was still hoping to implement uni-
formity on a global scale. In the process, it struggled to relativize Western
conceptions of proper social behavior, economics, personhood, gender,
knowledge, human-environmental relations, and much more.

On the face of it, it would seem, this relativizing mission was successful, at least to the extent that it helped transform the terms of intellectual
debate in the humanities and in much public discourse as well. But, as we
all know, relativism has raised as many problems as it has solved. For one

thing, it has made it evident how intellectual debate can live a life of its own, with very little impact on social, cultural, or political processes in the real world (cf. Bauman 1988). Relativism was to make us more tolerant of otherness, but is this really what we are seeing today? Relativism was to undermine the hegemony of ideologies and power structures founded on narrow perspectives, but has the discourse of Wall Street, the World Bank, and the World Trade Organization in its essentials been in the least perturbed by postmodernism? Rather the opposite, it seems. A recent estimate suggests that the 358 dollar billionaires in the world have assets equaling the annual income of the 45 poorest percent of the world's population, or about 2.7 billion people, and the gap between the wealthiest and the poorest is constantly widening. If such data would strike someone as being beyond the horizons of anthropology, I would not agree. Anything that can be bought for money is per definition a matter of global distribution, and this includes virtually everything that local people everywhere consider essential for a "good life": for instance, security, health, a clean environment, and not least the freedom to live their lives in accordance with their own *cultural definition* of a good life.

So, by and large, it seems that relativism has not posed any real threat to hegemonic power structures. What it *does* seem to have achieved, on the other hand, is to create dilemmas for the human rights movement and other movements driven by a genuine concern to make things better. Postmodern attitudes have in part disarmed movements advocating the use of legal and political institutions to try to *remedy* various kinds of human suffering—suffering generated by those very power structures against which, I believe, postmodernism was originally launched. In other words, the relativistic turn has had little effect where it could have served an emancipatory purpose, while it has been all the more efficient in paralyzing the emancipatory movements themselves. The important lessons to draw from this, I believe, have to do with the location of power. For one thing, power is able to elude deconstruction because we—even anthropologists—are unconsciously selective about the aspects of our world that we are prepared to deconstruct. We are happy to talk about other people's—as well as our own—cultural idiosyncracies in various areas of life, but it seems that the most powerful discourses of our time are those that present themselves as somehow above and beyond culture. These putatively "supra-cultural" discourses, I would argue, today pose one of the greatest challenges to anthropology as a science of culture. Even the claim to be "noncultural" should be subjected to cultural analysis. On one hand, it is important to critically scrutinize such claims of universality and transcendence in order to identify the guiding metaphors and other, tacit, cultural foundations of, for instance, politics, economics, and science. On the other hand, we would do well to remain open to some particular kinds of universalism, namely those that have to do with moral issues such as human rights.

But morality is perhaps ever-present, even in our cognitive practice, for the boundary between representation and morality is often difficult to determine. Let me use my struggles with "machine fetishism" as an example. As I have argued in this book, conventional images of technology and economics misrepresent unequal relations of global exchange as *external* to the technologies "themselves." But if these technologies can be shown to rely, for their very existence, on a net appropriation of resources from a global periphery—gauged in terms of physical parameters such as energy transfers—then I can conclude only that unequal exchange, thus defined, is *intrinsic* to—yes, a *part of*—the technology. It strikes me that this dimension of technology and "development" is being systematically obscured from view by the hegemonic vocabulary of economics: the tautological language of "utility," "willingness to pay," "output and demand," and so on. In fact, then, *even this vocabulary* becomes a part of the technology. Ultimately, it is these *words*—these culturally constituted categories—that keep our machines running and that give some privileged sectors of global society such a tremendous source of power, in every sense of the word. This really shouldn't be such an alien thought to anthropologists. Isn't this exactly the kind of thing that we have been observing about other, particularly non-European kinds of "material culture," namely that artifacts, social relations, and cosmology are embedded in each other and together constitute an integrated whole? Anthropology should be in a unique position to deliver equally revealing perspectives on the material infrastructures by which the urban West defines itself as "modern" and "developed."

But how to handle the power of the machine as a problem of anthropological research? I could, of course, have restricted my studies to the various ways in which machines are fetishized and subjected to ritual behavior in different local contexts. In Peru, for instance, I have seen sewing machines ritually baptized in much the same way as Michael Taussig observed money being baptized in rural Colombia. Rosa Huamaní de Huamán, mother of eight, and her friends in a Lima *barriada* in the early 1980s tied brightly colored ribbons onto their shining new Singer sewing machines and baptized them after their Swedish donors, hoping finally to have found a source of empowerment with which to transcend their marginality. Here again was an expectation of magical potency that merely made more concrete and culturally exotic the technological and economic fetishism of mainstream development discourse. Here again it seemed that anthropological observations in the periphery of the world system could help shed light on the taken-for-granted—yet thoroughly cultural—constructions of the center. But I also wanted to understand why the sewing machines did *not* bring their Peruvian owners the prosperity that they had hoped for, and the answer to that question had to be located far beyond the horizons of Rosa Huamaní de Huamán. Pursuing it meant constructing an alternative image of the machine, beyond its cultural guises in a *barriada* in Lima or a World Bank office in Washington, that would reveal its foundation in unequal exchange and global power structures. This in turn meant investigating conventional economic discourse not only as a cultural text but as an *ideology* involving specific strategies for rendering power and inequality either invisible or inevitable. However contrary it seems to the tenets of postmodern anthropology, I feel that we have to retain the right to identify *mis*representations, or at least *incompleteness* of representations, not only among our academic colleagues but even out there in the real world of politics and business.

The world is still dominated by a cultural model of economic processes that emerged in England at the height of its colonial power. It was originally a local perspective, designed by bankers such as David Ricardo to render meaningful and perhaps also morally justifiable the accumulation of much of the world's wealth in its privileged center. In creating a worldview in which the physical properties of the traded commodities became completely irrelevant, and that instead concerned itself exclusively with abstract exchange values, the founding fathers of economics managed to render invisible a basic mechanism of capitalist accumulation. Even hard mathematical sciences thus rest on assumptions about the world that are the products of cultural, meaning-making processes, and as such they are proper subject matter for anthropology, for one thing because their cultural aspects protrude most clearly precisely when juxtaposed with *other* cultural models, and for another because they are now rapidly being "globalized," as cosmologies have ceased to be territorially bounded phenomena, and European versus "non-European" are no longer very relevant cultural entities. For the moment, however, the point I want to make is that the retreat of economic science into objectivism and mathematics made invisible not only such cultural assumptions but also the *moral* dimension of human exchange. From within this discursive space, it became impossible even to *ask questions* about unequal exchange. It is only when we break out of this discursive space and acknowledge the material dimensions of world trade—the silent but continuous net transfer of productive capacity to the industrialized sectors—that its moral dimensions become visible.

In being able to draw on cross-cultural contrasts and parallels, anthropology has a crucial role to play in the defamiliarization of everyday power. I have tried to bring my point on "machine fetishism" across by comparing it with the fetishization of the Inca emperor. Like the machine, his fetishized office—and body—was a concrete reification of a wider system of material exchanges, and as such was attributed with autonomous productivity. We can now see how both these illusions of autonomous productivity are contingent on specific and unequal terms of exchange. The machine is a paramount symbol of modernity, and the notion of modernity evokes images of a machine-like society. The social condition of modernity has been defined in terms of a number of different features, including heightened reflexivity, an orientation toward the future, and a pursuit of rationally managed homogeneity. A common denominator of these and other features attributed to the modern condition is the pervasive inclination toward *decontextualization*—whether of artifacts, ideas, or human persons. To a large extent, such processes of disembedding, reembedding, and re-disembedding are a consequence of how market institutions operate, and thus ultimately a consequence of money. Commodities, knowledge, and human labor are regularly removed from their original context and shuffled around until recontextualized—if only temporarily—in a new setting. In effect, modernity can be visualized as a selective process in which those artifacts, ideas, and persons are selected for that are least dependent on context. Conversely, the more elaborately a notion, an object, or a human being is dependent on a specific, local context of understanding, the less likely it is to spread. In other words, the more local knowledge that is required to engage a certain item of culture, the less likely it is to become globalized.

What is the relation, then, between culture and modernity? Are not locally specific contexts of understanding, such as profound and long-term familiarity and complex codes of interpretation, in fact the very substance of culture? In this sense, it would seem that modernity does contain aspects that are fundamentally *opposed* to culture. Conversely, assertions of cultural specificity and *non*-interchangeability can be understood as strategies for resisting the mega-machine of modernity. This is exemplified by the Mi'kmaq struggle to safeguard a sacred mountain from being turned into a granite quarry.

I have tried to contextualize this struggle in terms of identity, personhood, and the polarization of the local and the global. This has given me occasion to try to bring together insights from different branches of anthropology that are now less in dialogue with each other than they are with other disciplines such as economics, ecology, and psychology. It has become apparent to me how much anthropology would have to gain from drawing together the fragmentarized pursuits of, for instance, ecological anthropology, economic anthropology, and psychological anthropology into the truly "holistic" inquiry that they could jointly add up to. The ambition of anthropology must be to resist the centrifugal forces of sectorized knowledge production. It is certainly important for anthropology to engage with, and demonstrate its relevance to, domains conventionally reserved for other disciplines, but the challenge is how to do this without losing the core of our own discipline as an integrated perspective on the human predicament.

When the Mi'kmaq opposed themselves to the prospect of finding Kluskap's sacred mountain turned into a granite quarry, almost any conceivable subfield of anthropology could have offered something relevant to say about it. An approach from ecological or environmental anthropology could have focused on the cultural and political dimensions of human-environmental relations, studying environmental negotiations as an arena both for the assertion of local autonomy and for the exercise of centralized power. An approach from economic anthropology could have reflected on the nature and operation of the capitalist world market and on the contrast between the inertia of its impersonal principles, on one hand, and the informal economic life on the reserves, on the other. A psychologically oriented anthropologist could have concentrated on identity and personhood, investigating how a sacred mountain can become a symbol of ethnic—*and* personal—identity strong enough to prompt local people to literally risk their lives to preserve it. Rather than choose *between* these discourses, my ambition has been to show how they are connected to each other. I am convinced that there are fundamental connections between how human beings relate to nature, to each other, and to their own selves, that is, between human ecology, exchange, and personhood. If there is any discipline that should be able to uncover these connections, it is anthropology.

The confrontation between the newborn Mi'kmaq Warrior Society and the mining company was a struggle at many levels, between the local and the global, between spirituality and capitalism, between identities anchored in uniquely meaningful places and identities anchored in boardrooms. It thus very much came to highlight the elusive but pervasive polarity between the modern and the nonmodern, not as periods in history or even sectors of world society but as *modes of life* into which we are *all* variously drawn. Kluskap's sacred mountain came to represent strong emotional and spiritual attachment to the concrete specifics of a unique *place*, and it was obvious how the primary threat to it—and to Mi'kmaq identity—was the very *language* that was imposed on it from the outside, aspiring to define it as an abstract assemblage of natural resources or quantifiable "ecosystem components." The Mi'kmaq were finally successful in reshaping the discursive space of these negotiations, so as to make it permissible to refer to the mountain as "sacred." The underlying message was that neither the mountain nor Mi'kmaq identity is negotiable. Ironically, however, in the process, what had been an argument grounded in the wordless phenomenology of local life-worlds became fetishized into formal, legal discourse, turning the mountain into a monument and the self-professed "traditionalists" into thoroughly *modern* activists. But perhaps this is an inevitable paradox whenever that which is to be rescued from modernity is drawn into the orbit of modern reflexivity precisely because it is recognized as worth rescuing. This is a fundamental paradox of our continuous concern with objectifying *culture*, expressed even more distinctly in the currently fashionable notion of "cultural property." The paradox is very obvious in the struggle to salvage "traditional" or "indigenous" knowledge systems, which are thus reified by the very structures that continue to marginalize them.

The last weekend of July every year since time immemorial, several thousand Mi'kmaq from all the reserves in the Atlantic provinces gather on a little island in the Bras d'Or Lake on Cape Breton that is said to have been a ritual center long before a French mission was established there in the seventeenth century. For several days, the participants immerse themselves in their own specificity, visiting relatives among the tightly packed cabins, drinking tea, gossiping, and sharing the atmosphere of this place so dense in lifelong memories. As an outside observer of such intensely meaningful events, I have felt convinced that a primary objective of anthropology should be to understand the very *relation* between the local and the disembedded. This would include not only local strategies of resistance—and accommodation—to modernity but also, crucially, those very supra-local processes and discursive practices through which local life-worlds are being encompassed, marginalized, and disempowered. The two parts of this book are meant to show that such processes and practices can be challenged either at the macro-level—in their own, rationalist terms—or at the micro-level, by asserting the irreducibility of local modes of being-in-the-world. Rather than entrenching their antagonism, approaches from political economy and phenomenology need to join forces in their parallel struggles to expose the power of the machine.

References

Adams, N. A. 1993. *Worlds Apart: The North-South Divide and the International System.* Zed Books.

Adams, R. McC. 1974. Anthropological Perspectives on Ancient Trade. *Current Anthropology* 15(3):239–258.

Adams, R. N. 1975. *Energy and Structure: A Theory of Social Power.* University of Texas Press.

———. 1978. Man, Energy, and Anthropology: I Can Feel the Heat, But Where's the Light? *American Anthropologist* 80:297–309.

———. 1982. *Paradoxical Harvest: Energy and Explanation in British History, 1870–1914.* Cambridge University Press.

———. 1988. *The Eighth Day: Social Evolution As the Self-Organization of Energy.* University of Texas Press.

Adas, M. 1989. *Machines As the Measure of Men: Science, Technology, and Ideologies of Western Dominance.* Cornell University Press.

Ahonen, P. 1989. The Meaning of Money: Comparing a Peircean and Saussurean Perspective. In R. Kevelson, ed., *Law and Semiotics,* vol. 3, pp. 13–29. Plenum.

Altvater, E., K. Hübner, J. Lorentzen, & R. Rojas, eds. 1987 [1991]. *The Poverty of Nations: A Guide to the Debt Crisis from Argentina to Zaire.* Zed Books.

Amin, S. 1974. *Accumulation on a World Scale.* Monthly Review Press.

Anderson, E. N. 1996. *Ecologies of the Heart: Emotion, Belief, and the Environment.* Oxford University Press.

Anderson, M., J. Deely, M. Krampen, J. Ransdell, T. A. Sebeok, & T. von Uexküll. 1984. A Semiotic Perspective on the Sciences: Steps toward a New Paradigm. *Semiotica* 52:7–47.

Apffel Marglin, F., & S. Marglin, eds. 1990. *Dominating Knowledge: Development, Culture, and Resistance.* Clarendon.

Appadurai, A. 1986. Introduction: Commodities and the Politics of Value. In A.

245

Appadurai, ed., *The Social Life of Things: Commodities in Cultural Perspective*, pp. 3–63. Cambridge University Press.

Apter, E., & W. Pietz, eds. 1993. *Fetishism As Cultural Discourse*. Cornell University Press.

Ardener, E. 1989. *The Voice of Prophecy and Other Essays*. Blackwell.

Århem, K. 1996. The Cosmic Food Web: Human-Nature Relatedness in the Northwest Amazon. In P. Descola & G. Pálsson, eds., *Nature and Society: Anthropological Perspectives*, pp. 185–204. Routledge.

Aristotle. 1962. *The Politics*. Penguin Books.

Baines, G. 1989. Conclusion: Issues in the Application of Traditional Knowledge to Environmental Science. In R. E. Johannes, ed., *Traditional Ecological Knowledge: A Collection of Essays*, pp. 67–69. IUCN, The World Conservation Union.

Banuri, T. 1990. Modernization and Its Discontents: A Cultural Perspective on the Theories of Development. In F. Apffel Marglin & S. Marglin, eds., *Dominating Knowledge: Development, Culture, and Resistance*, pp. 73–101. Clarendon.

Banuri, T., & F. Apffel Marglin, eds. 1993. *Who Will Save the Forests? Knowledge, Power and Environmental Destruction*. Zed Books.

Baran, P. 1957. *The Political Economy of Growth*. Penguin.

Bates, D. G., & S. H. Lees, eds. 1996. *Case Studies in Human Ecology*. Plenum.

Bateson, G. 1972. *Steps to an Ecology of Mind*. Paladin.

———. 1979. *Mind and Nature: A Necessary Unity*. E. P. Dutton.

Baudrillard, J. 1972 [1981]. *For a Critique of the Political Economy of the Sign*. Telos.

———. 1973 [1975]. *The Mirror of Production*. Telos.

———. 1976 [1993]. *Symbolic Exchange and Death*. Sage.

Bauman, Z. 1988. Is There a Postmodern Sociology? *Theory, Culture & Society* 5:217–237.

———. 1989. *Modernity and the Holocaust*. Polity Press/Basil Blackwell.

———. 1992. *Intimations of Postmodernity*. Routledge.

———. 1993. *Postmodern Ethics*. Blackwell.

———. 1998. *Globalization: The Human Consequences*. Polity Press.

Beanlands & Duinker. 1983. *An Ecological Framework for Environmental Impact Assessment in Canada*. Dalhousie University, Halifax.

Beck, U. 1986 [1992]. *Risk Society: Towards a New Modernity*. Sage.

Bennett, J. W. 1990. Ecosystems, Environmentalism, Resource Conservation, and Anthropological Research. In E. F. Moran, ed., *The Ecosystem Approach in Anthropology: From Concept to Practice*, pp. 435–457. University of Michigan Press.

Benton, R. 1982. Economics As a Cultural System. *Journal of Economic Issues* 16(2):461–469.

Berdan, F. F. 1989. Trade and Markets in Precapitalist States. In S. Plattner, ed., *Economic Anthropology*, pp. 78–107. Stanford University Press.

Berkes, F., & C. Folke. 1994. Investing in Cultural Capital for Sustainable Use of Natural Capital. In A. M. Jansson, M. Hammer, C. Folke, & R. Costanza, eds., *Investing in Natural Capital: The Ecological Economics Approach to Sustainability*, pp. 128–149. Island Press.

Berkes, F., C. Folke, & M. Gadgil. 1993. Traditional Ecological Knowledge, Biodiversity, Resilience and Sustainability. *Beijer Discussion Papers* No. 31. Beijer International Institute of Ecological Economics.

Bernstein, R. J. 1983. *Beyond Objectivism and Relativism: Science, Hermeneutics and Praxis*. University of Pennsylvania Press.

Bijker, W. E., T. P. Hughes, & T. J. Pinch. 1987. *The Social Construction of Technological Systems*. The MIT Press.

Bird, E.A.R. 1987. The Social Construction of Nature: Theoretical Approaches to the History of Environmental Problems. *Environmental Review* 11:255–264.

Bird-David, N. 1992. Beyond "The Original Affluent Society": A Culturalist Reformulation. *Current Anthropology* 33:25–47.

———. 1993. Tribal Metaphorization of Human-Nature Relatedness. In K. Milton, ed., *Environmentalism: The View from Anthropology*, pp. 112–125. Routledge.

Blaug, M. 1985. *Economic Theory in Retrospect*. Cambridge University Press.

Bloch, M. 1989. The Symbolism of Money in Imerina. In J. Parry & M. Bloch, eds., *Money and the Morality of Exchange*, pp. 165–190. Cambridge University Press.

———. 1994. Language, Anthropology, and Cognitive Science. In R. Borofsky, ed., *Assessing Cultural Anthropology*, pp. 276–283. McGraw-Hill.

Bohannan, P. 1955. Some Principles of Exchange and Investment among the Tiv. *American Anthropologist* 57:60–70.

Borgström, G. 1965. *The Hungry Planet*. Collier.

Bourdieu, P. 1990. *The Logic of Practice*. Polity.

Bourdillon, M.F.C. 1978. Knowing the World and Hiding It: A Response to M. Bloch. *Man* (N.S.) 13:591–599.

Braudel, F. 1979. *Le Temps du Monde*. Librarie Armand Colin.

Brewer, A. 1990. *Marxist Theories of Imperialism: A Critical Survey*. 2d ed. Routledge.

Brown, L. B. 1995. *State of the World '95*. Worldwatch Institute.

Bruun, H. 1997. *Transdisciplinary Challenges for Human Ecology*. Manuscript. Human Ecology Section, University of Gothenburg.

Bunker, S. G. 1985. *Underdeveloping the Amazon: Extraction, Unequal Exchange and the Failure of the Modern State*. University of Chicago Press.

Carrasco, P. 1982. The Political Economy of the Aztec and Inca States. In G. A. Collier, R. I. Rosaldo, & J. D. Wirth, eds., *The Inca and Aztec States 1400–1800: Anthropology and History*, pp. 23–40. Academic Press.

Cheney, J. 1989. The Neo-Stoicism of Radical Environmentalism. *Environmental Ethics* 11:293–325.

Chew, S. C. 1997. Accumulation, Deforestation, and World Ecological Degradation 2500 B.C. to A.D. 1990. *Advances in Human Ecology* 6:221–255.

Chisholm, M. 1990. The Increasing Separation of Production and Consumption. In B. L. Turner II et al., eds., *The Earth As Transformed by Human Action: Global and Regional Changes in the Biosphere over the Past 300 Years*, pp. 87–101. Cambridge University Press.

Codere, H. 1968. Money-Exchange Systems and a Theory of Money. *Man* (N.S.) 3:557–577.

Cohen, A. P. 1985. *The Symbolic Construction of Community*. Tavistock.

Corbridge, S., & N. Thrift. 1994. Money, Power and Space: Introduction and Overview. In S. Corbridge, R. Martin, & N. Thrift, eds., *Money, Power and Space*, pp. 1–25. Blackwell.

Corson, W. H. 1990. *The Global Ecology Handbook*. Beacon Press.

Costanza, R. 1980. Embodied Energy and Economic Valuation. *Science* 210:1219–1224.

Costanza, R., R. d'Arge, R. de Groot, S. Farber, M. Grasso, B. Hannon, K. Limburg, S. Naeem, R. V. O'Neill, J. Paruelo, R. G. Raskin, P. Sutton, & M. van den Belt. 1997. The Value of the World's Ecosystem Services and Natural Capital. *Nature* 387:253–260.

Crick, M. 1982. Anthropology of Knowledge. *Annual Review of Anthropology* 11:287–313.

Croll, E., & D. Parkin, eds. 1992. *Bush Base—Forest Farm: Culture, Environment and Development*. Routledge.

Cronon, W. 1983. *Changes in the Land: Indians, Colonists, and the Ecology of New England*. Hill and Wang.

———. 1991. *Nature's Metropolis: Chicago and the Great West*. Norton.

Crosby, A. W. 1986. *Ecological Imperialism: The Biological Expansion of Europe, 900–1900*. Cambridge University Press.

Crump, T. 1981. *The Phenomenon of Money*. Routledge & Kegan Paul.

Daly, H. E. 1992. *Steady-State Economics*. Earthscan.

Daly, H. E., & J. B. Cobb, Jr. 1989. *For the Common Good: Redirecting the Economy towards Community, the Environment and a Sustainable Future*. Beacon.

Dasmann, R. 1976. Future Primitive: Ecosystem People versus Biosphere People. *CoEvolution Quarterly* 11:26–31.

Dawkins, R. 1976. *The Selfish Gene*. Oxford University Press.

Debeir, J.-C., J.-P. Deléage, & D. Hémery. 1986 [1991]. *In the Servitude of Power: Energy and Civilization through the Ages*. Zed Books.

de Coppet, D. 1968. Pour une étude des échanges cérémoniels en Mélanésie. *L'Homme* 8(4):45–57.

Denys, N. 1672 [1908]. *Concerning the Ways of the Indians: Their Customs, Dress, Methods of Hunting and Fishing, and Their Amusements*. The Nova Scotia Museum, Halifax.

Descola, P. 1992. Societies of Nature and the Nature of Society. In A. Kuper, ed., *Conceptualizing Society*. Routledge, pp.107–126.

———. 1994. *In the Society of Nature: A Native Ecology in Amazonia*. Cambridge University Press.

———. 1996. Constructing Natures: Symbolic Ecology and Social Practice. In P. Descola & G. Pálsson, eds., *Nature and Society: Anthropological Perspectives*, pp. 82–102. Routledge.

Devall, B., & G. Sessions. 1985. *Deep Ecology: Living As if Nature Mattered*. Peregrine Smith.

Douglas, M. 1966. *Purity and Danger: An Analysis of the Concepts of Pollution and Taboo*. Routledge & Kegan Paul.

———. 1975. Environments at Risk. In *Implicit Meanings: Essays in Anthropology*, pp. 230–248. Routledge & Kegan Paul.

Douglas, M., & B. Isherwood. 1978. *The World of Goods: Towards an Anthropology of Consumption*. Penguin Books.

Dumont, L. 1986. *Essays on Individualism: Modern Ideology in Anthropological Perspective*. University of Chicago Press.

Earle, C. 1988. The Myth of the Southern Soil Miner: Macrohistory, Agricultural Innovation, and Environmental Change. In D. Worster, ed., *The Ends of the Earth: Perspectives on Modern Environmental History*, pp. 175–210. Cambridge University Press.

Ellen, R. F. 1982. *Environment, Subsistence and System: The Ecology of Small-Scale Social Formations.* Cambridge University Press.

———. 1988. Fetishism. *Man* (N.S.) 23:213–235.

———. 1993. Rhetoric, Practice and Incentive in the Face of the Changing Times: A Case Study in Nuaulu Attitudes to Conservation and Deforestation. In K. Milton, ed., *Environmentalism: The View from Anthropology*, pp. 126–143. Routledge.

———. 1996. The Cognitive Geometry of Nature: A Contextual Approach. In P. Descola & G. Pálsson, eds., *Nature and Society: Anthropological Perspectives*, pp. 103–123. Routledge.

Ellul, J. 1954 [1964]. *The Technological Society.* Vintage Books.

Emmanuel, A. 1972. *Unequal Exchange: A Study of the Imperialism of Trade.* Monthly Review Press.

Evans, R. B. 1969. *A Proof That Essergy Is the Only Consistent Measure of Potential Work.* Thesis. Dartmouth College, Hannover, New Hampshire.

Evernden, N. 1985. *The Natural Alien.* University of Toronto Press.

Feit, H. 1973. The Ethno-ecology of the Waswanipi Cree: Or How Hunters Can Manage Their Resources. In B. Cox, ed., *Cultural Ecology: Readings on the Canadian Indians and Eskimos*, pp. 115–125. McClelland and Stewart.

Fieldhouse, D. K., ed. 1967. *The Theory of Capitalist Imperialism.* Longman.

Flannery, K. V. 1968. The Olmec and the Valley of Oaxaca: A Model for Inter-Regional Interaction in Formative Times. In E. P. Benson, ed., *Dumbarton Oaks Conference on the Olmec*, pp. 79–110. Dumbarton Oaks Research Library and Collection.

Folke, C., & T. Kåberger, eds. 1991. *Linking the Natural Environment and the Economy: Essays from the Eco-Eco Group.* Kluwer Academic Publishers.

Foucault, M. 1971. *L'ordre du discours.* Collège de France.

Francis, D. 1992. *The Imaginary Indian: The Image of the Indian in Canadian Culture.* Arsenal Pulp.

Frank, A. G. 1959. Industrial Capital Stocks and Energy Consumption. *Economic Journal* 69:170–174.

———. 1966. The Development of Underdevelopment. *Monthly Review* 18:17–31.

———. 1967. *Capitalism and Underdevelopment in Latin America.* Monthly Review Press.

———. 1978. *World Accumulation 1492–1789.* Monthly Review Press.

———. 1995. The Modern World System Revisited. In S. K. Sanderson, ed., *Civilizations and World Systems: Studying World-Historical Change*, pp. 163–194. AltaMira.

Frank, A. G., & B. K. Gills, eds. 1993. *The World System: Five Hundred Years or Five Thousand?* Routledge.

Friedman, J. 1974a. Marxism, Structuralism, and Vulgar Materialism. *Man* (N.S.) 9:444–469.

———. 1974b. The Place of Fetishism and the Problem of Materialist Interpretations. *Critique of Anthropology* 1:26–62.

———. 1979. Hegelian Ecology: Between Rousseau and the World Spirit. In P. C. Burnham & R. F. Ellen, eds., *Social and Ecological Systems*. Academic Press, 253–270.

———. 1979 [1998]. *System, Structure, and Contradiction: The Evolution of Asiatic Social Formations*. 2d ed. AltaMira.

———. 1983. Civilizational Cycles and the History of Primitivism. *Social Analysis* 14:31–52.

Gadgil, M. 1991. Traditional Resource Management Systems. *Resource Management and Optimization* 8:127–141.

Gaggioli, R. A., ed. 1980. *Thermodynamics: Second Law Analysis*. American Chemical Society.

Gall, P. L., & A. A. Saxe. 1977. The Ecological Evolution of Culture: The State As Predator in Succession Theory. In T. K. Earle & J. E. Ericson, eds., *Exchange Systems in Prehistory*, pp. 255–268. Academic Press.

Geertz, C. 1983. *Local Knowledge: Further Essays in Interpretive Anthropology*. Basic Books.

Georgescu-Roegen, N. 1971. *The Entropy Law and the Economic Process*. Harvard University Press.

Giddens, A. 1990. *The Consequences of Modernity*. Polity.

———. 1991. *Modernity and Self-Identity: Self and Society in the Late Modern Age*. Polity.

Gills, B. K., & A. G. Frank. 1993. The 5,000-Year World System: An Interdisciplinary Introduction. In A. G. Frank & B. K. Gills, eds., *The World System: Five Hundred Years or Five Thousand?*, pp. 3–55. Routledge.

Glansdorff, P., & I. Prigogine. 1971. *Structure, Stability, and Fluctuations*. Wiley.

Godelier, M. 1969. La monnaie de sel des Baruya de Nouvelle-Guinée. *L'Homme* 9(2):5–37.

———. 1986. *The Mental and the Material*. Verso.

———. 1994. Mirror, Mirror on the Wall . . . The Once and Future Role of Anthropology: A Tentative Assessment. In R. Borofsky, ed., *Assessing Cultural Anthropology*, pp. 97–109. McGraw-Hill.

Goffman, E. 1959 [1969]. *The Presentation of Self in Everyday Life*. Allen Lane/The Penguin Press.

Grand Council of Mi'kmaq. 1987. *The Mi'kmaq Treaty Handbook*. Native Communications Society of Nova Scotia, Sydney.

Grove-White, R. 1993. Environmentalism: A New Moral Discourse for Technological Society? In K. Milton, ed., *Environmentalism: The View from Anthropology*, pp. 18–30. Routledge.

Gudeman, S. 1986. *Economics As Culture: Models and Metaphors of Livelihood*. Routledge & Kegan Paul.

Gudeman, S., & A. Rivera. 1989. Colombian Conversations: The Strength of the Earth. *Current Anthropology* 30:267–281.

Haas, J., S. Pozorski, & T. Pozorski, eds. 1987. *The Origins and Development of the Andean State*. Cambridge University Press.

Habermas, J. 1987. *The Theory of Communicative Action.* Vol. 2. Beacon.

Hajer, M. A. 1995. *The Politics of Environmental Discourse: Ecological Modernisation and the Policy Process.* Clarendon Press.

Hannerz, U. 1989. *Scenarios for Peripheral Cultures.* Symposium on Culture, Globalization, and the World-System. State University of New York at Binghamton.

Harries-Jones, P. 1993. Between Science and Shamanism: The Advocacy of Environmentalism in Toronto. In K. Milton, ed., *Environmentalism: The View from Anthropology*, pp. 43–58. Routledge.

Hart, K. 1999. *An Unequal World: Money As the Problem and the Solution.* Manuscript.

Harvey, D. 1989.*The Condition of Postmodernity.* Blackwell.

———. 1996. *Justice, Nature and the Geography of Difference.* Blackwell.

Hastings, C. M. 1987. Implications of Andean Verticality in the Evolution of Political Complexity: A View from the Margins. In J. Haas, S. Pozorski, & T. Pozorski, eds., *The Origins and Development of the Andean State*, pp. 145–157. Cambridge University Press.

Helms, M. W. 1981. Precious Metals and Politics: Style and Ideology in the Intermediate Area and Peru. *Journal of Latin American Lore* 7:215–238.

Hemming, J. 1970. *The Conquest of the Incas.* Abacus.

Hettne, B. 1990. *Development Theory and the Three Worlds.* Longman.

Hirschman, A. O. 1970. *Exit, Voice, and Loyalty.* Harvard University Press.

Hodder, I. 1986. *Reading the Past: Current Approaches to Interpretation in Archaeology.* Cambridge University Press.

Hoffman, B. G. 1946. *The Historical Ethnography of the Micmac of the Sixteenth and Seventeenth Centuries.* Thesis. Department of Anthropology, University of California.

Hoffmeyer, J. 1993 [1996]. *Signs of Meaning in the Universe.* Indiana University Press.

Holling, C. S., & S. Sanderson. 1996. Dynamics of (Dis)harmony in Ecological and Social Systems. In S. S. Hanna, C. Folke, & K.-G. Mäler, eds., *Rights to Nature: Ecological, Economic, Cultural, and Political Principles of Institutions for the Environment*, pp. 57–85. Island Press.

Horkheimer, M., & T. Adorno. 1944 [1972]. *The Dialectic of Enlightenment.* Seabury Press.

Hornborg, A. 1988. *Dualism and Hierarchy in Lowland South America: Trajectories of Indigenous Social Organization.* Uppsala Studies in Cultural Anthropology 9. Stockholm: Almqvist & Wiksell.

———. 1990. Highland and Lowland Conceptions of Social Space in South America: Some Ethnoarchaeological Affinities. *Folk* 32:61–92.

———. 1993. Panoan Marriage Sections: A Comparative Perspective. *Ethnology* 32:101–108.

———. 1998a. Mi'kmaq Environmentalism: Local Incentives and Global Projections. In A. Sandberg & S. Sörlin, eds., *Sustainability—The Challenge: People, Power and the Environment*, pp. 202–211. Black Rose Books.

———. 1998b. Serial Redundancy in Amazonian Social Structure: Is There a Method for Poststructuralist Comparison? In M. Godelier, T. R. Trautmann, &

F. E. Tjon Sie Fat, eds., *Transformations of Kinship*, pp. 168–186. Smithsonian Institution.

———. 1999. Comment on Nurit Bird-David, " 'Animism' Revisited: Personhood, Environment, and Relational Epistemology." *Current Anthropology* 40:1:S80-S81.

Hughes, J. D. 1994. *Pan's Travail: Environmental Problems of the Ancient Greeks and Romans*. Johns Hopkins University Press.

Hultkrantz, Å. 1961. The Owner of the Animals in the Religion of the North American Indians. In Å. Hultkrantz, ed., *The Supernatural Owners of Nature*, pp. 53–64. Stockholm Studies in Comparative Religion 1.

Ingerson, A. E. 1994. Tracking and Testing the Nature/Culture Dichotomy. In C. L. Crumley, ed., *Historical Ecology: Cultural Knowledge and Changing Landscapes*, pp. 43–66. School of American Research Press.

Ingold, T. 1979. The Social and Ecological Relations of Culture-Bearing Organisms: An Essay in Evolutionary Dynamics. In P. C. Burnham & R. F. Ellen, eds., *Social and Ecological Systems*, pp. 271–292. Academic Press.

———. 1986. *The Appropriation of Nature: Essays on Human Ecology and Social Relations*. Manchester University Press.

———. 1988. Tools, Minds and Machines: An Excursion in the Philosophy of Technology. *Techniques et culture* 12:151–176.

———. 1992. Culture and the Perception of the Environment. In E. Croll & D. Parkin, eds., *Bush Base—Forest Farm: Culture, Environment, and Development*, pp. 39–56. Routledge.

———. 1993. Globes and Spheres: The Topology of Environmentalism. In K. Milton, ed., *Environmentalism: The View from Anthropology*, pp. 31–42. Routledge.

———. 1996. Hunting and Gathering As Ways of Perceiving the Environment. In R. Ellen & K. Fukui, eds., *Redefining Nature: Ecology, Culture and Domestication*, pp. 117–155. Berg.

Isbell, B. J. 1985. The Metaphoric Process: "From Culture to Nature and Back Again." In G. Urton, ed., *Animal Myths and Metaphors in South America*, pp. 285–313. University of Utah Press.

Isbell, W. H. 1987. State Origins in the Ayacucho Valley, Central Highlands, Peru. In J. Haas, S. Pozorski, & T. Pozorski, eds., *The Origins and Development of the Andean State*, pp. 83–90. Cambridge University Press.

———. 1988. City and State in Middle Horizon Huari. In R. W. Keatinge, ed., *Peruvian Prehistory: An Overview of Pre-Inca and Inca Society*, pp. 164–189. Cambridge University Press.

Jackson, M. 1983. Thinking through the Body: An Essay on Understanding Metaphor. *Social Analysis* 14:127–148.

Jansson, A. M., M. Hammer, C. Folke, & R. Costanza, eds. 1994. *Investing in Natural Capital: The Ecological Economics Approach to Sustainability*. Island Press.

Johannes, R. E., ed. 1989. *Traditional Ecological Knowledge: A Collection of Essays*. IUCN, The World Conservation Union.

Johnston, B. R., ed. 1994. *Who Pays the Price? The Sociocultural Context of Environmental Crisis*. Island Press.

Jones, C. 1979. *Tikal As a Trading Center: Why It Rose and Fell*. Paper presented at the XLIII International Congress of Americanists, Vancouver.

Julien, C. J. 1982. Inca Decimal Administration in the Lake Titicaca Region. In G. A. Collier, R. I. Rosaldo, & J. D. Wirth, eds., *The Inca and Aztec States 1400–1800: Anthropology and History*, pp. 119–151. Academic Press.

Kåberger, T. 1991. Measuring Instrumental Value in Energy Terms. In C. Folke & T. Kåberger, eds., *Linking the Natural Environment and the Economy: Essays from the Eco-Eco Group*, pp. 61–75. Kluwer Academic Publishers.

Kay, J. 1985. Native Americans in the Fur Trade and Wildlife Depletion. *Environmental Review* 9:118–130.

Keatinge, R. W. 1981. The Nature and Role of Religious Diffusion in the Early Stages of State Formation: An Example from Peruvian Prehistory. In G. D. Jones & R. R. Kautz, eds., *The Transition to Statehood in the New World*, pp. 172–187. Cambridge University Press.

———, ed. 1988. *Peruvian Prehistory: An Overview of Pre-Inca and Inca Society*. Cambridge University Press.

Klymyshyn, A. M. U. 1987. The Development of Chimu Administration in Chan Chan. In J. Haas, S. Pozorski, & T. Pozorski, eds., *The Origins and Development of the Andean State*, pp. 97–110. Cambridge University Press.

Kopytoff, I. 1986. The Cultural Biography of Things: Commoditization As Process. In A. Appadurai, ed., *The Social Life of Things: Commodities in Cultural Perspective*, pp. 64–91. Cambridge University Press.

Körner, P., G. Maass, T. Siebold, & R. Tetzlaff. 1984 [1986]. *The IMF and the Debt Crisis: A Guide to the Third World's Dilemmas*. Zed Books.

Krech, S., ed. 1981. *Indians, Animals and the Fur Trade*. University of Georgia Press.

Larsen, T. 1983. Negotiating Identity: The Micmac of Nova Scotia. In A. Tanner, ed., *The Politics of Indianness: Case Studies of Native Ethnopolitics in Canada*, pp. 37–136. Memorial University of Newfoundland.

Lasch, C. 1980. *The Culture of Narcissism*. Abacus.

Lash, S., & J. Urry. 1994. *Economies of Signs and Space*. Sage.

Lathrap, D. W., D. Collier, & H. Chandra. 1975. *Ancient Ecuador: Culture, Clay and Creativity 3000–300 B.C.* Field Museum of Natural History, Chicago.

Leach, E. R. 1976. *Culture and Communication*. Cambridge University Press.

Lechtman, H. 1984. Andean Value Systems and the Development of Prehistoric Metallurgy. *Technology and Culture* 25:1–36.

Le Clercq, C. 1691 [1910]. *New Relation of Gaspesia with the Customs and Religion of the Gaspesian Indians*. Translated and edited by W. F. Ganong. The Champlain Society, Toronto.

Lee, R. B. 1988. Reflections on Primitive Communism. In T. Ingold, D. Riches, & J. Woodburn, eds., *Hunters and Gatherers*. Vol. 1, *History, Evolution and Social Change*, pp. 252–268. Berg.

Lescarbot, M. 1609 [1928]. *Nova Francia: A Description of Acadia, 1606*. Translated by P. Erondelle. George Routledge & Sons.

LeVine, R. A. 1984. Properties of Culture: An Ethnographic View. In R. A. Shweder & R. A. LeVine, eds., *Culture Theory: Essays on Mind, Self, and Emotion*, pp. 67–87. Cambridge University Press.

Lévi-Strauss, C. 1963. *Structural Anthropology*. Allen Lane/The Penguin Press.

———. 1969. *The Elementary Structures of Kinship*. Eyre & Spottiswoode.

Lithman, Y. 1978. *The Community Apart: A Case Study of a Canadian Indian Reserve Community.* Stockholm Studies in Social Anthropology 6. Department of Social Anthropology, University of Stockholm.

Löfgren, O., M. Harbsmeier, & M. Trolle Larsen, eds. 1990. *Consumption.* Culture & History 7. Akademisk Forlag.

Lomborg, B. 1998. *Verdens sande tilstand.* Centrum.

Luxemburg, R. 1913 [1951]. *The Accumulation of Capital.* Routledge & Kegan Paul.

Lyotard, J.-F. 1979 [1984]. *The Postmodern Condition: A Report on Knowledge.* Manchester University Press.

MacGaffey, W. 1990. The Personhood of Ritual Objects: Kongo *Minkisi. Etnofoor* 3(1):45–61.

Mackey, C. J. 1987. Chimu Administration in the Provinces. In J. Haas, S. Pozorski, & T. Pozorski, eds., *The Origins and Development of the Andean State*, pp. 121–129. Cambridge University Press.

Månsson, B. Å., & J. M. McGlade. 1993. Ecology, Thermodynamics and H. T. Odum's Conjectures. *Oecologia* 93:582–596.

Marcos, J. G. 1977/78. Cruising to Acapulco and Back with the Thorny Oyster Set: A Model for a Lineal Exchange System. *Journal of the Steward Anthropological Society* 9:99–132.

Marcus, G. E., & M. M. J. Fischer. 1986. *Anthropology As Cultural Critique: An Experimental Moment in the Human Sciences.* The University of Chicago Press.

Marglin, S. 1990. Towards the Decolonization of the Mind. In F. Apffel Marglin & S. Marglin, eds., *Dominating Knowledge: Development, Culture, and Resistance*, pp. 1–28. Clarendon.

Marsh, G. P. 1864 [1965]. *Man and Nature: The Earth As Modified by Human Action.* Belknap Press of Harvard University Press.

Marshall, D., A. Denny, & S. Marshall. 1989. The Mi'kmaq: The Covenant Chain. In B. Richardson, ed., *Drumbeat: Anger and Renewal in Indian Country*, pp. 71–104. Summerhill Press/The Assembly of First Nations.

Martin, C. 1978. *Keepers of the Game: Indian-Animal Relationships and the Fur Trade.* University of California Press.

Martinez-Alier, J. 1987. *Ecological Economics: Energy, Environment and Society.* Blackwell.

Martinez-Alier, J., & M. O'Connor 1996. Ecological and Economic Distribution Conflicts. In R. Costanza & O. Segura, eds., *Getting Down to Earth: Practical Applications of Ecological Economics*, pp. 153–183. Island Press.

Marx, K. 1867 [1976]. *Capital: A Critique of Political Economy.* Vol. 1. Penguin Books.

———. 1894 [1967]. *Capital: A Critique of Political Economy.* Vol. 3. International Publishers.

Masuda, S., I. Shimada, & C. Morris, eds. 1985. *Andean Ecology and Civilization: An Interdisciplinary Perspective on Andean Ecological Complementarity.* University of Tokyo Press.

Maturana, H. R., & F. J. Varela. 1987 [1992]. *The Tree of Knowledge: The Biological Roots of Human Understanding.* Shambhala.

Mauss, M. 1923–24 [1967]. *The Gift.* Norton.

May, E. 1982. *Budworm Battles: The Fight to Stop the Aerial Insecticide Spraying of the Forests of Eastern Canada.* Four East Publications.

McEvoy, A. F. 1988. Toward an Interactive Theory of Nature and Culture: Ecology, Production, and Cognition in the California Fishing Industry. In D. Worster, ed., *The Ends of the Earth: Perspectives on Modern Environmental History*, pp. 211–229. Cambridge University Press.

Merchant, C. 1989. *Ecological Revolutions: Nature, Gender, and Science in New England*. University of North Carolina Press.

Miller, D. 1987. *Material Culture and Mass Consumption*. Blackwell.

———. 1990. Persons and Blue Jeans: Beyond Fetishism. *Etnofoor* 3(1):97–111.

Miller, J. G. 1965. Living Systems: Basic Concepts. *Behavioural Science* 10:193–237, 337–379.

Millon, R. 1988. The Last Years of Teotihuacan Dominance. In N. Yoffee & G. L. Cowgill, eds., *The Collapse of Ancient States and Civilizations*, pp. 102–164. University of Arizona Press.

Milton, K., ed. 1993. *Environmentalism: The View from Anthropology*. Routledge.

Mommersteeg, G. 1990. Allah's Words As Amulet. *Etnofoor* 3(1):63–76.

Moran, E. F., ed. 1990. *The Ecosystem Approach in Anthropology: From Concept to Practice*. University of Michigan Press.

———. 1993. *Through Amazonian Eyes: The Human Ecology of Amazonian Populations*. University of Iowa Press.

Morris, C. 1978. The Archaeological Study of Andean Exchange Systems. In C. L. Redman, ed., *Social Archaeology: Beyond Subsistence and Dating*, pp. 315–327. Academic Press.

———. 1979. Maize Beer in the Economics, Politics and Religion of the Inca Empire. In C. F. Gastineau, W. J. Darby, & T. B. Turner, eds., *Fermented Food Beverages in Nutrition*, pp. 21–34. Academic Press.

———. 1982. The Infrastructure of Inka Control in the Peruvian Central Highlands. In G. A. Collier, R. I. Rosaldo, & J. D. Wirth, eds., *The Inca and Aztec States 1400–1800: Anthropology and History*, pp. 153–171. Academic Press.

Mumford, L. 1934. *The Myth of the Machine: Technics and Civilization*. Harcourt, Brace & World.

Munn, N. 1986. *The Fame of Gawa*. Cambridge University Press.

Murra, J. V. 1956 [1980]. *The Economic Organization of the Inka State*. Supplement 1 to *Research in Economic Anthropology*. JAI Press.

———. 1962. Cloth and Its Functions in the Inca State. *American Anthropologist* 64:710–728.

———. 1971 [1975]. El tráfico de mullu en la costa del Pacífico. In *Formaciones económicas y políticas del mundo andino*, pp. 255–267. Instituto de Estudios Peruanos, Lima.

———. 1972 [1975]. El control vertical de un máximo de pisos ecológicos en la economía de las sociedades andinas. In *Formaciones económicas y políticas del mundo andino*, pp. 59–115. Instituto de Estudios Peruanos, Lima.

———. 1982. The Mitá Obligations of Ethnic Groups to the Inka State. In G. A. Collier, R. I. Rosaldo, & J. D. Wirth, eds., *The Inca and Aztec States 1400–1800: Anthropology and History*, pp. 237–262. Academic Press.

Naess, A. 1973 [1989]. *Ecology, Community and Lifestyle*. Cambridge University Press.

―――. 1995. Industrial Society, Postmodernity, and Ecological Sustainability. *Humboldt Journal of Social Relations* 21(1):131–146.

Nöth, W. 1996. The Sign Nature of Commodities. In M. Meyer et al., eds., *Tangenten: Literatur & Geschichte*. Lit Verlag.

Odum, H. T. 1971. *Environment, Power, and Society*. Wiley-Interscience.

―――. 1988. Self-Organization, Transformity, and Information. *Science* 242:1132–1139.

Odum, H. T., & J. E. Arding. 1991. *Emergy Analysis of Shrimp Mariculture in Ecuador*. Working paper prepared for Coastal Resources Center, University of Rhode Island, Narragansett, Rhode Island.

Orton, D. 1992. *"Sustainable Development" and Conceptual Enclosure*. Occasional bulletin from the *Green Web*.

Pálsson, G. 1996. Human-Environmental Relations: Orientalism, Paternalism and Communalism. In P. Descola & G. Pálsson, eds., *Nature and Society: Anthropological Perspectives*, pp. 63–81. Routledge.

Parry, J., & M. Bloch. 1989. Introduction: Money and the Morality of Exchange. In J. Parry & M. Bloch, eds., *Money and the Morality of Exchange*, pp. 1–32. Cambridge University Press.

Parsons, E. C. 1925. Micmac Folklore. *Journal of American Folklore* 38:87.

Paulsen, A. C. 1974. The Thorny Oyster and the Voice of God: Spondylus and Strombus in Andean Prehistory. *American Antiquity* 39:597–607.

―――. 1977. Patterns of Maritime Trade between South Coastal Ecuador and Western Mesoamerica, 1500 B.C.–A.D. 600. In E. P. Benson, ed., *The Sea in the Pre-Columbian World*, pp. 141–160. Dumbarton Oaks Research Library and Collection.

Pease G. Y., F. 1982. The Formation of Tawantinsuyu: Mechanisms of Colonization and Relationship with Ethnic Groups. In G. A. Collier, R. I. Rosaldo, & J. D. Wirth, eds., *The Inca and Aztec States 1400–1800: Anthropology and History*, pp. 173–198. Academic Press.

Peirce, C. S. 1931–1958. *Collected Papers*. Vols. 1–6. Harvard University Press.

Pfaffenberger, B. 1988a. Fetishised Objects and Humanised Nature: Towards an Anthropology of Technology. *Man* (N.S.) 23:236–252.

―――. 1988b. *The Hindu Akama Temple As a Machine, or, The Western Machine As a Temple*. Manuscript.

Pietz, W. 1985. The Problem of the Fetish, I. *Res* 9:5–17.

―――. 1987. The Problem of the Fetish, II. *Res* 13:23–45.

―――. 1988. The Problem of the Fetish, III. *Res* 16:105–123.

―――. 1993. Fetishism and Materialism: The Limits of Theory in Marx. In E. Apter & W. Pietz, eds., *Fetishism As Cultural Discourse*, pp. 119–151. Cornell University Press.

Polanyi, K. 1944. *The Great Transformation*. Holt, Rinehart and Winston.

―――. 1957. The Economy As Instituted Process. In K. Polanyi, C. Arensberg, & H. W. Pearson, eds., *Trade and Markets in the Early Empires*, pp. 243–270. The Free Press.

―――. 1968. The Semantics of Money-Uses. In G. Dalton, ed., *Primitive, Archaic and Modern Economies: Essays of Karl Polanyi*, pp. 175–203. Beacon Press.

Ponting, C. 1991. *A Green History of the World: The Environment and the Collapse of Great Civilizations*. Penguin Books.

Pool, R. 1990. Fetishism Deconstructed. *Etnofoor* 3(1):114–127.

Posey, D. A., & W. Balée, eds. 1989. Resource Management in Amazonia: Indigenous and Folk Strategies. *Advances in Economic Botany 7*.

Prigogine, I., & I. Stengers. 1984. *Order out of Chaos*. Bantam Books.

Radetzki, M. 1990. *Tillväxt och miljö*. SNS Förlag.

———. 1992. Economic Growth and Environment. In P. Low, ed., *International Trade and the Environment*. The World Bank.

Radin, P. 1957. *Primitive Man As a Philosopher*. Dover.

Rappaport, R. A. 1968. *Pigs for the Ancestors: Ritual in the Ecology of a New Guinea People*. Yale.

———. 1979. *Ecology, Meaning, and Religion*. North Atlantic Books.

———. 1990. Ecosystems, Populations and People. In E. F. Moran, ed., *The Ecosystem Approach in Anthropology: From Concept to Practice*, pp. 41–72. University of Michigan Press.

———. 1994. Humanity's Evolution and Anthropology's Future. In R. Borofsky, ed., *Assessing Cultural Anthropology*, pp. 153–166. McGraw-Hill.

Rathje, W. L. 1973. Classic Maya Development and Denouement: A Research Design. In T. P. Culbert, ed., *The Classic Maya Collapse*, pp. 405–454. University of New Mexico Press.

Raymond, J. S. 1988. A View from the Tropical Forest. In R. W. Keatinge, ed., *Peruvian Prehistory: An Overview of Pre-Inca and Inca Society*, pp. 279–300. Cambridge University Press.

Rayner, S. 1989. Fiddling While the Globe Warms? *Anthropology Today* 5:1–2.

Rees, W. E., & M. Wackernagel. 1994. Ecological Footprints and Appropriated Carrying Capacity: Measuring the Natural Capital Requirements of the Human Economy. In A. M. Jansson, M. Hammer, C. Folke, & R. Costanza, eds., *Investing in Natural Capital: The Ecological Economics Approach to Sustainability*, pp. 362–390. Island Press.

Relph, E. 1976. *Place and Placelessness*. Pion.

Rival, L. 1997. Oil and Sustainable Development in the Latin American Humid Tropics. *Anthropology Today* 13(6):1–3.

Rosaldo, R. I. 1982. Afterword. In G. A. Collier, R. I. Rosaldo, & J. D. Wirth, eds., *The Inca and Aztec States 1400–1800: Anthropology and History*, pp. 459–464. Academic Press.

Rostworowski de Diez Canseco, M. 1977. Coastal Fishermen, Merchants, and Artisans in Pre-Hispanic Peru. In E. P. Benson, ed., *The Sea in the Pre-Columbian World*, pp. 167–186. Dumbarton Oaks Research Library and Collection.

Rowe, J. H. 1982. Inca Policies and Institutions Relating to the Cultural Unification of the Empire. In G. A. Collier, R. I. Rosaldo, & J. D. Wirth, eds., *The Inca and Aztec States 1400–1800: Anthropology and History*, pp. 93–118. Academic Press.

Ruyle, E. E. 1973. Slavery, Surplus, and Stratification on the Northwest Coast: The Ethnoenergetics of an Incipient Stratification System. *Current Anthropology* 14(5):603–631.

———. 1977. Energy and Culture. In B. Banardi, ed., *The Concept and Dynamics of Culture*, pp. 209–237. Mouton.

Sabloff, J. A., & C. C. Lamberg-Karlovsky, eds. 1974. *The Rise and Fall of Civiliza-tions: Modern Archaeological Approaches to Ancient Cultures.* Cummings.

Sahlins, M. D. 1972. *Stone Age Economics.* Aldine.

————. 1976. *Culture and Practical Reason.* University of Chicago Press.

Sahlins, M. D., & E. R. Service. 1960. *Evolution and Culture.* University of Michigan Press.

Sallnow, M. J. 1989. Precious Metals in the Andean Moral Economy. In J. Parry & M. Bloch, eds., *Money and the Morality of Exchange*, pp. 209–231. Cambridge University Press.

Salomon, F. 1986. *Native Lords of Quito in the Age of the Incas: The Political Economy of North Andean Chiefdoms.* Cambridge University Press.

Sanderson, S. K., ed. 1995. *Civilizations and World Systems: Studying World-Historical Change.* AltaMira.

Saussure, F. de. 1916 [1966]. *Course in General Linguistics.* McGraw-Hill.

Sayen, J. 1990. Ecological Ignorance: Why the Environmental Movement Was Still-born. *Glacial Erratic* 2(3):23–25.

Schacht, J. 1973. *Anthropologie culturelle de l'argent.* Payot.

Schreiber, K. J. 1987. From State to Empire: The Expansion of Wari Outside the Ayacucho Basin. In J. Haas, S. Pozorski, & T. Pozorski, eds., *The Origins and De-velopment of the Andean State*, pp. 91–96. Cambridge University Press.

Schrödinger, E. 1944 [1967]. *What Is Life? Mind and Matter.* Cambridge University Press.

Sebeok, T. A. 1994. *Signs: An Introduction to Semiotics.* University of Toronto Press.

Shimada, I. 1985. Perception, Procurement, and Management of Resources: Ar-chaeological Perspective. In S. Masuda, I. Shimada, & C. Morris, eds., *Andean Ecology and Civilization: An Interdisciplinary Perspective on Andean Ecological Com-plementarity*, pp. 357–399. University of Tokyo Press.

————. 1987. Horizontal and Vertical Dimensions of Prehistoric States in North Peru. In J. Haas, S. Pozorski, & T. Pozorski, eds., *The Origins and Development of the Andean State*, pp. 130–144. Cambridge University Press.

Shiva, V. 1991. *The Violence of the Green Revolution.* Zed Books.

————. 1993. *Monocultures of the Mind.* Zed Books.

Shweder, R. A., & E. J. Bourne. 1984. Does the Concept of the Person Vary Cross-culturally? In R. A. Shweder & R.A. LeVine, eds., *Culture Theory: Essays on Mind, Self, and Emotion*, pp. 158–199. Cambridge University Press.

Simmel, G. 1900 [1990]. *The Philosophy of Money.* Routledge.

Simmons, I. G. 1993. *Environmental History: A Concise Introduction.* Blackwell.

Singer, M. 1984. *Man's Glassy Essence: Explorations in Semiotic Anthropology.* Indi-ana University Press.

Sperber, D. 1985. *On Anthropological Knowledge.* Cambridge University Press.

Spyer, P., ed. 1998. *Border Fetishisms: Material Objects in Unstable Spaces.* Routledge.

Steiner, D. 1993. Human Ecology As Transdisciplinary Science, and Science As Part of Human Ecology. In D. Steiner & M. Nauser, eds., *Human Ecology: Frag-ments of Anti-Fragmentary Views of the World*, pp. 47–76. Routledge.

Stewart, K. 1988. Nostalgia: A Polemic. *Cultural Anthropology* 3:227–241.

Stover, C. F., ed. 1962. "The Encyclopedia Britannica Conference on the Techno-logical Order." Special issue of *Technology and Culture.*

Suzuki, D., & P. Knudtson. 1992. *Wisdom of the Elders: Sacred Native Stories of Nature.* Bantam.

Szerszynski, B. 1996. On Knowing What to Do: Environmentalism and the Modern Problematic. In S. Lash, B. Szerszynski, & B. Wynne, eds., *Risk, Environment and Modernity: Towards a New Ecology,* pp. 104–137. Sage.

Taussig, M. T. 1980. *The Devil and Commodity Fetishism in South America.* The University of North Carolina Press.

———. 1993. *Maleficium:* State Fetishism. In E. Apter & W. Pietz, eds., *Fetishism As Cultural Discourse,* pp. 217–247. Cornell University Press.

Thoden van Velzen, B. 1990. Social Fetishism among the Surinamese Maroons. *Etnofoor* 3(1):77–95.

Thomas, W. L., Jr., ed. 1956. *Man's Role in Changing the Face of the Earth.* University of Chicago Press.

Tönnies, F. 1887 [1963]. *Community and Society.* Michigan University Press.

Topic, J., & T. Topic. 1987. The Archaeological Investigation of Andean Militarism: Some Cautionary Observations. In J. Haas, S. Pozorski, & T. Pozorski, eds., *The Origins and Development of the Andean State,* pp. 47–55. Cambridge University Press.

Tucker, R. P. 1988. The Depletion of India's Forests under British Imperialism: Planters, Foresters, and Peasants in Assam and Kerala. In D. Worster, ed., *The Ends of the Earth: Perspectives on Modern Environmental History,* pp. 118–140. Cambridge University Press.

Turner, B. L., II, W. C. Clark, R. W. Kates, J. F. Richards, J. T. Mathews, & W. B. Meyer, eds. 1990. *The Earth as Transformed by Human Action: Global and Regional Changes in the Biosphere over the Past 300 Years.* Cambridge University Press.

Vayda, A. P. 1986. Holism and Individualism in Ecological Anthropology. *Reviews in Anthropology* (fall):295–313.

von Uexküll, J. 1940 [1982]. The Theory of Meaning. *Semiotica* 42:25–82.

von Uexküll, T. 1982. Introduction: Meaning and Science in Jakob von Uexküll's Concept of Biology. *Semiotica* 42:1–24.

Wachtel, N. 1982. The Mitimas of the Cochabamba Valley: The Colonization Policy of Huayna Capac. In G. A. Collier, R. I. Rosaldo, & J. D. Wirth, eds., *The Inca and Aztec States 1400–1800: Anthropology and History,* pp. 199–235. Academic Press.

Wackernagel, M., & W. E. Rees. 1996. *Our Ecological Footprint: Reducing Human Impact on the Earth.* New Society Publishers.

Wackernagel, M., L. Onisto, A. Callejas Linares, I. S. López, J. Falfán, A. I. Méndez García, & M. G. Suárez Guerrero. 1997. *Ecological Footprints of Nations.* Centre for Sustainability Studies, Universidad Anáhuac de Xalapa, Mexico.

Wagner, R. 1986. *Symbols That Stand for Themselves.* University of Chicago Press.

Wall, G. 1986. *Exergy: A Useful Concept.* Thesis. Chalmers Tekniska Högskola, Gothenburg.

Wallerstein, I. M. 1974. The Rise and Future Demise of the World Capitalist System: Concepts for Comparative Analysis. *Comparative Studies in Society and History* 16:387–415.

———. 1974–1989. *The Modern World System I–III.* Academic Press.

Wassén, S. H. 1972. A Medicine-Man's Implements and Plants in a Tiahuanacoid Tomb in Highland Bolivia. *Etnologiska studier* 32:8–114.

Watts, M. J. 1994. Oil As Money: The Devil's Excrement and the Spectacle of Black Gold. In S. Corbridge, R. Martin, & N. Thrift, eds., *Money, Power and Space*, pp. 406–445. Blackwell.

Webb, M. C. 1973. The Petén Maya Decline Viewed in the Perspective of State Formation. In T. P. Culbert, ed., *The Classic Maya Collapse*, pp. 367–404. University of New Mexico Press.

———. 1987. Broader Perspectives on Andean State Origins. In J. Haas, S. Pozorski, & T. Pozorski, eds., *The Origins and Development of the Andean State*, pp. 161–167. Cambridge University Press.

White, L. A. 1959. *The Evolution of Culture: The Development of Civilization to the Fall of Rome*. McGraw-Hill.

Whitehead, R. H. 1989. *Kluskap's Cave: Documentation of Micmac Oral Tradition*. The Nova Scotia Museum, Halifax.

Whorf, B. L. 1956 [1978]. The Relation of Habitual Thought and Behavior to Language. In *Language, Thought, and Reality*, pp. 134–159. MIT Press.

Wikan, U. 1990. *Managing Turbulent Hearts: A Balinese Formula for Living*. University of Chicago Press.

Wilkinson, R. G. 1973. *Poverty and Progress: An Ecological Model of Economic Development*. Methuen.

———. 1988. The English Industrial Revolution. In D. Worster, ed., *The Ends of the Earth: Perspectives on Modern Environmental History*, pp. 80–99. Cambridge University Press.

Winner, L. 1977. *Autonomous Technology: Technics-out-of-Control As a Theme in Political Thought*. MIT Press.

Wittgenstein, L. 1921 [1971]. *Tractatus Logico-Philosophicus*. Routledge & Kegan Paul.

Wolf, E. R. 1982. *Europe and the People without History*. University of California Press.

World Commission on Environment and Development [WCED]. 1987. *Our Common Future*. Oxford University Press.

Worsley, P. 1957. *The Trumpet Shall Sound: A Study of 'Cargo' Cults in Melanesia*. Macgibbon and Kee.

Worster, D. 1993. Ecological History. In C. Merchant, ed., *Major Problems in American Environmental History*, pp. 2–9. D. C. Heath & Co.

———, ed. 1988. *The Ends of the Earth: Perspectives on Modern Environmental History*. Cambridge University Press.

Yoffee, N. 1988a. The Collapse of Ancient Mesopotamian States and Civilization. In N. Yoffee & G. L. Cowgill, eds., *The Collapse of Ancient States and Civilizations*, pp. 44–68. University of Arizona Press.

———. 1988b. Orienting Collapse. In N. Yoffee & G. L. Cowgill, eds., *The Collapse of Ancient States and Civilizations*, pp. 1–19. University of Arizona Press.

Yoffee, N., & G. L. Cowgill, eds. 1988. *The Collapse of Ancient States and Civilizations*. University of Arizona Press.

Zerries, O. 1987. Lord of the Animals. In M. Eliade, ed., *The Encyclopedia of Religion*. Macmillan.

Index

True State of the World, The (Lomborg), 24
truth, 25
Tsembaga Maring, 178
Turner, B. L., II, 54

Unama'kik district, 213
underconsumption, 15, 37
underdevelopment, 11, 15–16, 26–27, 29, 37; technology transfer, 19–20
underpayment, 13, 37–38, 57–59, 69–70, 84
understanding, 63, 65–68, 165–66
unequal exchange, 2, 11–12, 18, 33; appropriation of energy, 44–48; conceptualization, 36–40; energy consumption, 28–29; fossil fuels and, 95–96, 99; growth of capital, 25–26; machines and, 44, 147–48; order, 93–95; prices, 148–49. *See also* center/periphery; exchange
Union of Nova Scotia Indians (UNSI), 217, 219
unions, 50
United Nations, 19, 21, 222
United Nations Department of Economic and Social Affairs, 19
United States:
oil imports, 82–83; triangle trade, 59–60, 63
universalism, 51, 90–92, 184, 238–39
universal selection theory, 163–64
urbanism, 79
use value, 86, 89–93, 103, 105–9
U.S.S.R. Academy of Sciences, 19
utility, 45, 86, 90, 105, 114–15, 124, 184; abstract, 91–92

vacuity, 170–71
value, 15, 84; early theory, 95–101; emergy and, 40–42; exchange value, 70, 86, 89–93, 105; labor theory of, 94–95; short-term *vs.* long-term, 170, 184; theories of, 38–42; use value, 86, 89–93, 103, 105–9
Varela, F. J., 179–80, 182
vertical economic systems, 72–73, 75

Victoria County Committee for Development, 216, 217
von Uexküll, Jakob, 183
von Uexküll, Thure, 183

Wassén, S. H., 72
Wackernagel, Mathis, 31, 56
wages, 58, 62, 69, 85–86
Wagner, R., 122
Wallerstein, Immanuel, 36, 37, 56, 60, 65
WCED conference, 21, 24, 26, 55
Weber, Max, 56, 194
West Africa, 59–60
Western concepts, 109, 112–13, 119, 130, 136, 181, 195–200, 236
West Indies, 63
White, Leslie, 95, 97, 98, 99–101, 176
White, Lynn, 19, 20
Wildlife Act, 213
Williams, Raymond, 51, 52
Wisdom of the Elders: Sacred Native Stories of Nature (Suzuki and Knudtson), 234–35
Wittgenstein, Ludwig, 116
Wolf, Eric R., 38, 65, 85
work, 12–14, 122
workers, 26, 36–37, 57–59, 85–86
work gates, 99
World Bank, 26, 49
world market, 10–13, 82–83
world-structure, 119–20
world system, 2–3, 25, 33–34, 36, 62, 214, 235–36; Andean exchange system, 71–76; energy consumption, 28–29; historical perspective, 53–57, 65; theories, 3, 37, 39–40, 42, 67, 108
World Trade Organization (WTO), 24
worldviews, 10, 18–21, 24–25. *See also* Marxism
Worster, D., 192

yanacona, 74
Yoffee, Norman, 46

zero-sum game, 24, 26, 27–29, 32, 53, 59, 149–50

About the Author

Alf Hornborg is an anthropologist and professor of human ecology at the University of Lund, Sweden. His major research interests include the social organization and ecology of indigenous peoples of South America, past and present. In recent years he has addressed the cultural and political dimensions of global environmental discourse. This has led him to investigate various negotiations of environmental issues to uncover underlying assumptions, power relations, and sources of identity. He has conducted fieldwork in Peru, Canada, and Tonga. He is the author of *Dualism and Hierarchy in Lowland South America* and co-editor of *Voices of the Land: Identity and Ecology in the Margins* and *Negotiating Nature: Culture, Power, and Environmental Argument*. He has also published a number of articles in international journals.